*Nashville's Songwriting
Sweethearts*

Nashville's Songwriting Sweethearts

THE BOUDLEAUX AND FELICE BRYANT STORY

★ ★ ★ ★ ★

Bobbie Malone and Bill C. Malone

UNIVERSITY OF OKLAHOMA PRESS : NORMAN

LIBRARY OF CONGRESS CATALOGING-IN-PUBLICATION DATA

Names: Malone, Bobbie, 1944– author. | Malone, Bill C., author.
Title: Nashville's songwriting sweethearts : the Boudleaux and Felice Bryant
story / Bobbie Malone and Bill C. Malone.
Description: [First edition.] | Norman : University of Oklahoma Press, 2020. |
Series: American popular music ; volume 6 | Includes bibliographical
references and index. | Summary: "As the first fulltime songwriters to move to
Nashville in the mid 20th century, Boudleaux and Felice Bryant played a
significant role in shaping the development of three genres of American music:
country, rock 'n roll, and pop, and in so doing, helped make their adopted
home Music City USA"—Provided by publisher.
Identifiers: LCCN 2019035614 | ISBN 978-0-8061-6486-1 (hardcover)
Subjects: LCSH: Bryant, Boudleaux | Bryant, Felice | Composers—Tennessee—
Nashville—Biography. | Lyricists—Tennessee—Nashville—Biography.
Classification: LCC ML390 .M237 2020 | DDC 782.42164092/2 [B]—dc23
LC record available at https://lccn.loc.gov/2019035614

Nashville's Songwriting Sweethearts: The Boudleaux and Felice Bryant Story is Volume 6 in
the American Popular Music Series.

1 2 3 4 5 6 7 8 9 10

For Del and Dane,
who carry on the Bryant legacy

And for our grandson,
Theo Sontheimer,
who loves all kinds of music

CONTENTS

PREFACE

You may not know the names of Boudleaux and Felice Bryant, but you probably know their music. Almost completely unknown when they first arrived in Nashville in 1950, they created a body of music that moved around the world, and they became the first independent songwriters the musical city had ever had. Songs like "Bye Bye Love," "All I Have to Do Is Dream," "Love Hurts," and "Rocky Top" inspired young musicians everywhere, not only during the decades in which they were written, but ever since.

Meet the Bryants

Boudleaux and Felice Bryant played a significant role in shaping the development of three genres of mid twentieth-century American music: country, rock 'n' roll, and pop. Contemporaries with greater name recognition—such as Hoagy Carmichael in pop, Hank Williams in country, and somewhat later, Chuck Berry in rock 'n' roll—gained greater visibility from performing as well as writing. The Bryants were the first people to move to Nashville solely to write songs and to make a living from the profession. Their mentor Fred Rose composed a multitude of fine and enduring songs, but he won admission to the Country Music Hall of Fame through the exercise of many other talents, including his cofounding of Nashville's first major publishing house, Acuff-Rose. Seeing his success and heeding his sage advice, Felice and Boudleaux recognized from the beginning that, although writing a country song is an art, success depends on persistent hard work, business acumen, and—equally important—luck.

The Bryants arrived at the right place at precisely the right time. Their son Del, who has spent his life in the music business, said that his own success benefited "from having parents who well understood both halves of

Boudleaux and Felice during their first decade in Nashville. Courtesy of the
Country Music Hall of Fame® and Museum.

the phrase 'music business.'"[1] Their emergence in the early 1950s coincided
with a similar rise by Nashville as Music City, USA, and their enormous
output of songs became a major factor in that transformation. Happily,
Felice and Boudleaux achieved commercial viability by freely combining
well-crafted lyrics and stylistic innovation. While they worked successfully

with older rural idioms, their collaboration with the Everly Brothers, beginning in 1957, moved country music toward fusions that lay at the heart of what we now call country-pop music. And their positive personal relationship and reputation as songwriting sweethearts only enhanced their appeal.

Meet the Malones

As an ardent fan and amateur singer of country music and a purchaser of journals like *Country Song Roundup Magazine,* Bill became aware of the Bryants' names when he was a teenager and young adult growing up in rural East Texas. Never permitting academic studies to interfere with his fantasies of being on the stage of the Grand Ole Opry, Bill continued to sing throughout his days as an undergraduate and graduate student at the University of Texas in Austin. He still has fond memories of many hours performing at parties and at the now famous bar in North Austin known as Threadgill's. "Country Boy" may have been the first Bryant song of which he became aware, but other songs like "Take Me as I Am" and "Making the Rounds," which permitted more nuanced emotional expression, became part of his repertoire. Years later, they became part of the body of songs that he and Bobbie perform. Ten years Bill's junior, and growing up in a middle-class San Antonio home where country music played no significant role as it did in Bill's, Bobbie never realized that the rockabillies she admired had country roots. But in 1957, when she was thirteen, she fell in love with the music of the Everly Brothers. Only years later did she learn that most of these songs were written by Boudleaux and Felice Bryant.

In his scholarship, including *Country Music, USA* (the first academic study of the subject), Bill has always acknowledged the Bryants' importance. But he feels he never adequately emphasized the major contributions they made to the music of the world. This present study, we hope, will help to rectify that situation.

Telling the Bryants' Story

We became engaged with the Bryants' story in the midst of spending four intensive and thoroughly enjoyable days in October 2017, in Walpole, New Hampshire. Bill had been actively participating as the historical consultant for the then forthcoming series titled *Country Music,* produced by Ken Burns, written and produced by Dayton Duncan, and produced by Julie

Dunfey. The Walpole team gathered consultants from various aspects of the country music business to critique the series before its final revision.

Del Bryant, recently retired from decades as head of BMI, was one of the other consultants attending with his wife, Carolyn. During a break the first morning in that stimulating setting, Bobbie engaged Del in conversation. As an avid Everly Brothers fan, she wanted to tell Del how much she appreciated his parents' providing the soundtrack of her early adolescence, as they did for many of her peers. Bobbie and Bill moved to Madison, Wisconsin in 1995, when Bobbie accepted a position at the Wisconsin Historical Society writing about the state for young students. From Bill's previous research, she knew that Felice Bryant was a native daughter of Milwaukee. In the midst of her conversation with Del, she proposed that she write an article on his mother for the *Wisconsin Magazine of History*. Del enthusiastically concurred. When Bobbie reported the interchange to Bill, he countered, "Why stop there? We could write their biography." When we approached Del with this greatly expanded proposition, he readily welcomed our decision to provide the full story of his parents' remarkable partnership and joint career.

Soon after we returned to Madison, Del sent us a copy of *All I Have to Do Is Dream: The Boudleaux and Felice Bryant Story*. Originally produced by the House of Bryant as a boxed set, the collection contains a colorful and beautifully produced short biography of his parents by Dane's wife, Lee Wilson; a generous sampling of their recorded songs and demos on CDs; and a DVD of filmed interviews with them and those who knew them.[2] The boxed set collection not only provided an overview of the Bryants' lives and careers, it also introduced us to its compilers, Del's older brother, Dane, and his wife, Lee. Since that time, Team Bryant—as Dane and Del referred to themselves and their folks growing up, and a term now including Lee and Carolyn—have been invaluable and unselfish in their assistance to us.

As we began our research and writing, we quickly discovered that, not only did Boudleaux and Felice make impressive contributions to the development of country music and to the emergence of Nashville as a major music center, but their dedication to their craft was undergirded by their own extraordinary love story. This songwriting duet's devotion to one another probably explains why their songs dealt almost exclusively with love, generally in its most positive aspects. The Bryants' songs seldom referenced the social, political, or economic realities of the decades in which

Boudleaux and Felice in Gatlinburg, early 1980s. Courtesy of the Country Music Hall of Fame® and Museum.

they wrote.[3] Nor did their songs often rely on any of the presumed topics of country lyrics described by David Allan Coe in his classic "You Never Even Call Me by My Name": Mama, getting drunk, prison, trucks, and trains. Journalist Franklin Bruno, in fact, wrote:

> If you're drawn to musicians who salvage their art from tragic romance, addiction, and other personal wreckage, you may as well turn elsewhere. The lives and joint career of Felice and Boudleaux Bryant offer few attractions for the rubber-necker. By all accounts, their forty-two-year marital and creative partnership was nearly idyllic, as Boudleaux acknowledged when asked to explain the optimism of many of their songs: "I suppose it's because we've had such a very wonderful relationship."[4]

Love *was* the motivating force behind most of their songs, and powered by the emerging Youth Revolution in America and throughout the world, Boudleaux and Felice pushed the boundaries of country music into the realms of pop and rock 'n' roll, building audiences as they built classic hits.

ACKNOWLEDGMENTS

As a long-married couple of historians writing this biography of a long-married couple of songwriters, we experienced what we liked to imagine as a similar joy of co-creating a work. Our many conversations with Dane Bryant and his wife, Lee Wilson, and Del and Carolyn Bryant, augmented by the tremendous number of primary sources they made available to us, helped us feel that we got to know Boudleaux and Felice Bryant as intimately as possible so many years after their deaths.[1]

Indispensable to the crafting of the biography was the Boudleaux and Felice Bryant Collection at Frist Library and Archives of the Country Music Hall of Fame as well as the transcripts of the oral histories of the Bryants conducted for the Hall of Fame, in 1975 by Patricia Hall, and in 1983 by John Rumble, also located there. Once we embarked on the research, the Frist Library and Archives staff were tremendously helpful to us, especially Lee Boulie, Brenda Colladay, Kathleen Campbell, Elizabeth Edwards, Bryan Jones, John Rumble, Kayleigh Shoemaker, and Alan Stoker.

Dane and Del generously allowed us to use the interviews that remain part of the House of Bryant Collection, which also proved extremely valuable. These interviews are recorded on CDs that remain in a private collection in Nashville. They also arranged for the majority of the interviews we conducted with other people who gave us additional insights into their parents.[2] We so appreciate the contributions of everyone who graciously participated in our research, including Leah Foster Alderman, Pete Balistrieri, Bobby Bare, the late Harold Bradley, Heather Bryant Creech, Jill Nabarro Douglass, Ralph Emery, Billie Foster, the late Fred Foster, Peter Guralnick, Jan Howard, Sue Johnson, Brent Maher, Gail Love May, Jim McCormick, Dennis Morgan, Graham Nash, Danise Bryant Nabarro, Sonny

Osborne, Sir Tim Rice, Thomas Schuyler, Paul Simon, Steve Singleton, Ray Stevens, Bud Wendell, and Martha Woods.

Our dear friends in Nashville, Heidi and Ron Addlestone, graciously hosted us during our many research trips; Dee Grimsrud guided us to genealogical resources in Milwaukee; Thomas Hemman directed us to the Italian historical papers at the Milwaukee Country Historical Society; Debra Hershkowitz, Christine Schelshorn and Nate Gibson offered critical insights, while Ann Boyer skillfully edited the entire manuscript. Our dear cousins, Bette and Jack Vexler, allowed us to sequester ourselves at their Monterrey Ranch in Tarpley, Texas, so that we could complete our biography. Of course, the Bryant family made the research both exciting and fun, and we could not have done this book without their full cooperation and support.

We chose the University of Oklahoma Press because of our close friend and acquisitions editor, Kent Calder, who had previously published books for both of us. His encouragement and support once again made us feel welcome and at ease. Emily Schuster and Stephanie Evans directed the editorial and production process, to which Pippa Letsky contributed her meticulous copyediting.

Felice wrote "We Could" for Boudleaux's birthday. The song might also stand as a metaphor for their careers as well as for their devotion to each other. Courtesy of the Country Music Hall of Fame® and Museum.

★ ★ ★ ★ ★

Chapter 1

LOVE AT FIRST SPLASH

Hailing from dramatically contrasting regions of the United States, two complete strangers from wholly different cultural paths had a chance encounter, sparking the love match that became the Boudleaux and Felice Bryant story. Small-town southern Georgia boy, Diadorius Boudleaux Bryant, meets Milwaukee native, Matilda Genevieve Scaduto (later known as Felice) of Sicilian American background. Although their childhoods and adolescence bore little in common, they grew up during the decades when commercial popular music and entertainment—propelled by radio, recordings, and movies—exploded in American culture. Boudleaux and Felice's intimate companionship ultimately blossomed into an unexpected songwriting partnership. In their long and mutually supportive career, they produced thousands of songs, of which more than nine hundred were recorded.

Diadorius Boudleaux was born in Shellman, Georgia, on February 13, 1920, the first of five children born to Daniel Green Bryant and Louise Parham Bryant. Daniel Green—always known by both names—gave his son the name Boudleaux as a tribute to Lucien Boudleaux, a French soldier. As Boudleaux Bryant told his sons throughout their childhoods, his father had been gassed while he fought in World War I and, presumed dead, was tossed in a pile with the bodies of other unfortunate soldiers. When the French soldier walked by the trench where the bodies were stacked, he saw a hand shaking, and realized that someone might still be alive. Boudleaux reached in and pulled Daniel Green free, got him to medics, and on to a hospital. Boudleaux kept up with Daniel Green in the hospital, visiting him several times. Grateful to Boudleaux for saving his life, Daniel Green told him that he would name his firstborn son after him.[1]

He and Louise may have given their children unusual names—daughters Lafontisse and Danise, and brothers Neruda Levigne and Jascha

Mascagni—to add luster to the otherwise pedestrian Bryant surname. Or the names may have sprung from Daniel Green's interest in classical and exotic cultures, suggesting his respect for the fine arts and, more broadly, Western civilization. Diodorus Siculus was an ancient Greek historian; Pablo Neruda, a famed twentieth-century Chilean poet; Jascha Heifitz, a Russian Jewish violinist; and Petro Mascagni, an Italian composer. Danise reported that her name was a combination of her parents' first names, but the origin of Lafontisse remains obscure. Perhaps it is a reference to the fables of La Fontaine.[2] The bestowing of unusual names may also hint at their parents' aspirations for their children's futures.

Ancestors on both sides of the Bryant family had lived in southwestern Georgia since at least the early nineteenth century; some were buried in the Bethlehem Freewill Baptist Church Cemetery in Shellman. Boudleaux was convinced that he had some American Indian ancestry, possibly Cherokee or Creek. He had heard of a paternal male ancestor's dalliance with an Indian woman, but no documentation confirms that speculation.[3] Located in southwestern Georgia not far from the Alabama border, the small agricultural community of Shellman had a population of just over one thousand people when Boudleaux was born, and that population has remained stable until today. Despite the presence of an old Confederate cemetery, the African American population has always exceeded the number of Anglos living in Shellman.

At the time of Boudleaux's birth, Daniel Green Bryant was a barber in a town far removed from the stereotypical image of the Roaring Twenties.[4] Dependent on agriculture, Shellman, like the rest of small-town and rural America, was already undergoing the severe economic downturn of the Great Depression. In the 1920s, while the boll weevil worked its way into Georgia's cotton fields, new fabrics such as rayon made the price of the staple plummet. Cotton's decline devastated the state's farmers, just as overproduction of other crops after World War I wreaked havoc on rural areas elsewhere. While the Bryants were not wealthy, they did own their land. They managed better than the poor white sharecroppers who worked about two-thirds of the farmland in the state, making next to nothing. Black sharecroppers fared even worse.[5]

Decidedly upwardly mobile, Daniel Green Bryant probably chose law as a more socially and economically promising alternative to barbering. Boudleaux was always proud to have been born in Shellman. But while he

Boudleaux at about two years old. Courtesy House of Bryant Publications.

was still a baby, the family relocated to Athens, where his father attended law school at the University of Georgia. After he became an attorney, the family settled permanently on the outskirts of Moultrie, about seventy-five miles southeast of Shellman. In addition to housekeeping, sewing, cooking, gardening, and canning, Boudleaux's enterprising and energetic mother, Louise, raised chickens, tended livestock, and cured pork for the smokehouse. Once he was old enough, Boudleaux (known as Diorius while he was growing up) did all the milking. The strength that milking by hand required probably contributed to the muscle control young Boudleaux brought to his fiddle playing.[6] Their home was close enough to Boudleaux's paternal grandparents to permit frequent visits, and Colquitt's county seat, Moultrie, offered more opportunities to an aspiring country lawyer.

About sixty miles north of Tallahassee, Moultrie is closer to Florida's capital than to Atlanta. Lying in the "Pine Barrens," Colquitt County lacked the rich soil around Shellman, which resulted in a different pattern of growth. Rather than cotton, the town depended on timber resources shipped out in the mid to late nineteenth century via the Georgia Northern Railroad. Dependent on a nonrenewable resource, the timber products boom was short-lived, however. By the dawning of the twentieth century, crops—from peanuts and sugar cane to cattle feed, corn, grains, and after 1925, tobacco—replaced timber-related production.[7] Moultrie's population over the years remained at around fourteen thousand, so it was still a small town, but not a hamlet like Shellman. It was a good place in which to raise children. Boudleaux considered Moultrie his hometown, having had his schooling there. And it was the place to which he returned often, both before and during his first years of marriage.

Although Daniel Green Bryant practiced law and was thoroughly professional, he maintained his strong musical interests. He also recognized the fine quality of his wife's singing. Their daughter Danise said that, while he was in law school, her father arranged for her mother to take voice lessons to further refine her style.[8] Louise Bryant was also a capable pianist. Daniel Green played mandolin, guitar, piano, trombone, and fiddle. He also taught in shape-note singing schools, generally ten-day schools where itinerant teachers taught a method of reading music through shapes rather than conventional notes on a staff. By so doing, he retained his links to a thoroughly rural society. Boudleaux described his father as "an itinerant teacher in the backwoods who went from church to church teaching the

Boudleaux at about three years old. Courtesy House of Bryant Publications.

country choirs how to read their hymn music." Daniel Green even penned at least one hymn, "The Sages," intended for the singing school repertoire.[9] Louise often accompanied her singing with guitar, and both parents encouraged their children's musical education—especially that of Boudleaux, who received a fiddle on his fifth birthday. A younger neighbor from the first farm down the lane of their rural neighborhood, Gail Love May, recalls the musicality of the family and the way they invited folks in to listen. "They would have family concerts, especially at Christmas time. They were all so talented. Lafontisse played piano by ear, and Mrs. Bryant would sing 'The Holy City.'"[10]

The fiddle was widely regarded as the king of instruments in the rural South, and it was played by both African Americans and whites. Georgia had long been a citadel of old-time fiddle music. The annual Old-Time Fiddlers Convention in Atlanta, held since 1913, was nationally famous.[11] Such contests were seedbeds of the commercial country music that emerged in the early 1920s. Boudleaux must have been aware of the hillbilly bands that proliferated on radio and recordings during the two decades preceding World War II. He undoubtedly knew that Georgia fiddlers, such as Fiddlin' John Carson, Gid Tanner, Lowe Stokes, and Clayton McMichen, played prominent roles in the early history of country music. When the first commercial country recordings were made in the 1920s, several Georgia string bands predominated—including the famous Skillet Lickers. A gifted and receptive young Boudleaux grew up in the midst of this vibrant tradition.

At first, his father taught Boudleaux what he knew. Fortunately, A. E. Goodwin, a former musician with the Boston Symphony, had retired in Moultrie. Although he no longer wanted to teach formally, he did agree to take Boudleaux on as a private student when he turned six. This relationship continued for the next decade. Boudleaux described himself as a "near-sighted youth who went about his violin lessons sadly, vowing to lay the fiddle aside when he came of age."[12] He may have lacked the enthusiasm that his father and Mr. Goodwin expected of him, but he profited in gaining proficiency with the instrument. Years later, he recalled that early music education:

I grew up in country music at the same time I was studying violin, fiddle, classical music. I was studying that about two days a week, practicing about four hours a day on fiddle, and at the same time, my dad was bringing home all these old-time fiddlers, and I was learning hoedowns by the gross loads, and we were going to all-day singings with dinner on the ground on Sundays. Every Saturday afternoon at the courthouse there were people that we used to call buskers. They were itinerant musicians that would come and get to playing on the courthouse lawn—fiddlers, singers of all kinds, and I think that was as important a facet of my training as anything I got in a formal way.[13]

Along the way, Boudleaux also learned the music of jazz musicians, such as Stephane Grappelli and Django Reinhardt, who contributed to his emerging style. Having absorbed both popular and classical styles since boyhood, he moved effortlessly from one to another as an adult.

All the Bryant children (except the youngest sister, Danise) were musical, and they spent at least part of their summer vacations on the road playing music. Boudleaux even termed his father "something of a summer nomad."[14] For several summers, the Bryants traveled around the South playing music. Daniel Green drove an automobile with a specially built trailer holding their instruments, personal possessions, and a few chickens. Their longest trip occurred during the summer of 1933 when they drove to the Chicago Century of Progress, with stops along the way. They repeated this routine in 1936 for the Texas Centennial in Dallas. The children were sometimes embarrassed when Daniel Green pointed out their abilities to the crowd. As they traveled, they occasionally held fiddle contests to attract an audience. Of course, Boudleaux often won them.[15]

Graduating from Moultrie High School in 1937 in the midst of the Great Depression, Boudleaux moved to Atlanta to study classical violin at the Leffingwell School of Music. He lived with his father's sisters, Aunts Maymee and Jewel. Since employment was scarce for all—especially those in the arts—Boudleaux was fortunate to play with the Atlanta Philharmonic during the 1937–1938 season. To help pay bills, he also played part-time with the WPA Orchestra, then with the Carl Pathe Concert Orchestra, and with Charlie Jarrell's Little Symphony on WSB, the city's powerful 50,000 watt radio station.

Because any music well performed appealed to Boudleaux, Atlanta introduced him to outstanding musicians beyond the symphonies. Danise

A teenage Boudleaux, looking confident with his fiddle. Courtesy of the Country Music Hall of Fame® and Museum.

remembered that her brother wanted to bring an African American jazz pianist and composer home to Moultrie. But, as she said, "That just was not done," and the family discouraged such a visit.[16] Boudleaux's intent, however, demonstrates his open acceptance of an interracial friendship based on the respect of one musician for the other.

Boudleaux was just as open to playing whatever his audiences wanted to hear. Not surprisingly, while studying and playing symphonic music in Atlanta, he also hung around a fiddle shop. There, in mid-1938, he met Lowry Eugene Stripling, who became a longtime Georgia radio personality and later made a successful transition to television. Hailing from Macon, Stripling was a dapperly dressed man with a pencil-thin mustache whose overall look resembled that of Clark Gable. Stripling had played on the WSB noontime *Cross Roads Follies* since 1937 as Uncle Ned of the Texas Wranglers (even though the entire group was from Macon, Georgia).[17]

Learning that Boudleaux could play hoedowns, Stripling hired him to play that night at a show. He made fifteen dollars for the gig (much more than he was earning with the symphony) and soon was hired as a full-time member of Uncle Ned and His Texas Wranglers, sponsored by Garner "Pop" Eckler. A veteran radio personality, Eckler gained modest fame by writing a song titled "Money, Marbles, and Chalk." The song became a hit in 1949 by Patti Page, as well as country artists such as Rex Allen. Boudleaux played with Uncle Ned on Pop Eckler's *Radio Jamboree*, on the *Cross Roads Follies*, and in Atlanta theaters. He could scarcely have foreseen that this initial foray into radio would herald the prominent role that radio shows and contact with radio personnel would play in his songwriting future.

Fiddlers knew more than old-time hoedowns. Hot or jazz-inspired country fiddling already existed in Georgia in the 1920s and 1930s. Clayton McMichen, for example, was as famous for his jazz licks as he was for his hoedowns. After he left the Skillet Lickers, he led a group called the Georgia Wildcats who played swing music. Musicians like Boudleaux were also aware of the country swing music being played in Texas and Oklahoma during the mid-1930s by Texas musicians such as Milton Brown with his Musical Brownies, and Bob Wills with the Texas Playboys.

After Boudleaux left Uncle Ned, he joined the most popular country swing band in the Southeast, a group called Hank Penny's Radio Cowboys. Herbert Clayton "Hank" Penny from Birmingham, Alabama, was apparently a strong-willed and opinionated man who grew up within the powerful orbit of the Grand Ole Opry but was no friend of hillbilly music. Boudleaux, however, found him to be "a very witty, funny man" and "a really sophisticated comedian."[18] Inspired by the music coming out of Oklahoma and Texas, Hank and his band performed a style of music that ultimately became known as western swing. These were string bands dominated by the fiddle that combined blues, ragtime, and jazz along with traditional country tunes. The musicians improvised their solo passages, and their obvious similarities to the big pop bands of the era led to their music being described as "swing." But in the 1930s, they were more often known as "hot fiddle bands." The term "western swing" only gained currency after World War II when Spade Cooley began using it to describe his band on the West Coast. Milton Brown and His Musical Brownies were probably the most crucial inspirations for the music made by Penny and His Radio Cowboys.[19]

Boudleaux enjoyed being a member of the band. He recalled that "We had just a bunch of good musicians, and we did a different type thing" on *Cross Roads Follies*. While most bands were playing traditional country fare, "we were doing this so-called Texas swing style." Even without any designated vocalists, Penny's musicians gave their shows the variety they needed. But according to western swing authority Rich Kienzle, classically trained Boudleaux had some problems adjusting to Hank's "simple music and songwriting." Kienzle quotes Hank's statement, "Boudleaux used to say, 'you're not writin' songs, you're writing *shit*! Music is written by the masters, Beethoven and Bach.'"[20] At this point in his life, Boudleaux could not have anticipated how radically his perspective on songwriting would change.

During approximately the year and a half between 1938 and 1940 that Boudleaux played with Penny, they traveled from the Gulf Coast up north as far as Norfolk and west to Roanoke in a 1937 cream-colored Packard that Pop Eckler bought for them. The band had an electrically amplified steel guitar, new at that time to eastern country bands. Noel Boggs, the steel player, was an excellent musician and a jazz fan, fond of Benny Goodman. But since they played quite often in schoolhouses and other venues lacking electricity, the instrument could not always be used in their performances.[21] Penny's most notable musician, however, was the fiddler and guitarist Sheldon Bennett. He and Boudleaux could play twin fiddles or exchange solo musical breaks. The band performed on radio stations in Birmingham, Chattanooga, Atlanta, and Greenville, South Carolina.

WSB eventually introduced a Saturday night hillbilly variety show, the WSB *Barn Dance*, inspired by the popularity of programs such as Nashville's *Grand Ole Opry* and Chicago's *National Barn Dance*. On this venue, bolstered by the station's 50,000 watt coverage, the Radio Cowboys attracted mail from all over the country. Years later, Boudleaux recalled that the Hank Penny

Boudleaux and Sheldon Bennett, "twin fiddlers" in Hank Penny's band. Courtesy of the Country Music Hall of Fame® and Museum.

band was capable of playing dinner hour at a "first-rate hotel or going out and playing a square dance, either one."[22]

During this period Boudleaux, Hank, and another musician played at a local jamboree in Charlotte, North Carolina. There, he met accordion player Kelland Clark, who was with the Tennessee Ramblers on the same show. They became lifelong friends. Kelland said, "Bryant and Penny lured me back to their dressing room and showed off in general." A few months later, he went down to Atlanta and joined the Hank Penny Band. Along with several other band members, Kelland and Boudleaux formed the Cracker Barrel Gang, and they did a program on WSB at half past seven each morning, which turned out to be extremely popular. "Most of the Nashville musicians listened to it. It was fun, although we all had other programs to do for the same money. Sometimes we got bonuses, depending on how many people came to the shows."[23]

Kelland remained grateful for Boudleaux's guidance as "mentor, teacher, and inspirer" during those early years. "In having taken me under his wing," Kelland reminisced, "we had a show on Saturday mornings at 7:00 AM, another at 1:00 PM, and that night at the WSB Barn Dance at the municipal auditorium. Boudleaux and I would sit in that studio and play out of my book of 'better music'"—jazz and classic selections that these two trained musicians enjoyed. They spent the morning and afternoon sharing their talents and conversation, taking a sandwich break at lunch, and "then going at it again until going to the auditorium to play hillbilly music." Conversation moved freely and easily, since interest in philosophical and mystical subjects—topics that remained central to Boudleaux's thinking—intrigued both young men.[24]

Boudleaux appeared on thirty recordings with Penny, from five sessions: two in Memphis in July 1939, and three in Chicago in 1940. Among the songs recorded in Memphis, Boudleaux wrote "Mississippi Muddle" and played on "Hot Time Mama," "All Night and All Day Long," and "Won't You Ride in My Little Red Wagon." Apparently, this was the first recording of "Little Red Wagon," written by Penny's old Alabama friend Rex Griffin, a hillbilly singer and songwriter. It became Penny's most popular performance.

In Chicago the following year, Boudleaux played on "Rose's Sister," "Oh Yes? Take Another Guess," "Hawaiian Honeymoon," and "Tobacco State Swing," another of his own instrumental compositions. Boudleaux exhibited a smooth, swinging, blues-inflected style on this and other songs. His sound sometimes reflected that of his hero Stephane Grappelli.[25] Although Hank Penny's band never recorded in Atlanta, WSB *Barn Dance* performers Doug Spivey and Marvin Taylor, known as the Pine Ridge Boys, did record there. In September 1941, they cut another of Boudleaux's compositions, "No Matter What Happens." At the time, Boudleaux did not consider himself a songwriter. One night in a café, he got the idea for the song, jotted the words and notes on a napkin, and thought little of it. When he showed it to the Pine Ridge Boys, however, they recorded it.[26]

Despite the success of his Radio Cowboys, Hank had other aspirations and broke up the band.[27] On his own now, Boudleaux began the life of a roving musician, playing in a variety of genres over the next five years and periodically retreating to Moultrie where he performed with the hillbilly band Gene Mills and the Twilight Playboys. In Washington, DC, he worked as part of a four-piece supper club combo for about eight months, before drifting back to Moultrie.[28]

This may have been the visit home that triggered a memory from Danise during an interview many years later. When Boudleaux got interested in a subject, he would read everything he could find about it. This time, he decided to try raising turkeys. He read that finding the right kind of feed was essential to the task. In one source, the author believed that termites found in rotting wood comprised the dream food. Boudleaux collected the termites, but the food did not do the trick. "Then the rains came and drowned all the turkeys." In the same interview, Dane couldn't resist chiming in: "I remember that whenever Daddy wanted to do something that my mom thought was ridiculous, she'd say, 'We're not going to have another turkey farm, Boudleaux.'"[29]

More positively, Felice often described him as a builder, a planner—a man who always had something on the side in addition to what they were doing as songwriters.[30] The turkey fiasco, however, may have caused him to pursue his musicianship more seriously. By the following early spring of 1942, Kelland had lured Boudleaux to Memphis.

There they worked at radio station WMC for a few months as part of the band Gene Steele's Sunny Southerners.[31] Already alcohol dependent, Boudleaux was drinking heavily during this period. One Sunday night—when they never played gigs—he called Kelland, asking him to come over to his apartment "'and stay with me awhile, because there's a big dog running around my bed.' When I went over there, there were no dogs, but there were plenty of gin bottles lying around. As much as he could consume, I never saw it to be detrimental to his work. Those were good days, not lucrative, but good."[32] Looking back on that period of his life during an interview years later, Boudleaux admitted that, up until he and Felice met, "I must say that I was just gallivanting around the country, having a hell of a good time part of the time, starving part of the time, goofing off, with no sense of direction or anything—just playing and goofing off."[33]

Detroit looked more promising, with all the defense projects attracting southerners to the city. Workers were looking for work and musicians were needed in the clubs and beer joints that boomtowns inevitably spawn. Boudleaux and Kelland quit their jobs and joined the migration north in April 1942. They had to check out of their hotel by eleven o'clock the morning they left, so with nothing better to do the two went down to the station to await their three o'clock train. They got so involved in a debate over the question, "Is there anything such as true altruism?" that they missed the train and had to wait for another one that evening.[34] Intellectual debate remained a lifelong passion for Boudleaux. One of Kelland's musician friends, Clinton Collins, joined with him and Boudleaux to form a band that included the bass player Bill Ballard and Ray Bush, an underage musician Boudleaux had met in Washington, DC. They enjoyed working in local clubs until the bombing of Pearl Harbor changed the lives of young men in Detroit and everywhere.

Like millions of young men, Kelland and other musician friends got drafted, a fate Boudleaux narrowly avoided, in this instance, through paperwork confusion during the medical examination. At other times when he received a draft notice, he used sporadic drunkenness to his advantage. Getting "wasted" the night before a draft board appearance proved to be an effective way to attain a desired 4F status. As he liked to relate:

> I was a heavy-duty drinker, and every time I'd go in to be examined, and I was examined all over the country—Atlanta, Memphis, Washington, DC, Detroit, etc. It was early in the morning, and I'd go in so hungover, they'd turn me down. But the funniest thing was, they'd turn me down for something different every time. One time it was my eyes; another time it was my slipped disc; the last time, it was the grandfather of all hangovers. And I couldn't think; I couldn't see straight; I couldn't do anything. So, this guy just talked to me a little bit, and put down "severe neurosis."[35]

In Detroit, he actually passed the eye exam, but the doctor forgot to initial the form. When he went back, a different doctor was in and refused to sign the form without examining Boudleaux himself. The second doctor turned him down. Boudleaux attributed this piece of good luck to his having lived "a charmed life." When Kelland left for basic training, Boudleaux became a "strolling gypsy fiddler" playing among tables in restaurants, a role he remembered as a "thankless" gig and "the most miserable job I ever had!"[36]

After that "thankless gig," he was making forty or fifty dollars a week playing "in a booze house" with some other musicians, when some friends who had come to hear Boudleaux invited him to join them in one of the "so-called Ford combos." Ford Motor Company put several such combos on a guaranteed salary of sixty-five dollars a week, which was a real bonus.

That the combos were on call twenty-four hours a day was the only draw-back to the arrangement. Boudleaux joined "a great little group—two violins and a couple of guitars and piano—an accordion guy that doubled on piano and bass."[37]

One of these musicians was Rome Johnson, whose friendship proved invaluable a few years later. Ford sent the groups whenever and wherever the corporation wanted a performance—playing dinner parties or Sunday morning "horse get-togethers," which included playing for square dances on horseback. They might play late into the evening for a more formal party, then rush out the next morning for a chuckwagon breakfast.[38]

By early 1945 Boudleaux was in Chicago, playing in a trio at the Palmer House, the Brass Rail, and other clubs. When the band members found themselves momentarily out of a job there, the booking agency suggested a job at the Schroeder Hotel in downtown Milwaukee. The band added one musician and became a quartet performing in the cocktail lounge.

The stresses of trying to make a living as a musician and moving around the country very likely contributed to Boudleaux developing—or aggravating—his serious drinking problem. He claimed that his bouts with alcohol began because he tended to get nervous before going onstage. A physician he consulted suggested that he swallow a "swig of whiskey" to take the edge off. But, as is often the case, one swig led to another. Before long, he became "notorious for the piles of empty liquor bottles that accumulated in the corners of his hotel rooms on the road."[39] Heading for the Schroeder Hotel, he was determined to stay on the wagon.

And if he hadn't been trying to slake his thirst with water instead of liquor during a jam session, he and Felice may never have met. At that propitious moment, the pert and attractive twenty-year-old brunette was working a shift as an elevator operator at the Schroeder when she caught a glimpse of the tall Georgia fiddler heading toward the water fountain. She recognized Boudleaux as, quite literally, the man she had envisioned in a dream many years before that fateful event, and she immediately acknowledged this as the romance she'd been anticipating. Apart from their love of music, Felice's life differed from Boudleaux's in almost every aspect until the moment they met. Her older sister, Kitty, was two when Felice—named Matilda Genevieve Scaduto—was born at St. Mary's Hospital in Milwaukee on August 7, 1925, to Salvatore Philip (Sam) Scaduto, aged thirty-one, and Katherine Terri Loverdi Scaduto, aged nineteen.[40] Felice's early life was

Kitty and baby Felice sitting on their father's knees. Courtesy of the Country Music Hall of Fame® and Museum.

more settled than Boudleaux's, but when she was eleven, her parents divorced, disrupting the childhood that had begun so comfortably within the confines of her urban Catholic family in one of Milwaukee's immigrant neighborhoods.[41]

Many of the Italians who emigrated to the United States at the turn of the century came from Sicily. The suave and captivating Salvatore, a barber from the village of Bagheria, arrived in Milwaukee in 1913. His fellow countrymen had been emigrating since the 1880s when the Sicilian economy was floundering. Milwaukee was already "a manufacturing powerhouse, with an abundance of entry-level jobs [that] made the city a magnet for immigrants." Most of the Sicilians who settled in the city actually came from the vicinity of Palermo, especially the interlocking hamlets of Porticello and Sant'Elia, or the small villages such as Aspra or Santa Flavia, that lay east of Palermo along the Mediterranean.[42] While Katherine was born in Scranton, Pennsylvania, her parents also hailed from Sicily.

Through his service in World War I, Salvatore earned his citizenship, applying for it as soon as he was discharged from the army. In 1921 his barber shop was located at 148 Huron (now Clybourn), just blocks from downtown Milwaukee and at the northern border of the Third Ward, the area of first settlement for Italian immigrants. While Boudleaux's educated father valued music and culture, according to family stories Salvatore flirted with the idea of becoming a member of the Mafia or Black Hand, which had moved along with Sicilian immigrants to bloom in American urban centers. His father used his influence to keep him out of organized crime, recognizing that his son's proclivity for braggadocio would be hazardous in that world. Later in life, Felice's older sister, Kitty, told interviewers that Salvatore's Uncle Toledo was part of the Mafia in Detroit, adding, "Daddy was in it, too, but he didn't do much. He was a water boy."[43]

Felice's maternal grandfather, Carmelo (James or Jim) Loverdi, was also a barber, and he sold bootleg whiskey during the Prohibition years. Felice recalled that her grandfather used a trapdoor under her bed to enter a tunnel leading to a basement across the street where he distilled liquor. She and Kitty both attended school at the nearby Polish Catholic St. Casimir's and were confirmed there. Catholicism may have been the family's religion, but folk traditions had their hold. Felice's sons recall stories about their grandmother Katherine holding seances as a kind of old-country "white witch"—someone with useful powers.[44]

The First Ward (now Riverwest), where Felice spent her earliest years, was settled in the 1880s by Germans, but their Polish neighbors soon began outnumbering them. They built modest single-story frame homes, often adding to the original structures by raising them to build basement apartments underneath. In both the Historic South Side (often referred to as Polonia) and in the First Ward, these houses with their additions became known as "Polish flats." By the 1920s, Italian families moved north from the Historic Third Ward to join the Poles of Riverwest.[45] Perhaps that is why Felice spoke of growing up "in a very Italian family in an *almost* Italian neighborhood." She remembered knowing the time of day by the smells, when she walked outside the Loverdi-Scaduto household: "In the morning, it would be garlic and scrambled eggs; at lunchtime, it would be garlic and peppers for, as my grandmother would say, 'samwiches.' In the evening, it would be garlic and steak, so I remember smells better than I do events."[46]

The Scadutos' address on the east side of Humboldt Boulevard may have had the configuration of a Polish flat. The family rented an apartment in the Loverdis' house, where father and grandfather also shared a barber shop at the time of Felice's birth. After her parents separated, Salvatore, once again, moved his shop closer to downtown, an area in which he continued to work.[47]

Growing up in this mixed immigrant haven, which included Hungarians and Bohemians, Felice listened to the different musical sounds that "would just filter out on the street in the summer."[48] Even though she picked up parts of all three languages and learned to cook "in both Polish and Italian," she liked to say that she was completely Italian before she met Boudleaux.[49]

Felice retained vivid memories of her early years, especially her love of the Italian songs that her extended family used to sing or play. Her grandfather played mandolin; her father, guitar; her mother, piano. All the others, including Felice, sang. She told an interviewer in 1994 how much she liked the sound of gut strings on a guitar. "My father and my grandfather, they played gut. My grandfather strung gut up on a mandolin. Pa loved the soft sound of it. Unreal. Pa would always be tuning it. He'd say, 'Sonofabitch, aahh, so beautiful.'"[50]

She laughed when she said, "With Italians, it's sing, eat, and play bocce." Although she may have joked about singing "'O Sole Mio' when the umbilical cord was cut," the Italian folksongs of those years were not the

Kitty and Felice in their First Communion dresses, standing by their mother.
Courtesy of the Country Music Hall of Fame® and Museum.

only influence that shaped her musical tastes.[51] Attending St. Casimir's
during the period when the parish population reached the peak of its
diverse demographic mix added additional layers to her sense of identity.[52]
Despite bragging about being completely Italian before meeting Boudleaux, Felice also easily absorbed, embraced, and adored the sources of

popular culture, saying "I imagine I'm a product of what I was around." And moments later, when Boudleaux was asked if he thought Felice's writing bore any ethnic influence, he replied, "She didn't mention that she also had the influence of the pop music of the day. You know that, of course, her family had a radio, and she had enough [of a musical gift] that she could hear a song through in a movie and come out of a movie singing the whole thing: lyrics, melody, and everything. All of those influences come to bear on her work, and her work is representative of all of them from time to time." She was thoroughly American.[53]

Felice's older sister, Kitty, on the other hand, "was the quiet one." Del and Dane agreed that she "stayed ghetto" by remaining insular and more closely tied to her mother.[54] She even spoke with a slight Italian accent throughout her life. In a 2005 interview, Kitty admitted to being her mother's favorite, so she "took advantage of me." She also mentioned that her mother and the rest of the family did not care for Felice's outspokenness. At some point when Katherine chastised her younger daughter, Felice retorted, "You're not gonna do me like you did Kitty."[55]

Felice also loved looking at her father's "beautiful hand" when she was too young to read or even to recognize letters. She recalled watching him as he wrote letters to his relatives, including his sister, Angelina, who remained in Sicily, only moving to the United States after her husband died. Felice also loved the scrolling on the letters he received from Sicily. Then her active imagination took over. Whenever she had paper, she would create "pages and pages of things that would look like writing."[56]

Then she proceeded to make up stories as she pretended to read those pages to others, entertaining her preschool neighborhood peers. As she grew older, she moved on to writing poetry and little songs. Salvatore's musical abilities and suave ways, unfortunately, may have enhanced his tendencies toward womanizing. When Katherine contracted gonorrhea after some of his dalliances, she threatened her unfaithful husband with a knife and demanded a divorce. And whenever twelve-year-old Felice angered her mother, Katherine would tell her younger daughter that she was just like her father. That was when Felice learned that her father had also made up little songs.[57]

Although her mother may have berated preteen Felice by comparing her songwriting and singing to her father's penchants for both, Katherine had aggressively promoted her younger daughter's talents when she was still a preschooler. Katherine entered Felice into talent contests, like the one Kitty remembered, which was held at the Oriental Theater. Felice won, even though she was so nervous during this and other performances, that her hands were wet.[58]

Winning provided her with the opportunity to sing on *Cousin Betty's Children's Hour*, broadcast from the Riverside Theater on WISN and on other radio kiddie shows on WEMP from the time she was five. Felice enjoyed being a natural "show-off," performing for other children in the neighborhood, and in kindergarten, always volunteering to take part in any play, singing, or recitation. As she herself said, "I would sometimes do original works, because what I couldn't memorize, I would make up."[59] When interviewed just a few years before she died, Felice laughed as she recalled, "I'd have a little sing song somewhere in the story. And we used to play theater in the back yard, hang up sheets, you know, and we'd produce one of my stories, and it'd be a musical or whatever."[60]

Beyond using and enjoying her skills as a creative performer, young Felice shared with Kitty the pleasures of a Milwaukee childhood. In the winter they used the tops of trash cans as sleds to slide down the slippery alley behind their home. In the summer, when they still lived on Humboldt, they would walk to the beach at McKinley Park on the shore of Lake Michigan, then go by an ice factory where each could buy a chunk of ice to lick on the way home. As they grew older, they went ice-skating on the pond across from their school. Kitty remembered that pretty Felice always had more than one boy walk her home.[61]

After Katherine and Salvatore divorced, Katherine's parents were so ashamed they would no longer let their daughter and her children live in their house. The combination of divorce and being forced from home anguished the Scaduto children and may have been the beginning of Felice's ambivalence about Catholicism. She loved the beauty of the music and the rituals of the church, but she deplored its treatment of women. As Felice later told her family, she resented the way priests told women that if they prayed harder, their wayward husbands would reform. From her own experiences, she knew this wasn't true. Her daughter-in-law, Lee Wilson, strongly feels that Felice "must have seen many women in her family and neighborhood victimized by these patriarchal attitudes. I believe she resolved as a girl never to be victimized in the same way and valued and relied on the strong love she felt for Boudleaux and he for her."[62]

The three left behind the close neighborhood where Kitty and Felice played with their friends and roamed at will. While Salvatore opened his own barbershop on the northern border of the Third Ward, childhood as the girls knew it had ended.[63] Details become vague, probably because Felice was trying to dismiss those unpleasant memories. Both of her sons insisted that she did not want to share stories about her "miserable" childhood and only liked talking about its creative, more glamorous aspects.[64] The girls spent some time in Duquesne outside of Pittsburgh where their father had family members in the produce business. Katherine, Kitty, and Felice may also have lived briefly in Chicago with another set of relatives. After Katherine's divorce, they lived with their mother at 1105 West Vliet, about two miles further south and west of their grandparents on North Humboldt. Katherine waitressed in between cooking jobs, and both girls briefly attended Clarke Elementary and North Division High School. Probably expecting her daughters to contribute to the household income, Katherine forced each to drop out of school after eighth grade, a decision Felice always regretted having been made for her. Kitty said that, although he did not live with his daughters, their strict father remained concerned for their well-being. After her daughters' marriages, Katherine remarried George Sokas, a Greek immigrant and professional gambler. Dane and Del were fond of both their biological and step maternal grandfathers.[65]

As Felice grew older, her mother became increasingly abusive and demanding. Her exploitation and commodification of her young daughter probably served as an early indicator of her later expectations that her children should shoulder part of the burden she felt in rearing them. Felice's son Dane claimed that "Grandma had seen Felice as a 'ticket' to wealth. Mom was special. After all, that was the era of Shirley Temple. [But] the 'ticket' had its own mind. Grandma couldn't cash it or control it."[66] Neither Felice nor Boudleaux ever felt entirely comfortable about performing onstage. Did that anxiety have anything to do with their displaying their talents before audiences from such young ages? Whatever the reason, as children they likely had no awareness of anything beyond their own aptitudes for music-making.

Felice had ways of avoiding her mother's volatile moods, being forced to drop out of school, and experiencing the changes in household locations: she immersed herself in music, poetry, and work. Although she was no longer the adorable little girl who entered talent shows, she became an

attractive, charming adolescent performing in live musicals at the Riverside Theater, where she also worked as an usherette during the war years.
Del said that his mother "loved show business and could sing like Ella
Fitzgerald. Her friends would always scratch enough money to send her to
the hottest new musical movie, and she could go and learn all the songs
and come out and sing them to everybody. For her, show business was a
magical escape from a rough childhood, and she was good at the escape."[67]

As a young girl she obtained a copy of *The Best Loved Poems of the American People* (1936).[68] Consisting of about 575 poems and songs, the volume
dealt exclusively with material written in the nineteenth century and
earlier. The anthology contained poetry that was largely sentimental and
nostalgic, ranging from Alfred Lord Tennyson to Ella Wheeler Wilcox.
The *Best Loved Poems* introduced Felice to the world of rhyme and metrics,
reaffirming her thoroughly American identity while grounding her emerging facility for narrative, emotion, and rhythm. The cherished volume
served her well as she evolved as a songwriter.

In 1983 Felice told an interviewer that she didn't get along with her
family, that she was "pretty much a recluse. Anything I could find to get out
of the house, I did, and the most legitimate thing was good honest work."
She reported elsewhere: "My home life was such that, if I had anything on
my mind, I couldn't spill it to anybody. And so, I wrote it."[69] When interviewed, Kitty confirmed Felice's perception. As teenagers, the two were not
close. Each had her own set of friends.[70] In addition to being an usherette,
Felice found employment as a soda jerk and, briefly, as a roller-derby skater.
During World War II, she also performed and directed shows at the city's
United Service Organization (USO), which offered hospitality to traveling
active duty servicemen and women and their families.

At the time Felice met Boudleaux, she was holding down three
jobs, working mornings as a file clerk for the Falk Corporation—one of
Milwaukee's leading manufacturers. In the evenings both she and Kitty
worked as elevator operators at the Schroeder Hotel (now the Milwaukee
Hilton). On weekends Felice worked in the hotel's drugstore. She also spent
off-hours sequestered in her room, writing poetry.[71]

In the meantime, Felice claimed that Katherine tried to engineer her
teenage daughter's social life, allowing her to date only one young man,
Wladziu Valentino Liberace. Liberace, who hailed from the working-
class suburb of West Allis, later became famous as a flamboyant pianist.

Felice as a young working woman. Courtesy House of Bryant Publications.

Katherine may have deemed him "safe" because of his ambiguous sexuality. At other times, she pushed Felice toward more affluent and successful older professional men whom she believed would make suitable husbands. Felice resisted Katherine's efforts. Finding a husband and leaving home would have meant getting away from her mother's intrigues. Yet marriage at eighteen to Michael Geraci, a young coast guard sailor, also from West Allis, did not prove to be a successful alternative. After the church wedding, Felice and her new husband moved to a base on the Texas coast where he was stationed. Almost immediately, she realized that the marriage was not going to work, and she returned to Milwaukee within two weeks.[72] Restlessness stalked her. She told her Recording Academy interviewer in 1999 that at the time she met Boudleaux two years later, "I was a caged lion, and I needed the Serengeti to run around in."[73] Their fateful meeting freed the lion within and, ultimately, gave her the strength to harness her pent-up energy in pursuit of a creative career for them both.

Boudleaux and the band began their stint at the Schroeder on February 13, 1945, his twenty-fifth birthday. The booking agency told the musicians that they would really enjoy being at the hotel for two weeks, staying in the penthouse there, with five bedrooms and bath, kitchen, and living room. The band's spirits revived when they arrived. The experience turned out to be even more promising than Boudleaux anticipated. Felice chimed in: "He was on the wagon this particular week, and rather than order water from the bar he'd come out to the water fountain, which was out at the elevators, and that's how we met."[74] It was Valentine's Day to boot.

One of Felice's favorite stories concerned the man in a dream she had when she was only eight. The two were dancing to what she believed was "our song," but only later did "our song" take on a new meaning. The dream man was tall, dark, and bearded, and dark-haired Felice was dressed in blue chiffon. When she saw Boudleaux walking toward the water fountain, she recognized him from the dream twelve years earlier. "I don't know if it was love at first sight or 'At last my friend! I was wondering when you'd come along.' He didn't know who the hell I was, but I somehow knew who he was." She told another interviewer, "The doorway was open to tomorrow, and I could see on the other side."[75]

Many years later, Boudleaux told an interviewer that when he was still playing with the Atlanta Symphony, a member of the orchestra introduced him to a theosophist group.[76] Always interested in things of a mystical nature, Boudleaux joined the circle. The leader was a woman who read his horoscope and told him that his chart was one of the most auspicious she had seen. It revealed that, sometime in the future, he would meet a woman about five years his junior. Although he would not have any money when they met, through their joint efforts the couple would become immensely wealthy.[77]

Boudleaux may not have shared the same sense of recognition when he first saw Felice, but he could not have resisted the pleasure of having this captivating young woman come up to him with the offer, "Can I buy you a drink?" When he replied affirmatively, she described the encounter as "love at first splash, because I turned on the water and drenched him. That water arced and messed up his tuxedo." They hit it off immediately. During the band's next break, Boudleaux introduced her to a friend as his fiancée. Some forty years later when an interviewer asked Felice if she and Boudleaux communicated telepathically, Felice replied, "Yes, we do it all the time." And she told another interviewer, that when she saw Boudleaux, she thought to herself: "There's my future. I didn't know what the future would be, but there it was."[78]

In 1975, when interviewed for the Country Music Foundation, Felice told Patricia Hall, "I met Boudleaux, and I met the band. I had tickets to the Ice Capades and took all the wives." They wound up at the penthouse where all were staying. Boudleaux added that the suite contained a "fantastic" ballroom with a piano where they rehearsed and "enough bedrooms for every couple."[79] This romantic setting seemed to promise a relationship that would be both fruitful and mutually reinforcing.

Felice was always the most direct and outspoken of the two. Interviewed by John Rumble for the Foundation again eight years later, the conversation went as follows:

> RUMBLE: So, you met Boudleaux there in the hotel. How long was it between the time you met and the time you got married?
> FELICE: Five days. In five days, we took off and we left it all.
> RUMBLE: You saw a good thing and you latched onto it, right?
> FELICE: [Laughs] Yes, I guess so.[80]

★ ★ ★ ★ ★

Chapter 2

"WHAT DID THE LITTLE LADY DO TODAY?"

Not long after they met, Boudleaux told his future wife that the name Matilda did not suit her. When she asked, "What suits you?" he responded, "Felice," since she looked so happy. Because of its French origin, Felice also sounded good when paired with Boudleaux. She agreed. According to her future daughter-in-law Lee Wilson, Boudleaux told Felice, a few days later, "We've got to do something about that 'Scaduto.'" Felice again asked, "What suits you?" and he replied, "Bryant." She liked to claim, "Boudleaux titled me."[1]

Becoming "Felice" signaled the major transformation in her life. Her relationship with Boudleaux would become legendary for its fervor and commitment, and their marriage soon developed into the songwriting partnership that neither previously would have envisioned.

When telling of his parents' nearly instantaneous mutual attraction, Del quoted lines from songwriter Billy Edd Wheeler's "Jackson": they "got married in a fever, hotter than a pepper sprout."[2] Sure enough, Felice and Boudleaux ran off together before she had even secured her divorce from Geraci, although it had been almost two years since they lived together. According to an article in *Billboard*, Felice said that she and Boudleaux had been "married by God" in their own private ceremony five days after they met. After the stint at the Schroeder ended, they relocated to Cincinnati where Boudleaux had a gig at the Florentine Room in the Gibson Hotel. For eight months, he entertained there during the dinner hour, then went "over to the Sidewalk Café that had a little postage stamp floor in the middle of it, and played there until midnight."[3]

While his family knew nothing, her mother was horrified. When Felice disappeared with Boudleaux, she told no one of her intentions, not even her sister. Katherine was so distraught when she found her daughter miss-ing that she contacted the FBI. According to the Bryant sons and Felice's sister, Kitty, Katherine tried to drag Felice by the hair from the hotel where the young couple were staying in Milwaukee, and she broke her daughter's nose in the process.[4]

When Felice refused to give up the relationship, Katherine, however, helped her obtain a divorce from Geraci. Five days after she received the decree, Felice and Boudleaux were married on September 5, 1945, in Cov-ington, Kentucky, just south of Cincinnati. Covington was known as a place where marriages could be performed quickly. Rev. Paul Eninger officiated. He was a preacher at Christ's Gospel Mission, who advertised his services with a neon sign. Felice and Boudleaux asked the cab driver who drove them for their blood tests and marriage license to serve as best man. The bride wore slacks; the groom wore his tuxedo, because he was performing later that night.[5]

Boudleaux may have insisted on renaming his wife, but Felice's effect on her husband was even more profound. As he mentioned time and again: "I'd still be playing the fiddle if it hadn't been for my wife. Without Felice, I'd be a complete nothing."[6] Boudleaux was on the wagon the week he met Felice, and she fully intended that he stay that way. Making sure he maintained his sobriety became her first major marital crusade. Meeting Boudleaux fulfilled her childhood dream—he even sported a goatee off and on to emulate the man she had long ago imagined. Felice strongly believed in her dreams, even if she had no idea where they might lead. Now that she had married Boudleaux, she knew those dreams were becoming reality.

Aside from the fierce love they shared, Felice's dreams of glamour waited to be fulfilled. During the eight months Boudleaux worked at the Gibson Hotel, the couple lived in a two-room apartment. Because Felice had little to occupy her other than cleaning their small quarters, Boud-leaux bought her a jar of glycerin. Bored, she spent hours blowing bubbles out the window, watching as they wafted brightly into the sunlight.[7] After the gig in Cincinnati ended, the newlyweds headed for Moultrie, where Boudleaux's parents and younger siblings still lived. Moultrie remained Boudleaux's safety net; he knew he could always pick up work there with Gene Mills and his band, the Twilight Playboys, earning sixty dollars for playing three nights a week and on the radio every weekday morning.

But meeting Boudleaux's definitely sexy young wife could not have been easy for his mother, Louise. She may have found her son's attraction to Felice threatening her own primacy in his life. Although her new daughter-in-law was already an excellent cook, Louise did not want to share her son's favorite recipes, and she rejected any help Felice offered in the kitchen. Their neighbor Gail Love May remembers the many afternoons her mother welcomed Felice in her own kitchen where they would "spend hours chatting." Gail thought Felice "so fiery and joyous." Perhaps that is why she believed Mrs. Bryant worried about her stealing "Boudleaux's thunder." On the other hand, Danise, the sister nine years younger than Boudleaux and still in high school when he and Felice married, was immediately drawn to her new sister-in-law. "I was happy with Felice when he brought her home," Danise commented. "I thought she was really pretty. She brought some clothes with her that she'd outgrown, a couple of suits, that my mother made over for me. I cherished those clothes." And Felice loved Danise's long eyelashes and showed her how to curl them. Closer in age, the two bonded and remained warmly connected, though geographically apart, the rest of Felice's life.[8]

For a city girl like Felice, the small southern town offered little entertainment. Boudleaux even admitted that his hometown was "kind of dull."[9] The couple rented a small apartment, and boredom dominated Felice's days and the nights when Boudleaux worked. Years later she told an interviewer that since she was cleaning a *three*-room apartment, "we were advancing." Of course, she also complained: "My God, it took half an hour to clean this damned apartment. There is nowhere to go. I mean, what could you do?"[10] Southern mores seemed both random and mysterious; Moultrie itself did not suit her. Like Louise Bryant, the town did not know what to make of this determined young woman. Felice went to the local pool room to try her hand at the game and many years later claimed to have been the only woman ejected from this typically males-only environment.[11]

After they had been married about a year, Felice found that reading alone provided little respite. When her well-worn *The Best Loved Poems of the American People* no longer completely sustained her, Felice said, "I went back to an old device when I got bored or lonely while he'd be away. I went to writing poetry. I loved to write. It didn't have proper rhythm; it was out of meter. But if it sounded right to me, that was all that mattered."[12] She asked her mother to send her the box full of poetry that Felice had saved, but her mother had already thrown it away. "She didn't care," Felice reported, once again realizing how Katherine had belittled or stifled her creativity. That recognition reinforced her idea that her life meant nothing before she met Boudleaux.[13] Her mother's actions did not deter her; she continued to write. When Boudleaux came home after a gig and asked, "What did the little lady do today?"[14] Did he mean the question to be condescending, or was that just the accepted parlance of mid-twentieth-century husbands and wives? Regardless of the intent, Felice was proud she had something to show him beyond their spic and span apartment. She told Ralph Emery in a television interview, "And, so he'd pat me on the head and say, 'Oh, that's good.' And he'd fix it up, and it got so it was *fun*. And it didn't cost a thing. . . . He knew I was writing, and then he decided to get in on it with me, and we had so much fun that he couldn't wait to get home at night to see what the heck we were gonna come up with."[15] Felice told another interviewer that, during these early months of songwriting, "It was ours. Our little pastime. Saved money and kept mama happy. It was our little thing. He [Boudleaux] didn't see it as a business."[16]

As Boudleaux said years later:

I have to give Felice full credit for getting us started on this because without her having written all this stuff and having had it available when I'd get home from the dance job at night, I'd never even thought about writing songs for a living or even trying to get into it. I thought it was a closed shop. But she would write while I was out working a job, and I'd come home at night, and she'd say, "Hey! Look what I wrote today," and it was pretty good, and I thought I'd better get in on some of this. I did get really interested in it, and the first thing you know, we were just writing songs by the gross loads. And in a very few months, we had about eighty songs. At that point we decided we ought to get serious about trying to be writers.[17]

Felice may have begun with poetry and some hint of melody, which Boudleaux polished, but very soon the roles became blurred. Both wrote lyrics and composed melodies. The Bryants were serious enough to begin copyrighting their songs, and the *Catalog of Copyright Entries, 1946*, lists at least twenty-two from Moultrie, with two under Felice's name alone. Ernie Lee and His Southerners, a popular Cincinnati group, recorded their

"1, 2, 3, 4, 5 foot 6," which was copyrighted on May 3, 1949. It was released on RCA Victor in 1949.[18]

Writing together enflamed the sparks already glowing between the two. Felice found that she "couldn't wait until Boudleaux got home." Although he often arrived in the wee hours of the morning, she was "wide awake" and ready to write. "Bless his heart," she recalled, "we'd get so carried away with this stuff, and he had a six o'clock [morning] radio show. So, he'd do the radio show and then come back and sleep. Since we didn't have money to go anywhere and we were having so much fun doing this, it really entertained us completely. On Sundays we'd go to his mother's and we'd sing our week's-worth of new tunes for the family."[19] Louise Bryant, however, hardly enjoyed these weekly occasions. She did not want to believe that Felice had initiated the songwriting. Louise wanted to emphasize her son's role in the material the young couple were producing, since she clearly resented Felice's input.[20]

While the couple had no idea how to find outlets for their efforts, Boudleaux began buying weekly copies of *Billboard*, a music and entertainment trade journal. The two would scour it for any names of music publishers, radio stations, or anyone with "the remotest connection to the music business." Boudleaux wrote from fifteen to twenty letters a week, hoping to get some positive response, but most of the requests were returned unopened.[21] They got some encouragement from Leonard Rienisch, whom Boudleaux had known from WSB in Atlanta. By this time, Reinisch was on the board of directors of the Broadcast Music Incorporated (BMI), a performing rights organization that ensures that songwriters, composers, and publishers get paid whenever their music is performed. He accepted one of their songs for the BMI Publishing Division, which was never recorded.[22] But Boudleaux and Felice refused to give up.

When Patricia Hall interviewed the Bryants in 1975, Felice told her that, although she knew Boudleaux had written an instrumental or two before they met, she had no idea he had actually had any material recorded. "This only showed up after, my God, after we were into writing," she reported. Then self-deprecatingly, she claimed, "I'm a simple writer. I could not elucidate. I would not be able to use flowery language. I would just say what I wanted to, and they happened to be song lyrics." Since Boudleaux had formal training as a musician, he was able to transcribe the tunes that Felice was humming, and then he added to them to enhance their musicality. He concluded, "The bulk of our songs have been written together."[23]

Hall wanted to know more about how the Bryants approached their collaboration. Boudleaux explained: "When we were working together, we'd throw ideas back and forth and each of us has to examine the idea and we discuss whether it's applicable, or whether or not it's the best way that we think [it] could be said, or whether it's too bookish, whether it has an easy conversational-type flow and, eventually, we come up with a line that we both agree on." Hall asked whether they "throw lines verbally to each other," and Felice responded: "I throw them in. He throws them out. [laughter] That's where we argue. Now bookish, I would never get bookish. Boudleaux would. The thing that we as writers, and all writers, have to watch out for is ego. Oh, wow! When you think you have got the message for the world, throw that thing away." The dialogue between Boudleaux and Felice proceeded with almost none of Hall's intercession, and their interrupting one another gives a real sense of the intimate comfort of their relationship:

> BOUDLEAUX: If you have a line that might express a thought and abso-
> lutely succinctly, exactly precisely—
> FELICE: But grammatically wrong.
> BOUDLEAUX:—and have the absolute—wait, that isn't what I mean.
> FELICE: Oh, there goes a line.
> BOUDLEAUX: The absolute right shade of meaning all the way, and yet
> there might be some word in there that is sort of an insecure word
> or the word that isn't used very much or a word that sounds just a
> little bit phony, even though it's a completely proper and excellent
> word, you would—we normally would—throw that word away.
> FELICE: We know this is—
> BOUDLEAUX: If it sounds in the least bit stilted—
> FELICE: This is where we argue. His idea of what sounds phony doesn't
> necessarily sound phony to me. Now we will have discussion on that.
> BOUDLEAUX: So then, we'll have—yeah.
> FELICE: This is where we go back and forth. Now, if it says it in poor
> grammar, very poor grammar, if it says it, I believe in leaving it.
> HALL: Do you believe in leaving it, too?
> BOUDLEAUX: If it absolutely expresses a thing or if it's in the vernacular
> of the rest of the song.

FELICE: Oh, see, there's another point, now. If it's in the vernacular of the rest of the song, which could be a perfect piece of grammar, but then all of a sudden, the words 'ain't got no time' wouldn't fit. We would argue because—

BOUDLEAUX: I think that if you're writing a song, whenever, especially, it's hopefully going to be a sophisticated type song, then you would want the whole thing to have that flavor. But if the song isn't that sort of song, then—

FELICE: But sometimes it's very human sounding, too, when it's going along in a sophisticated manner. If it becomes very human, you leave it alone.

BOUDLEAUX: What you're getting now is a very—

FELICE: If you stick to precise sophistication, you become phony.

BOUDLEAUX: What we're doing—

FELICE: Then the word "phony" fits.

BOUDLEAUX: What we're doing now is an example of exactly the way we write together.

FELICE: The way we write.

BOUDLEAUX: Except that there's no particular—in the case of song that we'd be writing, there would be something explicit. This, though, in general, is the way we work together.[24]

When Felice spoke to interviewer Greg Tornquist in 1994, he asked: "Where did the song ideas come from?" Felice replied: "From both of us, I guess. When we were working, we were working all the time. All the time. It's like exercise. Muscles happen if you're steady, and we had muscle. Ideas just popped into our heads."[25]

Betty Gallup, a publicist and writer who interviewed the Bryants, appreciated the chemistry between them:

Many times, during the afternoon, one would start to say something, and the other would finish it. Signals would flash, and one would subside so the other could talk. Boudleaux would start to say something, and Felice would start to interrupt, and he would hold up his hand and say, "Wait, let me finish this," and Felice would stop and sit quietly on the edge of her chair just waiting for him to finish his thought so she could jump in with her two cents the minute he did. Then Felice would say something, and Boudleaux would jump in, and she would hold up a finger and say, "wait, wait, I lost my thread. Wait a minute, I can see it dangling," and she would pick up her thought and continue. . . . They remind me of a mountain and a bubbling stream. Boudleaux stands like a tall and majestic mountain, and Felice is like a merry, bubbling stream, laughing and splashing her way down the face of the mountain and enjoying every minute of it.[26]

After living in the three-room apartment for more than a year, the Bryants decided to buy a small travel trailer and park it on Boudleaux's parents' property while he and Felice were in Moultrie. If he picked up a gig elsewhere, they could simply move their home with them behind their 1937 Oldsmobile without having to spend nights away from one another. They'd also avoid paying for nights on the road or for rent on an apartment. But even with Moultrie as a place to fall back on, the newlyweds did not have it easy. They spent some time in Chicago not long after they married, and they went through "rough sledding" there. At one point, Boudleaux had to stuff newspapers into his jacket as protection against the chill winds from Lake Michigan.[27]

By mid-1946, Boudleaux received welcome news far from the Windy City. A promoter in Los Angeles with whom Boudleaux had worked earlier was putting a trio together. He invited Boudleaux to join and asked him to find a third musician to complete the group. So Boudleaux wrote his friend Kelland Clark, who was living in Lincoln, Nebraska:

> [The promoter] has terrific contacts. He says that decent trios out there are getting $400 and more per week when they're fairly well known. He also says that he can get $325 for a trio to start and break it in, with bigger money later. I know him well. He is honest, fair, a swell singer and guitar man and a good guy. We would split the take evenly. He said that our transportation will come out of the first two weeks' salary (which adds up to him paying an equal share of our fare).
>
> You son of a bitch, I will really be p.o.'d if you ignore me this time. There is a chance to build into a "name" unit. He already has a good name in the cocktail field. He wants me to get a third man and for my money you're it. There will be good music to play, good money to make, good times to be had, ritzy joints to play in and a chance to make better dough and—no cowboys on the stationery.

And no 2 & 3 hundred-mile showdates. I don't know exactly when the deal will start. So, don't say anything yet. You'll have time to work a notice.[28]

Boudleaux's reference to cowboys suggests he was now unwilling to follow the western or hillbilly route that many entertainers traveled during the 1930s and early 1940s. Nevertheless, on many occasions he had indeed donned cowboy duds and had played whatever the market demanded; it was music per se that attracted him. So Felice and Boudleaux headed west in the travel trailer to Oakland, California. In the East Bay area, Boudleaux joined Doc Parker and Kelland Clark to form the Tri-Tones, playing in clubs in the Bay area, including El Cerrito's El Torro Club.[29] While living there Felice discovered she was pregnant with their first child.

When the Tri-Tones gig ended early in 1947, the couple returned to the Midwest. Despite the difficulties Felice always had dealing with her mother, having a baby in Milwaukee seemed most feasible because Boudleaux was hooking up with Ernie Newton and Herb Warner, playing around Chicago and Skokie as a nightclub band. Felice needed someone close in case she went into labor while Boudleaux was playing a gig.

In April Felice gave birth to their son, Dana, at St. Mary's Hospital, where Felice herself had been born. She and Boudleaux had originally decided to name the baby "Daniel" after Boudleaux's father, but somehow, Daniel became Dana, after her favorite actor, Dana Andrews. When Dana began elementary school and was teased for having a "girl's" name, he was so upset that his parents had his name changed legally to "Dane."[30]

By 1948 Boudleaux's nightclub band got a sponsor—So Easy Flour. When Roscoe "Curley" Coldiron joined them as emcee, they became the So-Easy Singers. Curley played bass; he led western swing bands out of Chicago for several years.[31] The band was paid $150 a week for doing fifteen minutes a day on the radio, which, years later, Boudleaux felt was "fantastic at that time." From Chicago they sent transcriptions of their radio shows around the country. Nine months of playing with the So-Easy Singers put the Bryants back on the road, doing two-to-three-week stints at radio stations in the South. During their travels Felice became pregnant with the couple's second child. Boudleaux told John Rumble: "We went from Selma [Alabama] to Meridian, Mississippi to Newton, Mississippi, to Andalusia, Alabama, and just all around a bunch of towns." Like Hank Penny and the Radio Cowboys, the So-Easy Singers performed on the

"Budlo" as part of the So-Easy Singers. Courtesy House of Bryant Publications.

"Kerosene Circuit," in country schools and other venues not yet electrified. Boudleaux observed: "Since we were doing some shows, and since Felice and I had already been writing some songs, we decided that we would try to write something for the act to do. And that's when we wrote 'Country Boy.' After we got that song written, we thought that that was a hit song for somebody."[32]

Boudleaux was always ambivalent when he tried to explain the meaning or origins of "Country Boy"—sometimes saying that it was a burlesque of country life but more often arguing that the song was a realistic tribute to rural people and their ways. It is true that popular music sometimes dealt with this subject—as shown in the popularity of songs such as "Feudin', Fussin', and Fightin'" and tunes heard in Broadway productions such as *Annie Get Your Gun* or *Oklahoma*. The Bryants were acutely aware of this music, but Boudleaux was also very familiar with rural life and tried to chronicle it in a faithful and loving way. He later told John Rumble: "It wasn't a self-parody. It is absolutely a faithful example of the people that were living out on farms at that time. The humor is as true to life as it was at that time on the farm, out in the country, down home."[33]

> I'm a plain old country boy
> A cornbread loving country boy
> I raise Cain on Saturday

> But I go to church on Sunday
> I'm a plain old country boy
> A cornbread loving country boy
> I'll be looking over that old gray mule
> When the sun comes up on Monday.[34]

Boudleaux and Felice were certain they had a good song, but they still lacked someone willing to record it. As the So-Easy experience came to an end, they headed back toward Moultrie in the spring of 1948 to await the coming of their second child. They passed through Cincinnati, parking their trailer across the Ohio River in Ludlow, Kentucky, for a few days. While there, they visited with Boudleaux's old friend Rome Johnson. Boudleaux had known Rome since their days in Detroit when, as staff musicians for Ford Motor Company, they performed at social functions for the industry, while also playing on WXYZ Radio. Rome was from Winchester, Kentucky, and had been making music since 1932 when he played for the Kentucky String Ticklers on WLAP in Lexington. By the time Felice and Boudleaux came through Cincinnati, Rome was working there on WLW Radio. Fortuitously, he was also under contract to Fred Rose, for whom he recorded such popular songs as "Waltz of the Wind" and "No One Will Ever Know."[35]

One night, Rome invited the Bryants over for supper. Even at that point, Felice told an interviewer years later, "Boudleaux still hadn't considered us writers." But while the two wives were cooking spaghetti, Rome asked Boudleaux what he had been doing. Felice piped right in and said, "Writing songs. Show him 'Country Boy, Boudleaux.'" Rome liked the song and wanted to record it. He called Fred Rose immediately with the idea and introduced him to Boudleaux. Rose asked for a demo, and they made one at Rome's dining room table, with a Wilcox-Gay wire recorder. When Rose received the demo, he told Rome that the song was good, but that it really didn't fit his pop baritone vocal sound. Instead, Fred started shopping it around to other potential singers.[36]

In the years that followed, Fred Rose became a mentor to the two budding songwriters and a father figure to Felice. Rose was born in Evansville, Indiana, in 1897, but he grew up in St. Louis. There he sang for tips in saloons as a child and dropped out of school by the fourth grade. He moved to Chicago in about 1917, where he made rolls for player pianos and performed in bars and saloons and as a silent-film pianist. In the 1920s he

Fred Rose, Boudleaux and Felice's cherished mentor. Courtesy Nate Gibson.

made a few recordings for the Brunswick label, generally accompanying his light tenor voice on the piano. He wrote such songs as "Deed I Do," "Honest and Truly," and "Red Hot Mama," the latter performed with great zest by Sophie Tucker.

Rose moved to Nashville in 1933 and did a daily radio show on WSM. Performing as "the Song Doctor," he capitalized on his ability to make up a song immediately when presented with an idea. In 1938 he began traveling between Nashville, New York, and Hollywood, where he collaborated with Gene Autry on at least seventeen movies. One of these songs, "Be Honest with Me," was nominated for the Best Song Oscar in 1941. During these years he became increasingly committed to country music, supplying songs for people such as Ray Whitley, Tex Ritter, Gene Autry, Bob Wills, and Roy Acuff. Some of these songs became perennials such as "No One Will Ever Know" (written with veteran song plugger Mel Foree); "Roly Poly" (still a standard in western swing); and "Blue Eyes Crying in the Rain" (revived and made an international favorite in 1975 by Willie Nelson).

In 1941 Rose returned to Nashville. The following year he established Acuff-Rose Publishing House with twenty-five thousand dollars in seed money from the famous country singer Roy Acuff; then he organized Hickory Records in 1954. By this time, he was spending much time as a producer and promoter of young talent. He mentored many singers and songwriters, most notably Hank Williams. Rose's close relationship with Mitch Miller of Columbia Records inaugurated the "crossover" of country songs into popular music.[37]

Rose did not make an immediate decision on "Country Boy," but he began negotiating with various performers. In sounding out singers such as Carson Robison and Tex Williams, he seems to have toyed with the idea of presenting the song as a recitation.[38] He eventually settled on Little Jimmy Dickens, an Opry performer who had previously recorded a hit version of "Take an Old Cold Tater and Wait," a song first used by some of the southern gospel quartets as comic relief.

Dickens was born in Bolt, West Virginia; he was noted for his diminutive size (standing four feet ten inches high) and big voice. He was a bundle of energy who became typecast as a singer of novelty songs with a rustic flair. Almost immediately, Dickens began singing "Country Boy" on road shows and at the Opry, where he was called upon to perform repeated encores. Felice later told an interviewer that the first time they ever heard anyone perform one of their songs was on their radio set in Moultrie: "Jimmy Dickens was on the stage of the Grand Ole Opry singing encores of 'Country Boy'. Fred Rose called down and said, 'Hey, we need more verses. This kid can't get out there and keep singing the same lines.' So, we wrote fourteen more verses for Jimmy. Listening to that on the radio was pure manna, truly." Rose had actually written Boudleaux on March 28, 1949, telling him that Jimmy Dickens "has tied up the Grand Ole Opry the last two Saturday nights with 'Country Boy,' and he needs about two more funny verses for the song. Will you get these to me so he can add them next Saturday?" Rose passed on this sage advice: "Be sure to keep them clean as the powers that be won't let him do them if they are the least bit shady." Boudleaux and Felice may have sent all fourteen verses to Rose and Dickens, and let them choose the two that they deemed most suitable. Then Rose conveyed the best news the Bryants could ever have hoped for: "Jimmy will record the song for Columbia within the next two weeks, and we will go after a quick release, so don't let anyone have this song until we get the Dickens record out, or it will mess up the deal."[39]

"Country Boy" may have been a good song—and one in which the Bryants had staked their dreams—but it did not generate immediate revenues for the struggling little family. The little family, in fact, grew from three members to four in the fall of 1948, when son Del was born in Moultrie on October 5. It was gratifying to learn of the song's warm reception on the Grand Ole Opry, but Dickens had not yet recorded the number. The future soon brightened when Boudleaux received a message from Rose asking him to come to Nashville. Recognizing the family's current economic difficulties, Rose paid Boudleaux's train fare to Nashville, put him up in the Noel Hotel, and gave him seventy-five dollars for expenses, assuring him that the money would not come out of future royalties. The morning after Boudleaux's arrival, Rose picked him up at his hotel. After a harrowing drive to Rose's home (he was both visually impaired and a careless driver), Rose listened to a small batch of songs that Boudleaux had brought. When asked, years later, whether Fred Rose was as Boudleaux had imagined him, he replied: "I didn't really know anything about the guy. I didn't know anything about his work. I didn't know what he'd written. I didn't know anything about songwriters except for Irving Berlin. He's the only one I'd ever heard of." And Boudleaux couldn't name one Fred Rose song.[40]

Rose loved the Bryants' songs and asked Boudleaux to send more. While Rose's response undoubtedly bolstered the couple's faith in their songwriting, they may not immediately have recognized the import of this meeting as the beginning of their lifelong career in country music. Jimmy Dickens recorded "Country Boy" on April 11, 1949, at the Castle Studio in the Tulane Hotel in Nashville. The song soon rose to No. 7 on the country charts. As Boudleaux later declared, it "opened the door."[41] When Nashville

DJ and songwriter Joe Allison interviewed Felice in 1989, he said: "You got a hit—the first thing you did was a hit, wasn't it?" To which, she replied: "We had the market cornered. And I thought we'd better run with it and run fast before someone else catches on."[42]

In the meantime, the Bryants were surviving on Boudleaux's gigs with Gene Mills and the Twilight Playboys and the good graces of his Moultrie parents. As a consequence, when their old friend Curley Coldiron told them about a job in Green Bay, Wisconsin, that would pay $150 per week, they decided to accept the offer.

In the late spring of 1949, while Felice stayed at Brice's Trailer Park taking care of the kids and the family dog, Boudleaux joined a group styled as Mack and Sandy's Traveling Tent Show, a rural vaudeville act. Mack and Sandy, who believed that their "whip act" was sensational, had grand ideas about taking their tent show to towns throughout the area covered by WBAY Radio. Unfortunately, audiences did not agree, and the troupe folded after two weeks. Boudleaux told an interviewer: "Here we are in Green Bay, we're stranded, we had put all our money in a trailer, and there was no way to leave Green Bay; we had no money." By this time, "Country Boy" was generating some sales in the South but was unknown in northeastern Wisconsin, where Boudleaux and Felice had to contend with polka music and songs like "Blue Skirt Waltz." Without seeing other income-producing options, Boudleaux decided that he and Felice would perform as a duo, doing the pop tunes of the day, with the sole accompaniment of his guitar.[43]

A local bar owner, Clifford R. "Popeye" Anderson (the proprietor of Popeye's Tavern), took Boudleaux at his word that he and Felice were a seasoned act and hired them on a trial basis for a weekend show at seventy-five dollars. Felice remembered Popeye saying to Boudleaux: "Well, looking at her, she's show business, but I don't know about you. You don't look show business." She elaborated: "People have mistaken Boudleaux for a professor or medical man all through the years; he just never looked like what they thought a musician looked like." In a House of Bryant interview, they remembered Popeye told the couple: "I'll try you here in the club for a week, or a couple of days, and if you work out I'll book you out of the club."[44]

Felice was actually mortified at the prospect of public entertaining, because she had done little singing since her childhood days in Milwaukee

Felice poses with sons, Del and Dane, in front of their travel trailer. Courtesy House of Bryant Publications.

performing on Cousin Betty's radio show. Boudleaux could easily sympa-
thize with her hesitation, since his guitar skills were rusty, and the two had
little experience singing together. The only songs Felice knew were old pop
standards. They would have to wing it. They bought a music stand and
several songbooks from local magazine racks. Performing three nights a
week, they sang both individually and as a duet, accompanied only by
Boudleaux's guitar. Years later, Felice told interviewers: "For lack of anything better to do, we invited the drunks at the bar to sing along with us,
and we had sing-alongs, and they loved it." To their surprise, the act went
over so well that Popeye began finding other places for them to play. Felice
claimed: "We became a hit. We were an overnight sensation. We even got a
radio show out of it."[45]

Pleased with the Bryants' act, Popeye managed to book a morning
show, the *Coffee Clutch*, on the local radio station, WBAY. Felice thought
that Popeye's showing the station manager *Billboard* ads for "Country Boy"
may have helped with their being accepted. Boudleaux, on the other
hand, believed that the folks in Green Bay may have been more familiar
with the Homer and Jethro cover of the song than with Jimmy Dickens's
original. Homer and Jethro, who had recorded the parody with June
Carter, were a well-established act in Chicago. Beginning for fifteen minutes, Felice and Boudleaux's show soon grew to a thirty-minute slot, which
finally expanded to an hour. Felice read recipes; she and Boudleaux sang
the hit songs of the day; and they had actors put on silly, hastily improvised,
and (in Felice's words) "dumbass skits." Making about seventy-five dollars a
week, the duo apparently became sensations in Green Bay. Fan mail began
to arrive, and the station even opened its doors for a live audience. Felice
said: "we weren't very good, but we were a hit. Don't ask how or why, but we
were a hit."[46]

Although the Bryants ultimately enjoyed the Green Bay experience,
which was financially life-saving, it only lasted about six months. They
never intended their stay to be more than a stopgap to tide them over until
the hoped-for song royalties began to roll in. As Felice said: "we didn't want
to spend the rest of our lives on a radio station in Green Bay."[47] When the
first portents of winter appeared, they reflected on the state of their non-
winterized Mississippi-made trailer and decided it could never withstand
the icy blasts off the bay. But as they headed back toward Moultrie, they
could take satisfaction in the money they had made, and Felice could take

Felice and Boudleaux were instantly popular as performers on WBAY. Courtesy of the Country Music Hall of Fame® and Museum.

pride in having finally tasted the thrill of successfully entering show business, even if it had occurred only at a small-town level.

When they reached the northern outskirts of Chicago, the Bryants' long-suffering trailer came loose from their car, left the highway, and became wedged between a telephone pole and a big tree. The real damage, though, came when the wrecker's dolly came loose and rammed through their trailer door. Luckily, no one was hurt, but they had to face the expenses of both an unpaid-for trailer and the damages inflicted upon it, as well as car payments. The Green Bay money soon vanished, and they faced the prospect of limping home with very little to show for their northern "successes."

Once again, Fred Rose came to their rescue. As they drove through Nashville, they could not have known it would soon be their home and the center of their eventual preeminence. In a phone call to Rose, they were told that they had made four hundred dollars from "Country Boy." They soon realized that they would have made even more—largely through the many performances made by Jimmy Dickens—if they had licensed the song through BMI instead of American Society of Composers, Artists, and Publishers (ASCAP). Against Fred Rose's advice, Boudleaux had registered the song with ASCAP because this prestigious company had been the home of such revered songwriters as Irving Berlin, Sammy Cahn, and George Gershwin. In contrast to BMI, though, ASCAP did not pay non-members performance money. This was a lesson well learned. At the time, however, Felice argued: "Four hundred dollars looked like four hundred thousand dollars."[48]

When they looked for a place to spend the night, the first trailer camp rejected them. The Bryants believed they had been refused because they looked like a family of gypsies. This perception perhaps was fed by the appearance of Felice and her two black-haired and olive-complexioned boys, and by Boudleaux, whose dark eyes and visage seemed to reflect his presumed part-Cherokee and Creek ancestry. Fortunately, they soon found refuge at the Rainbow Trailer Court on Dickerson Road, managed by good-hearted Lonnie Polk. He took Boudleaux's word that his backdated check would soon be covered by sufficient funds. Felice told Joe Allison: "We Stopped at the Rainbow, and Boudleaux didn't have a penny. And he wrote a check for fifteen dollars, and told Lonnie it wasn't any good, but it would be good in two weeks. Could he hold it? Lonnie thought he'd never heard such a story in his life. And he said, 'Yeah, Buddy, I'll cash it.' So, he cashed that fifteen dollars, and we made the rest of the way to Moultrie." Polk seemed to have sensed, almost at first glance, both Boudleaux's integrity and his family's desperate circumstances. Polk's generosity endeared him to the couple, and they remained lifelong friends. He even served as a pallbearer at Boudleaux's funeral many years later.[49]

As the Bryants finally rolled into Moultrie in the early fall of 1949, they arrived with the prestige of having written a country music hit. The home folks were highly impressed, particularly when Jimmy Dickens came to visit the Bryants. Neighbor Gail Love May, a teenager at the time, remembers the event with delight: "When 'Country Boy' came out, I got to meet Jimmy Dickens at the end of the lane."[50]

Boudleaux again found work with his old reliable friends, Gene Mills and the Twilight Playboys, but he and Felice could now also begin to do their own shows. They promoted themselves as the writers of "Country Boy" on posters they tacked up in towns where they were playing. Felice recalled the differences in the ways the two families responded to the couple's vocational choices. "My family thought we were bums, ramblers. They kept wanting us to settle down. When we went to Moultrie, the red carpet came out. We were 'world travelers' and were treated like celebrities. And we could leave the babies with Boudleaux's mom at night." With Grandmother Bryant now babysitting the boys, Felice and Boudleaux concocted a ninety-minute show playing from three to four nights a week at theaters and schoolhouses in Georgia and Alabama. They began making from sixty to eighty dollars a night.[51]

Although Boudleaux and Felice welcomed this performance money, it permitted only a humble style of life. The promise of greater economic security, as well as access to the country music industry, came in early 1950 when Fred Rose arranged an introduction for Boudleaux to the New York publisher Nat Tannen in Nashville.[52] During a meeting at the Andrew Jackson Hotel, Tannen, who for several years had been the distributor for Acuff-Rose material in New York, asked Boudleaux to be his southern representative. The salary was to be only thirty-five dollars a week, but it permitted Boudleaux to promote the Bryants' songs, and it allowed him to reserve some songs for Fred Rose. Nat Tannen had entered the music business as an employee for Irving Berlin, but he became involved in hillbilly music while working on the road for another New York publisher, Sol Bourne. Tannen became converted to the genre in Texas when he heard a couple of songs by Bob Wills, "San Antonio Rose" and "Steel Guitar Rag," which he brought into the Bourne catalog. He established his own business in 1947 with headquarters at 146 West Fifty-Fourth Street, the nerve center of country music in New York. He became the distributor for a score of publishers, circulated sheet music through his subsidiary Keys Music, and published his own songs. His building also housed the Rosalie Allen Music Store (named for its singing proprietor), the only significant country music retail store in New York City.[53] Hiring Boudleaux Bryant meant that Tannen was now ready to launch a nationwide campaign.

Boudleaux was already working hard for Tannen when he and Felice decided, probably sometime in early June 1950, that the time was ripe for a permanent move to Nashville. On the way, their 1937 Oldsmobile died in Macon, Georgia. After finding a place in a trailer court, Boudleaux got a job with a dance band headed by local WNEX Radio DJ and country singer Charles "Peanut" Faircloth. Born in Mitchell County, Georgia, he was afflicted with polio in childhood and only reached the height of four feet eight inches, the basis of his nickname.

By the time the Bryants arrived in Macon, Faircloth had become the host of *The Hoedown Party*, carried on WNEX on the Mutual Broadcasting System. Boudleaux got an immediate job as a fiddler in Faircloth's band, and Felice was soon taken on as a singer. Felice was still resentful many years later when she told John Rumble: "I did some singing. Everybody got me for nothing. Faircloth got me for nothing; all the shows they just paid Boudleaux. They got me for nothing. Free."[54]

The group played at small towns in the area, but also in a drive-in circuit. Peanut sang and served as guitarist, Boudleaux played the fiddle, and Felice sang. During this financially stressful time in Macon, Nat Tannen expressed his sympathy for the Bryants' plight: "I'm glad to hear that you have been playing with Peanut Faircloth. Believe me, Boudleaux, I have no objection if you were to play with some of the boys every night, as I am sure no one could realize better than I how difficult it is to work when there are financial problems hanging over your head."[55]

Peanut later said that Boudleaux was, in his opinion, "the greatest fiddle player that ever was. He could play the violin like Chet Atkins could play the guitar—playing rhythm and melody at the same time." At one appearance, "Peanut recalled that he was calling a square dance, and kept having trouble staying on the beat because of Bryant's unique fiddling style. He paused calling the dance to say, 'Boudleaux, you ——, you messing me up.' According to Faircloth, Boudleaux was 'playing the melody on the treble strings of the fiddle and the boogie woogie on the others. I couldn't call the dance.'"[56]

After spending approximately three months in Macon, Boudleaux and Felice hitched up their trailer again, this time to a newly purchased 1948 Buick and at last hit the remaining miles of the road to Nashville. Their short-lived days as public entertainers had ended. Although they would make a few recordings in their early years in Nashville, the Bryants' full commitment to songwriting had finally arrived, almost exactly five years to the day after their marriage in Covington.

$\star$ $\star$ $\bigstar$ $\star$ $\star$

Chapter 3

SPAGHETTI AND SONG-PLUGGING

The Bryants rolled into Nashville on September 1, 1950, towing their sea-soned but battered and road-weary trailer behind their new Buick. Like the boll weevil described in the Tex Ritter ballad, they were "just lookin' for a home."[1] They returned to Rainbow Trailer Court where Lonnie Polk had accepted them so warmly that desperate night about one year earlier. Rainbow and other related parks had already gained the reputation as "hillbilly heaven," because of the high number of country musicians living there. Felice joked that they included the "wannabes, would-bes, and weres." But one of the trailer parks once had been the residence of the "king of country music," Roy Acuff.[2] Such an environment allowed Boudleaux and Felice to find easy camaraderie among their fellow musicians, sharing potluck suppers and occasional drinks at the café and ballroom on the premises.

Boudleaux did not lack for work in their new city of choice, but from 1949 onward, the demanding job of song-plugging with Nat Tannen kept him away from home more than he or Felice might have anticipated. While no longer making one-night stands as a musician, he was often on the road. These grueling trips involved constantly visiting musicians, disc jockeys, and jukebox vendors in cities around the South, promoting records and soliciting new songs. Sometimes his itinerary took him through Moultrie where he could spend some time with his parents. But the longer and more punishing drives to places such as Louisville, Atlanta, Birmingham, Jacksonville, and even New York City, meant lonely nights in hotels—without the anchoring of family—and dealing with the temptations of alcohol when wooing DJs and prospective clients. Those temptations also existed in Nashville, since Boudleaux often found it necessary to provide alcoholic libations for local musicians and DJs. His expense accounts, for example, list bottles of whiskey for Cowboy Copas and Guy Willis, and a bottle of wine for Chet Atkins.[3]

The Bryant family about the time they moved to Nashville. Courtesy House
of Bryant Publications.

Nashville, though, would have presented a forbidding environment for
the Bryants without the presence of Fred Rose. In their first four years,
Rose became a constant confidant and mentor to Felice and Boudleaux,
introducing them to the vagaries and machinations of the music business
and giving them vital pointers about the way a song should be written. The
fact that both Boudleaux and Fred had been alcoholics gave them a special
way of relating to each other and understanding life. They spent many

hours discussing Rose's belief in the wondrous qualities of Christian
Science, the religious faith he credited both with saving his life during an
earlier suicidal period and with keeping him sober afterward.[4]

Felice did not meet Rose until he drove out to the trailer park to see
them, in late 1950 or early 1951. "My first impression of Fred was through
Boudleaux, so I loved what I was hearing. And then when I met the man,
well, that solidified it. I was in love. I never met a more beautiful person, next
to Boudleaux." In addition to his kindness, charm, and unselfishness, Felice
was also intrigued by Fred's sartorial elegance, by his tendency to wear
flannel slacks, a silk shirt, and a fedora. They trusted Fred so completely
that when Del and Dane were still preschoolers, the boys had to memorize
a telephone number—CY78591—that they should call if they were ever in
need of help when they were left in a babysitter's care. That phone number
was the office of Acuff-Rose.[5]

While these personal characteristics were endearing, Felice and Boudleaux felt that they also owed Rose a life-changing indebtedness. His
patient tutelage helped them identify and tailor songs that appealed to
the singers who needed them and their fans who welcomed them. They
had not earlier aimed their songwriting at any target audience, and some
other mentor might have turned their interests toward pop, Broadway,
or another form of music. Working with Rose's well-informed guidance,
they chose and helped to grow both country music and Nashville's identity
with the genre.

On the whole, Nashville was not an easy or welcoming city for blue-
collar musicians. With a population of 321,758 in 1950, the progressive city
nevertheless still exhibited marks of its rural past even as it struggled with
its evolving identity. One student of Nashville history, Benjamin Houston,
said "anyone looking to comprehend Nashville's history must hold these
tensions in place—rural and urban, polished elites and gritty common
folk, a backward-looking past, and a forward-looking gaze—to discern the
city's character."[6] The civic elite justifiably took great pride in the city's
educational and cultural assets. They proudly touted its fine universities
(both white and black) and the replica of the Parthenon, constructed in
1897 to grace the site of Tennessee's Centennial Exposition that was held
in Centennial Park. The same elite had mixed feelings about the influx of
country folk who gathered at the Ryman Auditorium every Saturday night
to enjoy an evening of hillbilly music, and about the entertainers who were

busily producing phonograph records that circulated throughout the nation. Remembering those early days in the city, and the people who looked down on both the music and those performing it, Felice said: "I thought Nashville was one great gigantic blue nose."[7]

In contrast to the high cultural aspirations held by many, the rustic and restless nature of the Rainbow Trailer Court indicated that Nashville, for all its pretensions to the contrary, housed a hardworking, hard-scrabble, and growing country music community with slender means—but big dreams. Like the Bryants, most of these music-making folks hoped to gain a more permanent foothold elsewhere in the city. To the bewilderment of the established cultural elites, these same hillbillies, in fact, were putting their city on the map. Thinking of the throngs who attended the Grand Ole Opry and of the recording sessions held in the city increasingly since 1949, announcer David Stone at WSM Radio had earlier described Nashville as Music City, USA, a title that heralded its prominence down through the years. Martin Hawkins, the most astute observer and chronicler of the emerging music scene in Nashville, has shown that small recording companies and producers had been hard at work since the late 1940s utilizing the talent of local musicians.[8]

In 1954 Owen and Harold Bradley inaugurated the era of Music Row—a cluster of studios that defined Nashville's prominence as a recording center—when they established their own operation on Sixteenth Avenue South. Songwriter Thomas Schuyler later commemorated this area, and the young men and women who sought fame there, in his song "Sixteenth Avenue." The lyrics describe these songwriters arriving "from the corners of the country, from the cities and the farms/with years and years of living tucked up underneath their arms."[9] But well before this time, people like Hank Snow, Eddy Arnold, Ernest Tubb, Carl Smith, Jimmy Dickens, Red Foley, Hank Williams, and other Nashville-based performers were already dominating jukeboxes across the country. Led by Hank Williams, they were beginning to see their songs "covered" by such pop entertainers as Joni James, Frankie Laine, Sarah Vaughan, and Tony Bennett.

The Bryants came to Nashville at exactly the right moment. They encountered a burgeoning country music community ripe and eager for professional songwriting, with only a handful of songwriters available—and none of these full-time. Nashville's country musicians tried to create their own material or they borrowed from an inherited storehouse of traditional songs and ballads or from those composed on Tin Pan Alley in New York City. They needed and welcomed the songs that Boudleaux and Felice had come to town to write. Once in Nashville, the Bryants realized more than ever that they were doubly blessed by their association with their mentor, Fred Rose, and with the relationship with Nat Tannen that Rose had successfully seeded on their behalf. The Tannen connection brought in a small check each week, but Boudleaux more than earned his keep. While he now had stationery that described him as "Boudleaux Bryant, Southern Representative, Tannen Music," traveling, song-plugging, and cultivating relationships kept him under a great deal of stress. Both he and Tannen fretted when DJs failed to send in their weekly reports to the *Billboard* charts, since that failure meant that singers, songwriters, and record producers were not getting their due or the chart recognition they otherwise would have received.[10]

Through these fortunate relationships and his earlier performances on WSB in Atlanta, Boudleaux was already pretty well known among musicians in Nashville. One of them, Chet Atkins, who arrived in Nashville that same year, was delighted to learn that Boudleaux was already there. Chester Burton "Chet" Atkins was living on a farm near Hamilton, Georgia, when he first became aware of the name and music of Boudleaux Bryant. Hearing the broadcasts of Hank Penny's Radio Cowboys on WSB in Atlanta, Atkins was impressed by the fiddling of one of Penny's musicians. This, he thought, was no ordinary hillbilly. Chet appreciated that Boudleaux played music with a tinge of Stephane Grapelli–inspired jazz. Atkins's introduction to Boudleaux's fiddling came "during the ASCAP radio war, when most music played was public domain material. Boudleaux would play the melody on a tune such as 'Jeannie with the Light Brown Hair,' and then he would play a chorus in a light swing fashion. This was brand new to my ears and nearly blew my mind."[11]

Born in Luttrell, Tennessee, on June 24, 1926, Atkins grew up in a very poor, but musically rich, family. His dad was a music teacher and his brother Jim a respected jazz guitarist. Living the life of an itinerant musician, Atkins made music in Knoxville and other cities throughout the South. He returned to Nashville in 1950 for a second stint as a fiddler and guitarist for the team of Mother Maybelle and the Carter Sisters. Declaring that he aspired to be like Fred Rose, Atkins soon built a versatile career as a highly desired sessions musician, producer, and oft-recorded

The Bryants with their close friend Chet Atkins. Courtesy of the Country Music Hall of Fame® and Museum.

solo guitarist, with an inventive finger and thumb style indebted to Merle Travis. Atkins's musical intuition and acquaintanceship with the styles of many musicians eventually led to his elevation to the vice presidency of RCA Victor's Nashville operations where he became one of the chief architects of "the Nashville Sound."[12]

Atkins had actually met Boudleaux during the latter's lengthy gig at the Gibson Hotel in Cincinnati. When he learned that the Bryants were living at the Rainbow Trailer Court, he made a beeline to their door. "It was just a thrill to meet somebody with that amount of talent. I don't think I'd ever run into anybody before who knew everything there is to know about playing a guitar or fiddle."[13] Before long he was a frequent visitor to the trailer camp, trading instrumental licks with Boudleaux and experimenting with song composition. Each appreciated the other's musicality, and these visits initiated the growth of a fruitful and enduring friendship. Chet and Boudleaux's collaboration produced a flurry of musical pieces, including a series of commercial jingles, and a few instrumental tunes such as "Fig Leaf Rag," "Hangover Blues," and "Downhill Drag." Three outstanding songs—"Midnight," "How's the World Treating You," and "Country

Gentleman"—won them great commercial success. Atkins also helped
Boudleaux to gain admission to the backstage scene at the Grand Ole Opry.
There, in the narrow and cramped dressing rooms of the Ryman Auditorium, the best country musicians in the world practiced and jammed while
their colleagues presented their music onstage to the Opry audiences.

This chaotic but exhilarating scene provided Boudleaux his first
important arena for the peddling of the Bryants' songs. And because her
husband's musicianship impressed those backstage, Felice said they
"couldn't believe Boudleaux gave up playing for writing. They thought this
was the dumbest thing they ever heard of," but this decision turned out to
be the smartest thing he'd done—besides marrying Felice. Those two deci-
sions were also the healthiest. According to their sons, Boudleaux could
not play the fiddle unless he'd had a drink. Ultimately, he gave up fiddle
playing completely to prevent falling off the wagon, once he'd been able to
get back on again. He acknowledged his addiction to alcohol, even though
he remained sober most of the time after the early 1950s. Dane and Del
credit both their father and their mother for keeping his alcoholism largely
under control. It did not disrupt the successful roles Boudleaux maintained as husband, father, and songwriter.[14]

Boudleaux and Felice began visiting the "mother church" of country
music very soon after their arrival in Nashville. Every Saturday evening, the
Bryant family became an integral part of the Opry community, and their
sons fondly remember being babysat by people such as the comedienne
Minnie Pearl, the ragtime pianist Del Wood, and the comedian David
"Stringbean" Akeman, while their dad made music and promoted the
couple's songs. Dane remembered the fun that he and his younger brother,
Del, had at the Opry. "We could go out front if we wanted to, or go backstage and Skeeter Davis or some other star—usually a female star—would
talk to us." And Del appreciated the fact that "everyone knew us; we knew
them. Mom was always running around and going out to the stage area and
scream and yell to the audience and hopefully encourage an encore,
because if you got an encore, your song was sung again. She would also exit
the stage and run around to the back of the auditorium, then go down into
the audience to push for additional encores. If you got three or four encores
on a song, it might take it to another level, so it could become a hit."[15]

Jamming with musicians like Grady Martin, Hank Garland, and Chet
Atkins was a pleasant diversion for Boudleaux, but peddling songs was his

real reason for being there. Musicians knew him because of his prior musical experience in Atlanta and elsewhere, but the popularity of "Country
Boy," which Jimmy Dickens was presenting to Opry audiences in multiple
encores, along with the additional verses provided by the Bryants, proved
that Boudleaux and Felice's songs were reliable commercial properties.
Opry singers did not need much encouragement to listen backstage to
their newly written material.

No one in Nashville had ever seen anyone quite like Boudleaux and
Felice Bryant. Songwriting had become their sole profession, and they pursued it relentlessly, night and day, promoting the songs from their gesta-
tion on the printed or written page to their final recording. They were
constantly writing songs, trading lyrics and melodies with each other, with
Boudleaux adding the musical notations. In the beginning, Felice tended
to be the idea person in the partnership, while Boudleaux shaped up and
perfected the resulting songs. They wrote melodies and words on any scraps
of paper that were available. This casual, if careless, practice sometimes
yielded unfortunate consequences. One day on a hasty trip to Fred Rose's
little recording studio during a heavy rainstorm, Boudleaux dropped several song manuscripts in a mud puddle. On another occasion some years
later, Boudleaux wrote a song on a grocery shopping bag. After excitedly
telling his boys on their return from school that he had written a great song
for Sonny James, he could not find the item. He asked the Bryants' longtime housekeeper, Martha Woods, if she had seen the bag, only to find out
that she had already incinerated it with other household trash.[16] Incidents
like this inspired Chet Atkins to advise them to find a more secure method
for saving their songs. Chet told them that Stephen Foster used business
ledgers to transcribe songs and suggested that they do the same.

Although the Bryants never abandoned their habit of writing on any
scrap of paper available, they nevertheless adopted Foster's practice and
eventually compiled seventeen legal-size, five-hundred-page ledgers. They
filled each with songs, lyrics, musical notations, doodles, titles, and data
concerning recordings of the songs. Some pages simply contained random
lines or melodies they might return to and develop. Boudleaux always
made a point to sketch out the melody of the song in the ledger, so it
wouldn't succumb to a faulty memory. When the boys got older and began
sharing their own song ideas with their father, he faithfully entered those
in the ledger as well.[17]

Felice and Boudleaux did make numerous demos, sometimes at home but often in Fred Rose's garage-studio on his two Ampex recording units, with Fred playing the piano and Boudleaux playing the guitar. Neither Bryant was ever completely happy with these efforts, and Felice said in fact that Boudleaux sounded "awful" before they obtained adequate equipment.[18] Boudleaux much preferred to present the songs in person, so when people started asking if he had any songs, he'd tell them: "Well, why don't you come out to the house, we'll have some spaghetti, and we'll just sit around and listen to songs. And that's the way most of those early records came about." Although the couple may have accidentally stumbled upon their successful song-plugging strategy, from their earliest days at the Rainbow Trailer Park they pushed their songs by inviting performers over to engage in what became a tried-and-true experience. First, Felice built a warm and comfortable mood with her spaghetti and other Italian dishes. She said that this cuisine was still relatively new in Nashville or, as songwriter and singer Ray Stevens said, it "was pretty exotic to a bunch of hillbillies."[19] Felice saw it that way, too. "Italian cuisine was new to those people. They were not traveled. The country field was quite innocent. We were big fish in a little pond. We turned out to be big fish because we were novel."[20] While playing his guitar after dinner, Boudleaux pitched the Bryant songs to people they'd met at the Opry, among them Cowboy Copas, Carl Smith, and Kitty Wells.

Since the trailer had no strictly segregated living spaces other than the couple's bedroom, Felice would chime in from the "kitchen" from time to time with a song suggestion or bit of harmony. The living room couch doubled as their sons' bed, but on song-plugging evenings the boys were put to sleep in their parents' room. Listening in close proximity to the musical interchange, Dane and Del absorbed what they were hearing and grew up believing that everyone's parents either wrote songs or made music. After the guests left with a song or two to record, Boudleaux and Felice carried their sleeping boys back to the front of the trailer where the couch again became their bed. Many years later, when an interviewer marveled that the Bryants were able to write and deal with their little boys in such a cramped space, Felice told him: "It got so they knew how to play in and out of what we were doing and we knew how to write over what they were doing."[21]

According to Boudleaux, during their third year in Nashville, Fred Rose thought that the Bryants needed to buy a home. The couple chose an affordable "basement house" on North Gallatin Road, in the suburb of Madison, approximately fifteen minutes north of Nashville. A contractor had begun building the house before World War II, but when the war began, materials were no longer available to finish the job. The basement of what would have become a five-room house rose about three-to-four feet above the ground, with square windows all around the top. The builder roofed the basement and was selling it as such. Rose approved and told Nat Tannen, "We ought to front them money to buy the house." Each man put up three thousand dollars, which was, as Boudleaux stressed, not a loan, but an advance on royalties. Felice explained the situation to an interviewer: "We didn't have the kind of credit set up that we could borrow for a house on our own."[22]

The cozy house had no front door, so visitors entered through a door at the back. The living room was an all-purpose space, serving as an office, a casual seating area, a recording studio, and a library. Del spoke fondly of the many times that he and Dane sat in the kitchen window, talking to their mother as they dangled their feet over the sink. Or they would leave for school by climbing out of a window, as their mother stood on the couch watching them go. Even as youngsters, they already felt great pride in their

Dane and Del playing outside of their basement house. Courtesy of the Country Music Hall of Fame® and Museum.

roles as part of "Team Bryant." With their folks working at home, the boys overheard lyrics being vetted, melodies being born, and conversations about records being made and marketed. As the boys got a little older, when their parents put them to bed, Felice would polish their shoes and lay out their clothes, and then she and Boudleaux would write all night long. After the boys went off to school, the Bryants slept until the boys came home.[23]

Small and intimate spaces like the trailer and basement house nevertheless facilitated easy social fellowship and musical interchange, with good eating as an accompaniment. Felice and Boudleaux simultaneously established a relationship of trust with other musicians, which often resulted in long-term friendships and additional song placements. Best of all, the Bryants' working situation allowed them to be easily available to their boys as involved parents. In 1986, when the Bryants were named to the Songwriters Hall of Fame by the National Academy of Popular Music, Dane penned a note saying: "When the rest of the kids my age were going to sleep with their radios turned down low or tucked under their pillows, Del and I got to leave our bedroom door open and hear music that the world still talks about."[24]

While the Bryants managed an equitable working relationship within their family, beyond the confines of their home Felice found it difficult to navigate the country music business community. As Kitty Wells said in her southern country phrasing: "It was kindly [sic] hard for a woman back then because men ruled the music and recording industry." It's not surprising that Felice experienced the same frustrations: "That was one of the reasons I stayed home a lot because it aggravated the good ol' boys, and you sort of tried pretty much to stay out of their way, because you were an uppity woman, whatever the hell that was! What I did at home was my business, and I'm glad Boudleaux worked at home. It became a business, but it started out a hobby. It became our livelihood, but I still had to stay out of the way of the boys."[25]

It therefore took some time before the music industry and community understood that Boudleaux and Felice Bryant were true collaborators. Felice said that, in the beginning, the misconceptions began with Boudleaux's family, who accepted the stereotype that "The man makes the living." Then at the Opry, she claimed she was perceived as "some cute, little, exotic-looking thing, a new type of one of Solomon's strange women. They'd never seen anything with my whatever-it was, and this guy [Boudleaux] can talk the dictionary to you." At this point Boudleaux broke into the dialogue with the interviewer: "Don't get the idea that she was in this subservient position all the time because she made it her business *not* to be." To which Felice retorted: "But it was tough as hell."[26] In a 1994 interview, seven years after Boudleaux's death, Felice was even more blunt: "I'd work on something, and it would come out on the record, 'Boudleaux Bryant,' and I'd say, 'Boudleaux!?' and he'd just say, 'That's the way it is.' And I'd say, 'Don't let them do that!'" The interviewer asked, "[so] they'd start putting Felice on there?" You can almost hear her sigh, as she responded, "Finally."[27]

Del mentioned that he didn't believe that "Mother minded Dad working with Chet as they were the closest, closest of friends and fiendishly musical, crazy musicians." But Felice had worked on the lyrics of a couple of the songs they wrote, "and because Chet only wanted to write with Dad, any credit of hers was omitted. You can imagine how this kind of upset her." And when Chet's wife, Leona, "wrote a song or so with Dad, I know that Mother wasn't happy with that," although that only happened "once or twice." But turnabout was not fair play in Boudleaux's eyes, since "Dad was somewhat mildly jealous at the thought of mother writing with someone else. It would've usually been a male." Del recalls "Dad absolutely shutting down Mother writing anything with Roy Orbison. Our parents both loved Roy; it's just that Dad wanted the first crack at anything Mother was coming up with."[28]

Other writers sought out Boudleaux as a writing partner, and Felice commented that sometimes she'd work with Boudleaux, but the other writers "didn't want to go three ways. So, the work I did went unnamed. It was almost understood in the business that it was the man, the men's business. I was considered the 'cut in.' I had to break the women's line back then."[29]

Felice wanted their songwriting to succeed, whether she played a direct role in a particular song or not. According to Del: "the only thing that was a continuous problem for Mother, was when someone else was in the room addressing Dad rather than Mother, as if she were invisible!" Felice and her strong women friends—Delores Denning (a top background singer), and songwriters Cindy Walker and Marijohn Wilkin—always referred to the "Good Ol' Boy" network, which meant tiptoeing carefully when around them. Boudleaux "could always open that door and keep it open. That was great, and he had plenty of respect for Mom, and he knew how serious

Mother was."[30] When asked if there were times that she *did* feel creatively left out, Felice replied: "Oh, I did. But I didn't let it kill me. We would discuss it, and it would make me mad, but *they* never knew it. *We* knew it. And as long as *he* knew what I did, it was ok. I would get teed off about it though."[31] Elsewhere, she said, "If a woman thinks she is good enough to do something, she has some sonofabitch brow-beating her because it's stepping into his kingdom. But Boudleaux loved to see things bloom and grow. He was the best tree planter you ever saw. He never lost a tree that he stuck in the ground."[32] And bloom, the Bryants did.

Felice's daughter-in-law Lee Wilson wrote that "Felice felt that she could function as she wished at home and participate in song pitches by vocalizing melodies and charming people who were likely to cut one of the Bryants' songs, so that became their standard practice. This is in addition to the fact that they kept their song ledgers at home. I think Felice employed what she had—her abilities as a cook, her personality, her home—to achieve her ends, much like Loretta Lynn sewed her own stage costumes." Or as Felice self-deprecatingly told an interviewer later in her life: "Boudleaux stayed out of the kitchen, and I stayed out of the business."[33]

Songs poured out of the Bryants' fertile imagination. In Felice's words, "with a belly full of spaghetti and ears full of songs," singers in both Nashville and on the larger national music scene began adding Bryants' songs to their repertories.[34] From the beginning, the Bryants showed a remarkable ability to tailor their songs to the individual styles of singers and musicians, ranging from the rustic to the urbane. That quintessential country boy, Jimmy Dickens, profited repeatedly from the contributions of Boudleaux and Felice. But in writing for Dickens, the Bryants had to deal with an unpleasant side of the music publishing industry: the use of "cut-ins."

In September 1950, Nat Tannen wrote Boudleaux that, after recording two of the Bryants' songs, Jimmy Dickens was looking for cut-ins from songwriters on forthcoming records. This was a situation with which Felice and Boudleaux had not yet had to contend. A cut-in meant that the singer would get credit for the song along with those who had actually written it, and that song credit guaranteed that the singer would also share in any profits made from that recording. Advising that the Bryants "should go along with him, as well as some of the other artists who are doing this," Tannen argued, "I think this is one of the reasons why we have been missing out on some of the big recording artists." Leaving the decision up to Felice and Boudleaux, he went on to explain: "Of course, this is just between you and me and I wouldn't make it generally known." If the Bryants didn't agree, Tannen would simply "try to dig up some material for him [Dickens]."[35]

Boudleaux told an interviewer in the mid-1980s that "I'm Little but I'm Loud" was the Bryant song to which Tannen was referring. In the fall of 1950 right after the Bryants had moved to Nashville, when they desperately needed the money, they agreed to include Jimmy's name, which meant giving up half their royalties. And Felice added: "They wouldn't just give him one third. They looked at us as *one*." The interview took place over thirty years after that incident, but one could still hear the resentment in her voice. Boudleaux said that Jimmy was cut in on about four other songs. But then one day, he called to say that he was looking for more material. Boudleaux replied, "No more cut-ins," which he considered "a form of theft." By then, the Bryants felt financially secure enough that they no longer had to comply with such requests. Jimmy told them that he wouldn't record any more of their songs. But, as Boudleaux pointed out, "after a couple of years, he didn't have any hits. And then he called back and said he wanted to look at songs." When Boudleaux told him that there still would be no cut-ins, Jimmy replied, "That's all right." And sure enough, the Bryants provided him with additional hits.[36]

Such songs as "Bessie the Heifer" and "Out Behind the Barn" again demonstrated Boudleaux's understanding of and sensitivity to the folkways of the rural South. "Out Behind the Barn," for instance, was a wonderful example of the tradition of country songs, like "Down by the Railroad Tracks," that chronicled the mostly forbidden pleasures that awaited country kids who strayed from parental supervision. The refrain, "out behind the barn" tagged each line in the song, as in the first stanza, "I met a pretty girl one day . . . she taught me how to sing and play." She also taught him how "to kiss and pet . . . a game" that he "could not forget," because they "still play that same game yet," followed by the tagline. Saturday night Opry audiences, along with listeners everywhere, still had bittersweet memories of life in the country and could easily identify with the song's lyrics. The Bryants' former Moultrie neighbor, Gail Love May, remembers that "this was just the way it was in our little community."[37]

Jimmy Dickens's facility with these songs, generally perceived as novelties, typecast him in the minds of many as a singer of comic songs. Over the years, however, he became famous as an interpreter of serious love songs—heart songs, as they were often called. He readily expressed his gratitude to Felice and Boudleaux, which they reciprocated, for supplying him with several of their most poignant compositions: "Take Me as I Am," "Making the Rounds," "Where Did the Sunshine Go," and "We Could."

On the other hand, in the midst of their success with downhome country fare and heart songs, the Bryants could also write songs with an urban feel that presaged the country pop impulse. For instance, "Have a Good Time," popularized by pop icon Tony Bennett, reflected the sophisticated mood and tenor of city life. "How's the World Treating You," cowritten with Chet Atkins in 1953, first began circulation as a recording by the Beaver Valley Sweethearts (Colleen and Donna Wilson, Pennsylvania-born sisters who performed on the WLS National Barn Dance). This song went on to win enormous popularity on a recording by Eddy Arnold, launching its tenure as one of country music's most enduring love songs. Songs of this kind would engulf the country music world in the late 1950s. And it didn't hurt that in 1956 Elvis included "How's the World Treating You" on his second album.

> Do you wonder about me, like I'm hoping you do?
> Are you lonesome without me, have you found someone new?
> Are you burning and yearning, do you ever get blue?
> Do you think of returning, how's the world treating you?

Scores of musicians, great and small, made recordings from the Bryant canon, a body of work that eventually numbered more than nine hundred recorded songs. While some of these, inevitably, were immediately forgettable, a remarkably high percentage made the country popularity charts. Boudleaux and Felice recognized that most songs were evanescent, and that there was no way to know which ones would endure, or indeed whether a few might be newly recorded in later years. Their solution was to turn out songs in great profusion, almost on a daily basis. Reflecting later on his parents' approach to songwriting, Del said:

> You didn't make a lot of money just writing songs. You make a lot of money only if the songs are recorded. And to get enough songs recorded to make a living, you've got to get a lot of songs recorded. You've got to get a *whole* lot of songs recorded. And to get enough songs to pitch to get enough songs recorded means you've got to

write a helluva lot of songs. They had a specific formula, and it was called *quantity.*[38]

By 1953, the Bryants' formula was beginning to work so well that they could pay cash for an Oldsmobile after they moved into the basement house, having earlier replaced their first Buick with a second. Boudleaux's salary from Tannen was up to sixty dollars each week, but as he told an interviewer: "you could have a lot of songs cut and not be earning any money from them, if you're only being paid twice a year by a publisher. But now," he continued, "We were just getting to the point where this thing was going to start to snowball."[39]

Lloyd "Cowboy" Copas and his daughter Kathy scored with "Copy Cat." The veteran Texas honky tonk singer Ernest Tubb recorded "Somebody's Stolen My Honey," which reached No. 9 on the country charts, but strangely, he never recorded another Bryant song. Kitty Wells (born Muriel Deason), who was just beginning her career as "the Queen of Country Music," recorded a few Bryant songs including "A Change of Heart" and her answer to Carl Smith's "Hey Joe." Clyde Julian "Red" Foley, who had enjoyed great exposure as host of the NBC segment of the Grand Ole Opry, and who was comfortable with any style, recorded a No. 1 hit with "Midnight." Aubrey "Moon" Mullican, best known for his rollicking barrel house piano playing, won success with "Sugar Beet." Well before his prime, the future superstar Ray Price recorded songs like "You Weren't Ashamed to Kiss Me Last Night" and "Don't Tempt Me." Over the duration of his career, Price contributed significantly to the popularization and preservation of the Bryants' catalogue.[40]

A few Bryant songs were trivial at best. For example, June Carter did a harmless little novelty song called "Winkin' and a-Blinkin'," and Elton Britt performed the inelegantly titled "Jackass Blues." Boudleaux called the latter "a song of ours that nobody's heard of to amount to anything really, but it sold several hundred thousand copies because Walter Winchell [a nationally syndicated columnist] wrote that it was risqué." Although many stations refused to play it, "all of a sudden the thing started selling like hot cakes. You know it's the old 'banned in Boston' syndrome."[41]

A wide range of country singers recorded Bryant songs, but two performers did the most to make the music community aware of the commercial potential of their material: Eddy Arnold and Carl Smith. The legendary

Tennessee Plowboy, Eddy Arnold, had built a glittering career by the time the Bryants moved to Nashville. He had already taken his songs to lounges, supper clubs, network radio shows, and other venues that were still alien to most country singers. As one of Boudleaux's favorite singers, he dipped frequently into the Bryant song bag to record songs such as "How's the World Treating You," "I've Been Thinking," and "I'm the Richest Man in the World." He was also the first to record "Christmas Can't Be Far Away."

Carl Smith was born in 1927 in Maynardville, Tennessee, the same mountain town that claimed Roy Acuff as a native son. Smith's style, though, was far different from that of Acuff. Smith was a country crooner with a taste for western attire, and as a lean, good-looking young man he was popular with the women. In fact, he married two of country music's leading ladies: June Carter and Goldie Hill. Smith was already a seasoned and popular performer before recording any of the Bryants' songs and had served an apprenticeship on WROL in Knoxville before joining the Grand Ole Opry in 1950. But beginning in 1952, when he recorded "It's a Lovely Lovely World" and "Our Honeymoon," Smith cut a succession of hit songs written by the Bryants. These dominated the jukeboxes everywhere: "Just Wait 'til I Get You Alone," "Back Up Buddy," "Orchids Mean Goodbye," and "Hey Joe." All of these songs won places on the Top Ten country chart, but "Hey Joe" garnered the Bryants their greatest commercial acclaim as their first No. 1 song and their first major foray into the world of pop music.

Since 1948, when "The Tennessee Waltz" broke down the fragile barriers that supposedly separated country and pop, country songs had begun to move more frequently into the repertories of pop singers. This phenomenon occurred in large part as a consequence of a collaboration between Fred Rose and the New York producer Mitch Miller. Mitchell William Miller cut a striking figure with his dark Van Dyke beard and ever-present cigar. He was best known to the American public through *Sing Along with Mitch*. This forerunner of karaoke was first presented on Columbia Records in 1958, then transferred to television in 1961. Listeners were encouraged to sing along with Miller's singers on such vintage songs as "You Are My Sunshine" and "Yellow Rose of Texas." Designed to popularize and preserve the old songs in the face of the threat posed by rock 'n' roll (which Miller detested), *Sing Along with Mitch* masked the reality of a very complex and urbane musician.

Miller was much more than a promoter of musical gimmicks. Classically trained as an oboist at the Eastman School of Music in Rochester, New York (where he was born), he had played with musicians as diverse as George Gershwin and Frank Sinatra. He made his lasting mark, though, as a record producer for Mercury and Columbia, where he shaped and furthered the careers of a staggering array of mid-twentieth-century pop stars, including Rosemary Clooney, Doris Day, Frankie Laine, Guy Mitchell, and Tony Bennett.

Miller was not afraid to think outside the box, and he was receptive to experimentations with other forms of music such as Latin, calypso, blues, and country. Collaborating with Fred Rose, Miller became the chief architect of what became known as the "Crossover." At the time, this practice was somewhat controversial. Some traditionalists did not mind country songs being recorded by pop artists, but they resented country stars crossing over into pop music. The promotion of crossovers placed country and other vernacular songs in the repertoires of pop singers, hoping that they would find new and commercially lucrative markets.[42] While Miller also brought pop songs to Acuff-Rose that could work for country artists, he more often found success with the country songs written by Hank Williams and recorded by Tony Bennett and other pop stylists. Songs like "Cold Cold Heart" and "There'll Be No Teardrops Tonight" were not initially embraced by Bennett and his pop contemporaries until they exhibited marked commercial viability, but, according to music journalist Chet Flippo: "Mitch Miller and Hank Williams together forever changed the public concept of country music." A body of music that had been largely insular and regional, became "transformed into a broad national and even international phenomenon."[43]

A few of Felice and Boudleaux's songs became part of the pop music catalogue, starting as early as 1951 with Tony Bennett's rendition of "Sleepless." The next year both Bennett and Billy Eckstine scored again with "Have a Good Time." The crying vocalist, Johnnie Ray, recorded "Gee, but I'm Lonesome," and the great jazz stylist Sarah Vaughan found some success at the end of the year with "Time." In 1954 Peggy King, vocalist for the George Gobel television show, recorded "Burn 'Em Up." Easy-listening, jazz-inflected songs like these, written only a few years after the success of "Country Boy," underscore the Bryants' eclecticism and facility for writing for differing stylists and markets.

"Willie Can," written in 1956, also provides a hint of the inspirations behind the Bryants' songs. While passing through New Orleans on the way to Florida, Felice saw a garbage truck with the name "Willie Cook" painted on the side. Always thinking of wordplay and silly rhymes, she asked Boudleaux, "I wonder if Willie Cook can cook." Playing around with the possible answers to the question, they wrote the song and soon saw it become an international hit.[44] Boudleaux made a demo of the song for Miller, who was apparently the first to record it, performing with a big band arrangement including guitar, drums, bass, flute, and a group of unnamed vocalists. The demo somehow wound up in Australia and came into the possession of a disc jockey who, in turn, gave it to his friend in England, the singer Alma Cogan (born in London as Alma Angela Cohen). Her version reached No. 13 on the charts in the United Kingdom. Billed as "the Girl with a Giggle in Her Voice," she bears the distinction of being the first foreign-born singer to produce a chart-making record of a Bryant song.[45]

While these songs brought great satisfaction and considerable commercial reward, "Hey Joe," a lusty ode to masculine competitiveness, was the Bryants' first real ticket to national and international fame. The song contained some of the clever rhyming schemes that distinguished the couple's best songs, such as descriptions of the rival's girlfriend as that "pearly girly," such a "jolly dolly," with skin that looked so "creamy dreamy," eyes that appeared so "lovey dovey," and lips like "cherry berry wine." Carl Smith's version won the Bryants their first No. 1 country hit in the United States and remained on the charts for eight weeks. Later that year Kitty Wells recorded a popular cover, from a woman's perspective. "Hey Joe" also served as a perfect vehicle for the aggressive style of pop vocalist Frankie Laine. His over-the-top pop arrangement with the backing of Paul Weston and His Orchestra and the Norman Luboff Choir reached No. 1 on the UK Singles Chart. Recognizing its strong commercial potential, Felice and Boudleaux had hit the road to promote it among as many radio disc jockeys as they could contact. The song's success on both sides of the Atlantic suggests that the Bryants' reach extended well beyond the traditional country audience.

Although they had been promoting songs for Tannen at radio stations before this time, none of these tours had approached the magnitude of the "Hey Joe" enterprise. Leaving the boys under the loving care of their Georgia grandparents, which meant "biscuits every morning, good quality country life, and all the food you could eat," the Bryants drove up and down the Atlantic Coast along US Highway 1 (from Savannah to New York), and into the upper South, carrying a load of records and visiting radio stations, large and small.[46] Although Dane liked to joke that, if his parents saw a radio tower, they made a mad dash to visit the station to which it was attached, Boudleaux planned the trip with the same systematic care that he devoted to other enterprises. This was a far cry from the undisciplined young man who, prior to his union with Felice, had moved through life with no plans but plenty of booze.

For their extended trip up the East Coast, Boudleaux read the appropriate travel books, charted the maps, and took careful notes of the radio announcers that they might meet. This unprecedented practice by a songwriting team caught the attention of the music industry and was noted in *Billboard* magazine. Future superstar Loretta Lynn and her enterprising husband, Mooney, promoted one of her early records, "Honky Tonk Girl," by making a similar radio station tour. According to Bryant family members, Loretta and Mooney very likely had been inspired by what they read in *Billboard*.[47]

During his earlier tenure with Tannen, Boudleaux had come to recognize the crucial role disc jockeys played in the making of the emerging country music industry. He visited radio stations regularly, making contacts and maintaining relationships even when he did not have a specific record to promote. The Bryants' early Nashville career emerged during the heyday of the hillbilly radio disc jockey, the era between the decline of live radio programming and the advent of the depersonalized and automated radio station. When many of the DJs organized the Country Music Disc Jockey Association in 1952 (the forerunner of the Country Music Association), Boudleaux became an active participant in its annual conventions in Nashville. He welcomed the opportunity to network among the members. The disc jockeys formed a varied and colorful group of personalities who held sway on stations large and small throughout the nation. Fortunately, their independence allowed them the freedom to refuse to be ruled by tight playlists, and they selected the records that they played. The jockeys had to be all-purpose announcers, typically reading the news and weather reports, answering requests and other types of fan mail, interviewing visiting performers, and physically working the turntables that spun the old 78 rpm and 45 rpm records.

Some of these personalities, like Nelson King in Cincinnati and Randy Blake in Chicago were smooth-talking urbane announcers. Others, like Eddie Hill in Nashville and Wayne Raney in Cincinnati, spoke with a southern down-home patter and accent and occasionally affected the near grotesque demeanor of hayseed characters. In spite of differences in style, they all loved country music or at least were convincing in their enthusiastic embrace of the genre. Many of the DJs were as popular as the country entertainers whose records they played. A few, like Jim Reeves and Charlie Walker, went on to become singing stars. Everywhere, certain disc jockeys made individual contributions to country music in the 1950s. These included Dewey Phillips in Memphis, who gave Elvis his initial music exposure; Tom Perryman down in East Texas, who earnestly promoted the early recordings of Jim Reeves; Don Owens in Virginia, who contributed directly to the popularization and naming of the emerging bluegrass genre; and Paul Kallinger in Del Rio Texas ("your good neighbor along the way") whose broadcasts from powerful XERF popularized and kept alive hillbilly music all over America.[48]

One of Boudleaux's first and most crucial DJ contacts was Walter Ralph Emery, at that time a young and ambitious announcer who eventually became one of the most influential radio and television personalities in the nation. Emery served as an emcee in a tribute to the Bryants in 2007, where he recalled the first time he met Boudleaux: "I was twenty years old, and I was playing records on a radio station in Franklin, Tennessee, the summer of 1953. The phone rang, and it was Boudleaux. I didn't know him, and he said he'd been listening to my program and asked me if I had the new Eddy Arnold record, 'How's the World Treating You.' He said, 'Chet Atkins and I wrote that, and would you please play it'?" Emery told him he had the record, "which was extraordinary, since we were a brand-new radio station and didn't have many records." He got to know Boudleaux and Felice better through Fred Rose, when he stopped by Acuff-Rose to pick up free samples.[49]

Emery, who was born in McEwen, Tennessee, worked at several small stations in his home state before finally settling down in Nashville, first at WMAK and WSIX, and then at powerful 50,000 watt WSM Radio. At WSM between November 1957 and 1972, Emery hosted an all-night show—*Opry Star Spotlight*—that made him one of the most powerful and influential personalities in the country music business. Extending an open invitation to all country music performers, Emery visited each night with people like

Marty Robbins, Tex Ritter, and Merle Haggard, eliciting both personal and professional gossip, and welcoming impromptu jam sessions with them. Performers could not have hoped for better public exposure.

Boudleaux visited the show often, cultivating a relationship that put him in contact with just about everyone in the music business. Emery, on the other hand, was surely taken aback when Boudleaux and Felice appeared as his guests on one of his very early morning television shows on Channel One. After the band played the show's theme, Ralph said, "Good morning, Felice," and she responded, "How'd you like a rap in the mouth?" meaning that she hated to be up so early. Interviewed years later, Ralph described her "fierce" personality, but not in a derogatory way.[50] While Boudleaux was quiet and laid-back, Felice did not hold back. They balanced one another as if their weights on a seesaw were equal.

By the end of 1954 Boudleaux and Felice felt the need to assert greater control over their catalogue. During a visit to Nat Tannen in New York, they suggested a renegotiated contract. After Tannen proposed a partnership, Boudleaux shocked him with a counterproposal. He asked for a contract granting the Bryants full ownership of their copyrights after ten years. Tannen agreed with a handshake, or at least Boudleaux believed that he did. When Tannen heard his lawyer's vehement objection to the proposal, he then rejected the idea.[51] The Bryants left Tannen soon after that.

The Bryants picked up the ten-year-reversion idea from Frank Loesser, the celebrated Broadway composer who was famous for such productions as *Guys and Dolls*. Ironically, Loesser kept an office in the building owned by Nat Tannen. Not quite as well known was the fact that Loesser also liked country music, an affinity that seems to have developed during his military service when he headed a special operations unit. Loesser in fact wrote a few country-flavored songs such as "Ballad of Rodger Young," "I Got Spurs That Jingle, Jangle, Jingle," and the enduring love song, "Have I Stayed Away Too Long."[52]

Felice and Boudleaux had learned about Loesser when he made an unheralded visit to Nashville. One evening, while watching the local news on television, Felice saw Loesser being interviewed at the Nashville airport. She was shocked when he said that he had come to see the Bryants. During their subsequent meeting, Loesser tried to convince them to move to New York to become part of his team of writers. Although Broadway had been one of Felice's lifelong dreams, as well as a goal cherished by Boudleaux, they turned the offer down, feeling that life in Nashville had become too stable and comfortable to be discarded. Their two boys were already deeply invested in school and their local playmates. Even more significantly, Fred Rose had warned them of the personal dangers posed by the aggressive and competitive world of New York show business. Cognizant of Boudleaux's problems with alcohol, Rose strongly asserted that he could not survive in that environment without suffering severe blows to both his ego and his health. When interviewed by Joe Allison after Boudleaux had died, Felice was very honest about the temptations of New York and the dangers it posed for someone with a drinking problem: "'Boudleaux,' I said, 'you know how you are.' I said, 'You know how I am. I'm just a little old housewife. I wouldn't know how to hack that thing, if you decided to disappear from the scene; I couldn't work with those people.' And so, we both thought it would [be] best for us to stay with a low profile. And that's what happened there. [Fred] suggested that Boudleaux pretty much stay away from all that intensity. He said, 'Boudleaux, you wouldn't live to be fifty.'"[53]

Instead, they stayed in Nashville and organized Showcase Publishing Company, the vehicle between 1954 and 1956 for their newly published songs. A desk in the living room served as their office. The arrangement allowed the Bryants to maintain a steady and high-quality level of production during these years. For a very short time at the beginning of the endeavor, they took on a partner, Lester Vernice "Vic" McAlpin, who presumably joined them as a song-plugger. Hailing from a tiny town in East Tennessee, McAlpin was a veteran songwriter who had written scores of good songs for artists such as Eddy Arnold and Roy Acuff. He was also a fishing buddy of Hank Williams, and the two of them were rumored to have cowritten songs on which they took turns putting their names. The Bryants recognized very soon, however, that McAlpin was not dedicated and disciplined enough as a songwriter and song-plugger. They realized they did not actually need a partner, and that their own work ethic served as a more frugal and efficient investment.[54]

All of the songs that bore the Showcase imprint came solely from the pens of Boudleaux and Felice. They wrote a wide variety of material during this period that achieved both popularity and lasting fame—such as "Where Did the Sunshine Go" and "Take Me as I Am" for Jimmy Dickens. But at least three songs from Showcase deserve individual recognition: "Hawk-Eye," "The Richest Man in the World," and "We Could."

"Hawk-Eye," inspired by the novels of James Fenimore Cooper, was recorded, first, by Bobby Lord and, later, by Frankie Laine. Lord, a big-voiced singer from Sanford, Florida, had already hosted television shows in his native state when Boudleaux heard one of his demos and recommended him to producer Don Law at Columbia Records. Given the lusty performances of both Lord and Laine, the song could have been the theme song of a television western.

Eddy Arnold's recording provided "The Richest Man in the World" with its distinctive sound, performed in his inimitably self-confident style. This song updated the theme heard earlier in "Country Boy." It now seemed ready-made for a big, bold Broadway production. "The Richest Man in the World" gave a sophisticated twist to the old southern theme of "poor but proud":

> I don't have much bank account; my cash on hand is small,
> But tell me, what are riches, but contentment after all?
> Other folks may think I'm poor, but I know it's not so,
> Cause when I count my blessings I'm the richest man I know!

Felice alone created "We Could" as a birthday present for Boudleaux. She told Dorothy Horstman that "we were working in the basement house. He was laying on the couch; he likes to lay on the couch when he's working. I was sitting in the chair directly across from him, and he fell asleep. I kept looking at him and thinking, 'How precious,' and I thought, if anyone could make this old-world whistle, we could, we could." Touched by this scene of domestic contentment, and thankful for the profound happiness they both enjoyed, she wrote this widely beloved tribute.[55] Recorded first by Jimmy Dickens, it has been revived repeatedly with great success by entertainers such as Jim Reeves, the Louvin Brothers, Charley Pride, and Al Martino. It has been a gift that keeps on giving:

> If anyone could pray each night,
> And thank the Lord that all is right,
> We could, we could, you and I.

Felice told an interviewer that "We Could" was the only song that Boudleaux "left alone" because it was his birthday present. "That's why he didn't put his mark on it."[56]

Although the Showcase years were highly satisfying, the Bryants' joy was tempered by the death, on December 1, 1954, of their dear friend and mentor, Fred Rose. Pappy, as they called him, was their reason for being in Nashville, and while they did not always follow his advice to keep their songs simple, they proudly recognized the profound influence that he had exercised over their lives. Felice, especially, was devastated. "Fred was our mentor. He was our guardian angel. He was the whole schtick. And he had to be a part of our lives, or we wouldn't play." She told another interviewer that when Rose died, "I didn't cry for my parents like I cried for that man. When you went out to his studio and did a night's work making demos and showing tunes, you just floated home. You could live on an evening with Fred for months. He was just so wise."[57] And to yet another interviewer, Felice mentioned that when their names were to be put in the sidewalk of the original Country Music Hall of Fame and Museum at 4 Music Square East, she wanted to know if her name and Boudleaux's could be placed next to Fred's. "And that's where it is. That man is long gone, but has never left. He's still here. I have paintings hanging around the house, but don't have pictures around the house. But that man's picture is in the house."[58]

Fred's son, Wesley, succeeded him as president of Acuff-Rose. Wesley had worked as an accountant for Standard Oil in Chicago. Although he had experience in the business offices of Acuff-Rose, his expertise in the musical end of the operation was uncertain at best. Because Boudleaux and Felice felt an allegiance to Fred's memory and were concerned for the future of the publishing house, they were determined to help the son of their old friend. For these reasons, they decided to disband Showcase and return to an affiliation with Acuff-Rose. The specific deal maker came when Wesley Rose agreed to a contract that contained the ten-year reversion Nat Tannen had rejected.[59]

The contract with Acuff-Rose, extending from January 1957 through 1966, was unprecedented in the Nashville music industry. With the exception of their international copyrights, the Bryants were assured that all of their songs published during the period would return to their complete control after a decade, with all unrecorded songs returning within one year after the expiration of the agreement. This stipulation proved providential, since their magical relationship with the Everly Brothers began in 1957. Very soon, Bryant songs, as well as the Bryant name, would be known all over the world.[60]

At the beginning of the Acuff-Rose years the Bryants had much to be thankful for. Their preeminence as songwriters was already widely acknowledged, and they had even made a few records of their own. Largely through the suggestion of Fred Rose, who thought they might have some commercial appeal as singers, on June 17, 1951, they had gone to the Castle Studio in the Tulane Hotel and recorded four songs for the MGM label.

It is now impossible to know the motivations that lay behind these recordings, since the Bryants had little time or energy to promote themselves as artists. Were their recordings made solely as a diversion or to comply with Rose's wishes, with no real hope that they would be commercial hits? When performing as Boudleaux and Felice Bryant, they added another vehicle to publicize their names, creating more public awareness of their songs. But this explanation does not hold for the recordings they did as Bud and Felice Bryant. The net gains they may have anticipated from these sessions remain mysterious. Nevertheless, the songs were well performed and deserve some critical acclaim. For example, "Overweight Blues," from this first session, is a clever boogie tune that resembles the songs recorded by Tennessee Ernie Ford and Kay Starr during that era. "Pepper Pickin'" and "Buttercup Valley," from the same session, reveal the Bryants' signature achievement of stylistic diversity. In the first song Felice injects some playful spice similar to comedienne June Carter's, and in the second song she and Boudleaux create a sweet homey sound reminiscent of the National Barn Dance lovebirds Lulu Belle and Scotty (Myrtle Eleanor Wiseman and Scott Wiseman). Almost one year later, they returned to the same studio and recorded four more songs, this time as Bud and Betty Bryant.[61]

The Bryants also could now easily measure their success by improvements in their material life. They began taking vacations in Gatlinburg and the Smoky Mountains. As good an environment as it had been for writing songs, they were now ready to leave the basement house. On the first morning that property could be bought, Boudleaux stood in line with other aspirants and made a down payment on a five-acre lot he had already carefully selected on the as-yet-unbuilt Old Hickory Lake in Hendersonville, Tennessee. He later bought an additional five acres adjacent to the original plot. Old Hickory Lake is a reservoir on the Cumberland River built and maintained by the US Army Corps of Engineers about twenty-five miles upstream from Nashville. Construction had begun in January 1952, and the final dam closure was completed in June 1954. During construction of their house, the Bryant boys took great pleasure in seeing the water gradually fill to the lake's present banks. Boudleaux went to the building site every day, often taking Felice and the boys and devoting the same kind of meticulous attention to detail that he had shown in the writing and marketing of their songs.

He and Felice sought to build a structure that would serve as the nerve center for Team Bryant. It had to be comfortable for the family, conducive to the writing and performance of songs, and aesthetically expressive of the heritage of central Tennessee. Consequently, they assiduously selected sturdy recycled material with which to build their home—beams from the Maxwell House in downtown Nashville, poplar and chestnut logs from an old log house in Cottontown, Tennessee, and large cedar logs and "antique" bricks from the chimney of a stagecoach inn in Lebanon, Tennessee, where Andrew Jackson had stayed. These cedar logs became a main feature of the house. They hired the only man in the area who knew how to build a traditional log structure, a Mr. Henley, a craftsman highly skilled in pioneer architecture. Boudleaux relished watching him utilize those skills as he built their residence.[62] Dane and Del were even employed to clean the soft mud mortar from the bricks. Their father explained that the two-pennies-per-brick payment that they received for their labor was similar to the royalties that writers and publishers received for their recordings.[63]

The residence that finally emerged was located at 215 Neptune Drive in a new Hendersonville subdivision, on a northeastern point of Old Hickory Lake. It was eventually surrounded by a multitude of tall trees that Boudleaux and the boys planted; he expressed regret when anyone in the community cut trees down. Describing the house in 1970, the journalist Teddy Bart said that "the outside of the Bryant home is of logs, bricks, and redwood" and "it commands a gorgeous view from its porch at the top of a rise from the lake." The two-story home had a spacious front porch. Bart described the setting designed for songwriting: "Their den was a den of everything. It was enormous, with a large bar, a modern kitchen, a reading-relaxing-talking room with subdued lights, and comfortable furniture."[64]

A recollection made several years later by a former guest noted that "the large country kitchen was the center of activity. A coffee table and couch faced the cooking island where Felice seemed to spend most of her time." Boudleaux placed guitars at either end of the couch, in case inspiration conjured up a verse or an idea for a song. And Chet Atkins described a visit there quite vividly: "You'd go into their house, and Felice would be cooking supper. Boudleaux would be on the guitar trying to get a melody for a song he was writing. And she'd yell from the kitchen, 'That sounds like something else, Boudleaux; don't use that melody!' And he'd never talk back to her, but he'd change that melody until he got something she approved of. They complemented each other very, very well in their efforts to write songs."[65]

During the twenty years and more in which the Bryants lived in this house, it became the scene of constant songwriting and social interaction—a domestic center of the Nashville music scene. They enjoyed the conviviality and convenience of the structure; it was the creative nexus of their lives. Felice pointed out: "We would take artists home to teach them our songs, because we were already signed up with Acuff-Rose, and we'd have the musicians there, the arrangers, and we'd work on the whole recording in my Dutch tavern kitchen, which was ideal for rehearsal."[66]

★ ★ ★ ★ ★

Chapter 4

"BYE BYE LOVE"
AND HELLO WORLD
The Everly Explosion

A s a perfectionist, Boudleaux never lost an opportunity to shape and
polish the songs he and Felice were in the process of writing. Every
day on the way to the site of the new lake house, "arriving at the same
time the carpenters showed up," Boudleaux's mind was tuned to songwriting as well as overseeing the progress of the house construction. "Well,
on the way, I'd have a little piece of paper, and I'd jot down ideas and
titles. On this particular morning, the boys were in the backseat of the
car, and Felice and I were just trying to get ideas on the way to the house
site." Everyone in the family could re-create the scene as he or she remembered it. According to Dane, they were just passing the new dam. Del said,
"There was a light drizzle, and the windshield wipers were going, and Dad
started 'Bye Bye Love' to the rhythm of the windshield wipers."[1] As Felice
recalled:

> Boudleaux says, "Boy, have I got a hell of an idea for Johnny and
> Jack." [Johnny Wright and Jack Anglin were famous for their
> up-tempo and Latin-beat country songs.]
> We're turning the corner off the blacktop into this new devel-
> opment where they had just scraped out roads, and it was muddy
> as hell. So, he stops the car. "Now all I've got is the chorus":
>
> Bye bye love
> Bye bye happiness
> Hello loneliness
> I think I'm gonna cry.
>
> Bye bye love
> Bye bye sweet caress

Hello emptiness
I feel like I could die.

[Felice continued] And I thought, "Great. Fine." I said, "That's it?"
He said, "Well, it isn't finished yet." So, we worked on that song
then and there, and we worked on it at the house site, and when we
got home that night, we put together what we had and finished it
up. And it was a good song, but he was so up in the air for it. He
said, "It's going to be a hit. I just know it. I can feel it in my bones."
And I said, "Well, that's nice."[2]

"Bye Bye Love" appeared on pages 94 and 95 of Ledger 3, which Felice had
presented to Boudleaux as a belated birthday gift on March 23, 1956. Del
pointed out that this particular ledger was "so special because the folks
were building the lake house, and Dad was worried about how much it cost,
so they were writing like mad." At the time Boudleaux may have had a pre-
monition of the song's success, but he could never have imagined that "Bye
Bye Love" would usher in a new chapter in their lives and transform the
course of both American and British music.[3]

Still, the hit that Boudleaux felt in his bones did not immediately take
off like a rocket. Like the Bryant family, Johnny and Jack liked the song,
but they were among at least thirty artists who rejected it, asserting that the
selections for their next album had already been chosen. Although the
song was eventually recorded by scores of entertainers, even in the first
year of its commercial birth—when people like Webb Pierce and Ray Price
covered it in the United States, and Rory Blackwell and his Blackjacks did it
in England—it may have originally sounded a bit too youthful and "bub-
blegummy" for the tastes of many country singers. Perhaps inadvertently,
the Bryants were beginning to get in step with the youth revolution that
American music had been undergoing since 1954 when Elvis made his
debut. The Bryants were not alone in writing songs that seemed directed
toward a youth audience. In the year before "Bye Bye Love," for example,
Sonny James with "Young Love" and George Hamilton IV with "A Rose and
a Baby Ruth" had done their part to bring country music into the youth
orbit. Almost simultaneously with the appearance of "Bye Bye Love," Marty
Robbins recorded his chart-busting version of "A White Sports Coat."

The recording of such songs indicated that a youth culture had begun
to take shape in the aftermath of World War II and was reaching fruition at

"Bye Bye Love" as Boudleaux captured it in one of the famous ledgers. Courtesy of the Country Music Hall of Fame® and Museum.

Boudleaux and Felice with Wesley Rose at Acuff-Rose Publishing. Courtesy of the Country Music Hall of Fame® and Museum.

the end of the 1950s. The popular culture industry and other agents of burgeoning capitalism began to treat young people as separate and special entities. Not only did this constituency now possess a purchasing power far beyond that of earlier generations of their peers, young people believed that their interests were being ill-served by the pop songs of the day. Either through a sense of deferred obligation held by parents who had been away during the war or through a genuine desire to give their kids the material advantages they had never experienced, American adults in the 1950s became increasingly generous with their financial resources. Simultaneously, young people were beginning to find ways to satisfy their longings independent of their parents' wishes. The move to the cities contributed to the emergence of alternative peer groups and influences, and popular culture became pervasive through the growing availability of automobiles, radio, movies, and television. Popular youth-oriented actors such as James Dean, Montgomery Clift, and Marlon Brando provided role models, if not sources, of rebel lifestyles. White youth dipped increasingly into the forbidden zones of popular culture to find excitement. In the realm of American music, this meant exploring and sampling African American styles.

Long before Elvis Presley successfully exploited such musical experimentation, African American music had been attractive to curious white listeners. From at least the emergence of ragtime, blues, and jazz in the early twentieth century, white youth looked for and discovered musical forms and their allied cultures that provided vital alternatives to the styles favored by their parents. Country music since the 1920s had always included entertainers—such as Jimmie Rodgers, Jimmie Tarlton, Cliff Carlisle, Bob Wills, and Hank Williams—who moved outside the mainstream to embrace and experiment with styles or songs born in black culture. Sometimes on radio stations that catered to black musical tastes but, more often, through the profusion of new record labels emerging after World War II, African American styles easily reached a broad audience.

Out of the exploration of these forms and their fusion with country and other styles, Elvis and his generation of country musicians created a body of music that eventually came to be described as rockabilly—the fusion of hillbilly sounds with the rocking beat of black music. Like other labels in American music such as bluegrass, western swing, jazz, and country blues, the term "rockabilly" emerged over a period of years and its origins cannot be precisely dated. However these hybrid musical offerings might be defined, youthful fans eagerly embraced the rockabillies, as their record sales and sold-out personal appearances indicated.

The young men who brought Felice and Boudleaux Bryant into the world of rockabilly music were a couple of well-scrubbed white youngsters named Don and Phil Everly. Of course, the fact that the Everlys themselves had not yet been defined as rockabillies lends an ironic twist to this emerging odyssey. By the time the Everly Brothers met the Bryants in 1957, Don and Phil were already seasoned veterans of traditional country music, singing with their impeccable brother harmony. While living in Shenandoah, Iowa, even as young children—"Little Donnie," aged eight, and "Baby Boy Phil," aged six—they had begun performing on their parents' live radio program, *The Everly Family Show*, on KMA.

Their father, Ike, who taught his boys to play guitar and sing was on the staff at the station. Their mother, Margaret, often joined in, creating four-part harmony on country songs. Isaac Milford "Ike" Everly (1908–1975)—a former coal miner from Muhlenberg County, Kentucky—used a style of guitar picking, with thumb and fingers, to fashion a long-lasting radio career that took him and his family all over the Upper South and into places like Hastings, Nebraska, Shenandoah, Iowa, and Evansville, Indiana. The brothers' different birthplaces—Brownie, Kentucky, for Don and Chicago for Phil—reflected their family's extensive travels. Ike's Muhlenberg-style guitar playing, though, was rooted in the county of his birth in Kentucky and was featured by an outstanding array of guitar players, including Arnold Schultz, Merle Travis, Kennedy Jones, and Mose Rager, who knew and learned from each other.[4]

By late 1953 the era of live radio programming was coming to an end. Ike Everly and his family band's performances on Cas Walker's show on WROL in Knoxville, Tennessee, had been earning them ninety dollars a week. Now they were making their final appearance. Still struggling to make a go of it, the Everlys moved from Knoxville to Chicago, seeking work.

Four years later Ike Everly gave up music entirely, training as a barber while Margaret trained as a beautician. They settled in Nashville, where he worked as a barber and their boys finished high school. Luckily for the Everlys, Chet Atkins had already become not only one of their biggest fans but a friend of the family as well.[5] Don and Phil, however, were still trying to create lasting performing careers for themselves, and Daddy Ike never lost an opportunity to tell his customers how well his boys could sing.

Coincidentally, Boudleaux Bryant was one of those customers. While Ike praised his sons on multiple occasions, Boudleaux tended to pass his remarks off as the predictable and exaggerated boasts of a proud father. But Chet did his best to further the careers of the brothers and managed to get them a short-lived recording contract with Columbia Records and a writer's contract for Don Everly with Acuff-Rose. Don placed "Thou Shalt Not Steal" with Kitty Wells and "Here We Go Again" with Anita Carter, but the brothers' few Columbia releases made no waves.

The association with Acuff-Rose proved to be one of the vehicles that launched them to international fame. In early March of 1957, Archie Bleyer came to Nashville looking for artists to record for his new Cadence label. Bleyer had been bandleader for the Arthur Godfrey show in New York, but with little experience in country music, he was ready to lean on Chet Atkins's and Wesley Rose's knowledge of this art form. Rose recommended three acts to Bleyer—Anita Carter, Gordon Terry, and the Everly Brothers—and had prepared audition tapes for each of them. Boudleaux Bryant was also there in his familiar guise, promoting his songs to anyone who would listen. Anita Carter, the beautiful daughter of Maybelle Carter, accepted Boudleaux's "Blue Doll." But it took Jim Reeves, who later recorded it as "Blue Boy," to turn the song into such a big hit that he named his band the Blue Boys. Gordon Terry, a handsome man with the looks of a bodybuilder, was a former bluegrass fiddler who was now trying to build a solo career as a vocalist. He became one of the many people to turn down "Bye Bye Love," asking Boudleaux if he had something stronger. Even Brenda Lee and Porter Wagoner are said to have rejected the song. After the song won success, however, Del recalls his mother remarking: "Porter came to us and said, 'Listen, you write me two and a half minutes of silence and I'll record it.'"[6]

When the Everlys, desperate for a hit, heard "Bye Bye Love," they believed it worth the gamble. Boudleaux was elated, expressing his otherworldly sense of the song's destiny: "It was turned down by exactly thirty people. I was about to lose my confidence in it. But then I showed it to the Everlys. It was the first thing I showed the Everlys and the first song they ever cut on Cadence. The Fates were with us. It was right for the Everlys, and the fates made everyone else turn it down." Don was twenty, and Phil was eighteen. Phil later said: "We would have sung anything. We were going to get a chance to record, and we were going to make $64, and $64 sounded really good to me at the time. Boudleaux designed that harmony, and I just sang it." Telling an interviewer in the mid-1980s about the day Boudleaux sang the first lines of "Bye Bye Love" to his family, Felice remarked: "Boudleaux is a harmony freak, and that's why it was inevitable that Boudleaux and the Everlys would get together. He can hear everything in his head. We didn't *know* we were starting with rock 'n' roll. Boudleaux has an ear for harmony and loves duets."[7]

The Everlys met for their historic first session on March 1, 1957, at the RCA Victor studios in the Methodist Television, Radio and Film Commission at 1525 McGavock Street. While Boudleaux and a few others looked on, the Everlys launched into their first take accompanied by some of the cream of Nashville's musical crop: guitarists Ray Edenton and Chet Atkins, steel guitarist James Clayton "Jimmie" Day, drummer Buddy Harman, and bass player Floyd Taylor "Lightning" Chance. Bleyer acted as the producer, and the ace recording engineer Bill Porter made sure that both musicians and vocalists received the best technical sound support available. The first session began rather sluggishly though, with no one completely satisfied with what was being recorded.

During recording lulls Don Everly practiced some riffs on his guitar, and according to Felice, "Boudleaux said, 'What is that?' Don told him it was a lick that he had borrowed from the African American rhythm-and-blues legend, Bo Diddley [born Ellas Bates McDaniel]. Boudleaux asked him to repeat it. Then [Boudleaux] said, 'Put that on the front of "Bye Bye Love."' And Boudleaux sat down with him, and they went through it, and it worked."[8] This was the famous riff that introduces and punctuates "Bye Bye Love." Don had used the riff on his earlier Columbia release, "Give Me a Future," but with no apparent success. Employed here, however, it gave "Bye Bye Love" its spark and vitality, the magic that brought the Everly Brothers out of obscurity. Don Everly had used an open G tuning on his guitar that his dad had taught him (and, coincidentally, that Bo Diddley also employed), "to get a real wide sound." Ray Edenton, a much-recorded Nashville musician who played guitar on the session, said that when Don Everly would play one of his riffs and hold up his guitar to do so, Edenton employed a high third, which effectively doubled Everly's efforts.[9]

While the Bo Diddley phrases were crucial to the sound heard on this first recording, the song itself conveyed an irresistible excitement. The lyrics captured the torment of unfulfilled teenage romance, proving to be the perfect vehicle for the Everly Brothers' clear, precise harmony—the inimitable quality that set them apart from the other acts in the incipient rockabilly revolution. The Everlys were heirs to the southern tradition of brother harmony singers that dated at least to the mid-1930s when the Monroe Brothers (Charlie and Bill) and the Blue Sky Boys (Bill and Earl Bolick) performed throughout the southeastern states. And immediately before the Everlys hit the charts, the Louvin Brothers (Ira and Charlie) had reached the peak of their performing careers with such hits as "When I Stop Dreaming."

Recorded at the very beginning of March, "Bye Bye Love" debuted on *Billboard*'s country charts on May 13, and two weeks later climbed to No. 1. It simultaneously reached No. 2 on the pop charts, and No. 5 in rhythm and blues—the first Bryant song to achieve recognition in all three categories. Even before the song hit No. 1, *Billboard* was already singing the Everlys' praises: "The Tennessee teen-agers have a distinctive, appealing sound and could click big in the pop as well as the c & w [country and western] field.

'Bye Bye Love' is a plaintive Boudleaux Bryant blues with an unusual rhythm pattern." In Paula Bishop's fine dissertation about the Everly Brothers, she noted that, in their initial hit song, "The sound had a character of its own: warmer, close-miked vocals with less echo and reverb in the ambient sound and a calmer energy in the rhythm instruments. The sonic result underscored the vocals, rather than competing with them, making melody and harmony the prominent characteristics of the Everly Brothers' recordings." When the Everlys were inducted into the Rock & Roll Hall of Fame in 1986, Kurt Loder interviewed them for *Rolling Stone.* He aptly describes their signature appeal: "In the beginning, with their crisply thrumming guitars and vibrant harmonies, the Everlys conjured a world of shimmering innocence eternally on the verge of experience." And the nation and world quickly picked up on these attributes.[10]

None of this exciting information, however, reached the Everlys as they went out on the road down through Alabama and Mississippi with a country package act headed by the veteran bluegrass musician Bill Monroe. To their dismay they soon learned that country singer Webb Pierce had recorded his own Decca version of the song. Mel Tillis, who was also on the tour, gave them the news, predicting that it would kill their version because Pierce was such a hit-making machine. Webb Pierce's recording did reach No. 7 on the country charts, but that was far below the mark established by the Everlys. Imagine their surprise when they found themselves on top!

In early May, "Bye Bye Love" moved onto *Billboard*'s Top One Hundred chart, and the Everly Brothers appeared on the stage of the Opry for the first time, singing their fast-climbing song. Furthermore, and most crucially, because of the song's popularity with rock 'n' rollers, the brothers soon began to be invited to join the expansive tours in the North sponsored by Cleveland disc jockey and rock-and-roll promoter Alan Freed. Almost immediately, the recording began to affect the music of fledgling musicians in wondrous ways. In far off Queens, New York, thirteen-year-old Paul Simon, already trying to hone his songwriting skills, heard the song on the family radio and immediately seized upon it as a potent model. Although 78 rpm records cost a dollar, Paul spent an hour riding two buses across town to get a copy at Triboro Records in Jamaica, Queens. Returning home, he played the record over and over, until he accidentally scratched it with the needle. He then made the two-bus trip back to Triboro Records to obtain another copy. In an interview years later, Simon said that this experience with the Everly Brothers marked the first time that he examined a record to find out who had written the songs. And he was enchanted with the names, Boudleaux and Felice, especially in combination with the Everly Brothers, that seemed "so exotic to a New Yorker like me. They brought me into that tradition." And he and his good friend Art Garfunkel, with whom he had already started singing, began imitating the Everlys as closely as they could. As Art put it: "Well, this is the best harmony I've ever heard in my life. And from that moment, I was on the train called Everly Brothers. What came before that was music that was so tame. This stirring things up was much more subversive."[11] What talented teenager wouldn't respond to such provocative stimulus?

When "Bye Bye Love" crossed the Atlantic, the Bryants' names that Paul Simon had found so romantic gained currency as well. This transatlantic passage was not their maiden voyage. Earlier forays had occurred in the 1950s—Alma Cogan's hit with "Willie Can" and Frankie Laine's rendition of "Hey Joe." But these recordings paled before the reception that awaited the engaging combination of the Everlys' impeccable harmony embedded in Felice and Boudleaux's song once it reached England.

Graham Nash—of the future Crosby, Stills, and Nash vocal team— talked about growing up in a working-class neighborhood in Salford, a suburb of Manchester. The devastation in England following World War II left him and many teenagers restless, with nothing to do. At sixteen, his experience upon hearing "Bye Bye Love" for the first time replicates the rapture Paul Simon felt. Graham and his best friend since the age of six, Allan Clarke, had just entered the hall of a girls' school where a dance was being held. Both friends had their eye on the same girl across the dance floor and were making "a beeline toward where she was standing, when all of a sudden a sound came blasting out of the speakers: the first stanzas of 'Bye Bye Love,' stopped us both dead in our tracks." When interviewed, he said, "the power of 'Bye Bye Love' was just outstanding. It changed my life." And in his memoir, *Wild Tales: A Rock & Roll Life*, Nash elaborated on just what that experience meant to him: "That moment was incredibly important . . . it was like the opening of a giant door in my soul, the striking of a chord, literally and figuratively, from which I've never recovered. From the time when I first heard the Everly Brothers, I knew I wanted to make music that affected people the way the Everlys affected me. That was *it* for me. I can trace it to that night at St. Clement's."[12] Since Graham and Allan "were already well interested in music," they immediately began incorporating "Bye Bye Love" into their performances, imitating the Everlys' harmony "as best we could."[13]

For Felice and Boudleaux, the "Bye Bye Love" phenomenon was both an unexpected and overwhelming surprise. They just happened to have a song on hand that not only perfectly fit the style of the Everlys but also meshed with the upsurge of interest in teen-oriented songs. In a sense, then, they were unprepared for the acclaim that ensued. But when the Everlys met for their second Cadence recording session in August 1957, the Bryants were more than ready for the challenge. They now wrote specifically with the Everly Brothers in mind. As Boudleaux told an interviewer: "For every song that we got cut by the Everly Brothers, we must have written 25 or 30 for them—and aimed specifically at their style of singing."[14] One early morning, in the living room of their incompletely furnished lake home, Boudleaux was strumming his guitar and singing verses from an unfinished song. As Felice described the morning: "We'd just moved into our new house, and it hadn't been carpeted yet. And the acoustics were fantastic in that living room."[15] Boudleaux's singing wafted easily to the second floor where Felice had not yet arisen. Excited by the sounds that awakened her, she hurried downstairs to be present at and part of the creation, explaining that she "wanted to get a piece of this." Hearing a song about two teenagers who fell asleep on a date and afraid it was becoming too risqué for its intended audience, she added some crucial lyrics:

> The movie wasn't so hot,
> It didn't have much of a plot.
> We fell asleep; our goose is cooked,
> Our reputation is shot.
> Wake up, little Susie
> Wake up, little Susie
> We gotta go home.[16]

But the lyrics still seemed suggestive enough to create a stir, and they were allegedly banned in Boston, which only helped increase intense interest in the song—and sales soared.[17]

To take advantage of the exciting touch provided earlier by Don's Bo Diddley riff, Boudleaux left enough space between vocal phrases for the guitar to deliver its magic. Paul Simon's reaction to "Bye Bye Love" was only the opening salvo of a similar response to the "Susie" song by musicians in England and around the world. Within a few short weeks of its issue, "Wake

Wake Up Little Susie — Boudleaux Bryant
Felice Bryant

Wake up little Susie   Wake up
Wake up Susie   "   "

We're both been sound asleep
weep   Wake up little susie and weep
heap   The movies over It's four oclock
leep   And we're in trouble deep
                Wake up Little Susie
Susie open up your eyes
You're in for a big surprise

What are we gonna tell your mama
"   "   "   "   "   "   pa
What are we gonna " our friends
when they say Ooh la la
    Wake Up Susie

Cut by Everly Bros   Cahrace
         Boudleaux Bryant   Monument
    Joe McCoy   Hickory
         R.&B. record — Merc. 1967
A.R. 10   Soul Riverboat Soul Band Merc, 1967
         Simon & Garfunkel 1952 (W. Bros)

"Wake Up Little Susie" ledger page. Boudleaux liked to add those who cut the songs to the ledger page. Courtesy of the Country Music Hall of Fame® and Museum.

Up Little Susie" had reached the No. 1 position on the three major music charts: country, rhythm and blues, and popular.

Coming as it did when fears of teenage pregnancy were heightened by the rise of youth culture, the song inspired at least one critic to believe that it was a deliberate expression of social commentary. Cultural historian Rickie Solinger, whose work focuses on reproductive politics, argued that "the words of that song are about the imputation of guilt, which was a key component in unwed pregnancy at the time. This young girl thinks her association with imagined sexuality will doom her." Bob Greene, columnist for the *Chicago Tribune*, asked Felice many years later to respond to Solinger's analysis. Felice answered in her typically frank and spirited way: "If she said that, then she's off in tutu land somewhere." She added, "It was just a song. The Everly Brothers had a session coming up, and it was a job we had to get done."[18]

Felice and Boudleaux continued to write songs specifically designed for the Everlys during their spectacular commercial ascent until the early years of the 1960s, when the brothers left the management of Wesley Rose. The Everlys never used material exclusively from the Bryants; they wrote many fine songs on their own and sometimes borrowed numbers from contemporary musicians and from the past. But the Everlys recorded thirty-one songs from the Felice and Boudleaux catalogue, amounting to nearly three-fourths of their singles released on Cadence, including several that remain among their greatest hits. They, in fact, recorded a few songs—like "Love Hurts" and "Sleepless Nights"—that did little for their career but that became major hits when recorded later by other entertainers. Their earliest Cadence recordings, though, established a pattern that remained constant throughout the Everlys' tenure with that label, coupling a slow song with a faster and more novelty number, such as "All I Have to Do Is Dream" with "Claudette" (written by Roy Orbison) and "Devoted to You" with "Bird Dog." These songs and others created for the Everlys demonstrated the strong skills the Bryants continued to perfect throughout their career: crafting their songs to the singer or singers' particular style or need. The Bryants could write a light but cleverly constructed song, like "Bird Dog," which humorously captures the jealously felt toward a romantic competitor whose defects should have been recognized and rejected by one's girlfriend:

> Johnny sings a love song (like a bird)
> He sings the sweetest love song (you ever heard)

But when he sings to my gal (what a howl)
To me he's just a wolf dog (on the prowl)
Johnny wants to fly away and puppy-love my baby
(He's a bird dog)

Boudleaux recalled sitting around the house one morning:

just thinking and trying to be creative, trying to come up with
something, and I was thinking of the schoolroom situation. I
remembered that my father used to call people that he thought
were a little bit mischievous, or a little bit slick or rascally, but yet
likeable, he'd say, "Oh, he's a bird." Well, immediately the thought
came, "Well, that same son of a gun, if he were such a rascal, he's a
dog, too," you know. And then "bird dog," the two words came
together and lit my head up, and I said, "Man, what a title, 'Bird
Dog!'" And the things just kind of almost started happening pretty
easily, and within about an hour, I guess it was written.[19]

The folk revival emerged after 1958, in the wake of the Kingston Trio's
huge success with "Tom Dooley." The Everlys contributed to the movement
with their own memorable album, *Songs Our Daddy Taught Us,* the second
album on Cadence Records, released in December the same year. Both the
revival and the Everly LP may have indirectly inspired "Take a Message to
Mary," which Felice worked out one day when she was running the vacuum.
Felice mentioned to an interviewer that the lake house had a chipped marble roof, and "a piece of that marble got in the vacuum cleaner, and it's
going 'chink, chink, chink, chink,' and I'm starting to sing this thing. And
I realized I've got something. And so I called Boudleaux. Boudleaux and I
always knew where we could put our fingers on each other. And so, I called
him down at Acuff-Rose, and he wrote it down for me because he knew that
I'd lose it."[20] Although Boudleaux had purchased portable tape recorders
for Felice, when she couldn't get one to work, as with this instance of "Take
a Message to Mary," she knew that Boudleaux would "write the lead notes
down and then he'd put my initials by it cause he knew I'd have the lyrics
as long as I knew the tune was trapped somewhere. Thank goodness, Boudleaux had it because, by the time he got back home, I didn't know what the
hell the melody was."[21]

Although both Bryant sons reiterate that their father was the keeper of
their song ledgers, "Take a Message to Mary" seems to have been an excep-

Wesley Rose and Boudleaux with the Everly Brothers at the height of their careers. Courtesy of the Country Music Hall of Fame® and Museum.

tion. Felice may have wanted posterity to know that she was the composer of the song because she wrote the original version in blue ink on page 273 of Ledger 3. In the pencil he always favored, Boudleaux eventually wrote the recorded version with music notation on another page in the ledger.[22] Attending the session when "Take a Message to Mary" was recorded, Archie Bleyer felt that the song "wasn't strong enough," and he suggested a new opening that Boudleaux wrote during a break in the session. It was his only contribution to the song:

> These are the words of a frontier lad
> Who lost his love when he turned bad.

At the recording session, Felice recalled, Archie Bleyer thought something else was missing in getting the song to work. "And then he said, 'Get a Coke bottle.' The screwdriver was right there on the engineer's board. 'Boudleaux,' he says, 'get out there and hit this Coke bottle like this.' And that's

While there's still time to play dam dance
time to

Take a Message To Mary   F. Bryant

Take a message to Mary But don't tell her where I am
Take a message to Mary. But don't say I'm in a jam
You can tell her I had to see the world
You can tell her my ship at sail
You can tell her anything you tell her
But don't tell her I'm in jail
Oh. Don't tell her I'm in jail

Take a message to Mary — But don't tell her all you know
take a message to Mama (Oh how I love my sweet Mary)
Make up some kind of story — I don't want to hurt her so
You can tell her I've gone to Tim-buck-too
Tell her that searching for gold.
Don't tell her that we'll never meet again
until we're both grown old
Oh Lord this jail is cold.

Mary ——— Mary
don't tell her I'm in jail

original version by F. B.

Felice's proud handwritten copy of her lyrics for "Take a Message to Mary" on the ledger page. Courtesy of the Country Music Hall of Fame® and Museum.

what he heard. He heard that damn thing in the vacuum cleaner." The interviewer asked whether Archie had heard the sound on the demo, but Felice replied: "No, he didn't hear it on the demo. It was never on the demo. It was mental. Definitely mental. Because I didn't tell them that's where the idea came from."[23] And one distinctly hears Boudleaux hitting the Coke bottle with the screwdriver in the original recording.

The country music industry as a whole had responded to the folk revival with a body of music known as "saga songs"—story songs that depicted the experiences of both historical and fictional characters.[24] "Take a Message to Mary" spins the tale of a young man who tried to hide the news of his prison sentence from his sweetheart. Songs like this, along with their novelty pieces, were easy for the Bryants, but the couple really demonstrated their genius on the slower romantic songs, where Boudleaux could exhibit his lyric facility and his love of harmony.

Harmony had been an interest of his since his early days studying violin. He could easily write it in the couple's songs, and the Everlys excelled in the duet style. Don Everly said "their stuff fit us like a glove, because it was designed to fit. A lot of Boudleaux's songs were written because he was getting inside our heads, trying to find out where we were going, what we wanted, what words were right." His brother Phil, whose tenor singing style remains unsurpassed in country and popular music history, further asserted that "they were masters. Anybody would be a fool not to watch how they did it. I learned more from them than from anybody." Phil especially admired the Bryants' discipline. He had already purchased a ledger book when he was attempting to write songs: "What I learned from Boudleaux and Felice both is that you *go to work*. To this day, if you really want to be a writer, you have to go at it and *produce*."[25]

When interviewed by Patricia Hall, Boudleaux talked about the way he perfected the lyrics that he and Felice were writing since, as son Del said, his father was the "finisher":

> I'd sooner go to some word that doesn't look like an attempt to make it a rhyme, go to something that has no rhyme whatsover, not in any part of the word, than to have a rhyme like that, "time" and "wine." See, if you're supposed to be rhyming a word, the words should rhyme. They should rhyme perfectly. If it's an attempt to rhyme, if you fail in the attempt, then you aren't craft-

ing a song. You're not a craftsman, that's all. If you're going for a
good song and you don't make it, that's understandable, because
you can't always write a good song. But if you're going for a rhyme
and don't make it, that is really inexcusable as far as I'm concerned
because rhymes are available, or else you can change the structure
around and change your other word. You don't have to use the
first word. You can find a way around it. There is always a way to
find a different solution.[26]

Del said that his father explained: "When you write a song, you want a rhyme
that the listener can anticipate even before it is heard. In that way, you are
making the listener, in essence, a co-writer. Then the listener can think of it
as 'my' song. The rhyme comes into one's unconscious mind first."[27]

The Bryants had exhibited a genius for succinctly couching lyrics in
the language of teenage angst. Think, for example, of the punctuating
complaint—"only trouble is, gee whiz, I'm dreaming my life away"—
registered in "All I Have to Do Is Dream." These same sentiments also struck
remarkably adult and universal chords. Years later, Boudleaux explained
that when they used the words, "gee whiz," he and Felice were not writing
lyrics to sound the way *they* might speak. "When we write songs, depending
on who we're writing for, we try to project into that situation, that milieu, so
that they at least fit the style or period that they're supposed to represent."[28]

When the internationally famous lyricist for Andrew Lloyd Webber, Sir
Tim Rice, was interviewed about his admiration for the Bryants' songwriting, he specifically mentioned the way "gee whiz" adds "the spice that
makes that line so memorable." In fact, he asserted, it was "genius."[29] Virtu-
ally all of their songs dealt with the pangs of heartbreak or longing but a
few, like "Devoted to You," were positive expressions of affection. "Devoted
to You," recorded at their July 10, 1958, session, would vie with "All I Have
to Do Is Dream" as the most beautiful song in the Everly repertory. Introduced by the tremolo of Chet Atkins's electric guitar and marked by the
exquisite singing of Don and Phil, the song also seems, for Felice and
Boudleaux, quintessentially autobiographical:

> I'll never hurt you, I'll never lie
> I'll never be untrue
> I'll never give you reason to cry

I'd be unhappy if you were blue
Through the years our love will grow
Like a river it will flow
It can't die because I'm so
Devoted to you.

The Everlys' exceptional talents—Don's superior guitar playing and Phil's peerless harmonies—gave Boudleaux the opportunity to move beyond songwriter Harlan Howard's depiction of country music's penchant for "three chords and the truth" and incorporate more complicated chord progressions and harmonies.[30] The Bryant-Everly combination worked wondrously, majestically boosting the fortunes of both couples. British youth had initially been swept away by American rhythm and blues, and then by rock 'n' roll as early as Elvis and Chuck Berry. The Everlys, however, offered something new with the Bryants' songs and their pristine harmony. And after that formula for success made it to the United Kingdom, it inadvertently helped fuel the British invasion as it boomeranged back across the Atlantic.

In the early 1960s the British childhood actor, singer, and future producer Peter Asher began his career with Gordon Waller as Peter and Gordon when they were both still students. They were smitten with the Everlys, learning everything they could from their records, reading whatever they could find, imitating their style, and singing their songs. And when Peter and Gordon saw "the little names in parentheses on the record label: Boudleaux and Felice Bryant," they thought, "What amazing names! Who are they? We thought they were totally magic writers who could write song after song. All the great songs would be Boudleaux and Felice Bryant. We loved all those and we sang them all. And the Everlys learned from the Bryants when they emerged as successful songwriters themselves."[31] In 1964 Peter and Gordon recorded their first Bryant-penned Everly Brothers song, "Sleepless Nights."

Sir Tim Rice was a young teenager in 1957 when he heard "Bye Bye Love" at a roadside café and played it on a jukebox about nine times in a row. And he remembers that "all of us kids" were soon buying up the Everlys' singles. The Everlys remained popular in England long after their popularity began waning in the United States, nurturing the young British acts who inhaled their harmonies and songs before writing, singing, and recording their own. Peter Asher feels that British youth had "fallen in love with American music" and may have "treated rock 'n' roll with more deference and even more respect," perhaps because it was foreign and harder to get, before British groups began "selling it back to you." For the teenage Graham Nash, "Boudleaux and Felice's melodies were so simple that if you were a kid just beginning to play guitar in England, the chords were simple enough to follow." Peter Asher, at the same point in his early career, found the songs "so easy to learn" with lyrics sounding "familiar and melodically simple in a good way." The Rolling Stones' Keith Richards summed up the Everly phenomenon as the result of a harmonious relationship between songwriters and singers: "I can never think of the Everly Brothers without thinking of the others who were involved. There were really four of them: the Everly Brothers and Boudleaux and Felice Bryant, who wrote all of those beautifully written songs so well suited to the boys' voices."[32]

Before the Everlys, the Bryants were already making an exceptionally good living as the most successful songwriters in Nashville. The Bryant-Everly collaboration proved even more financially significant. The Everlys and those producing them earned the lion's share of the money from the enterprise. While the songwriters' share of the total profits was only a fraction, Patrick Fabbio, an accountant for BMI at that time, said that Boudleaux was their highest earner in 1958 and 1959. Even in 1957, according to Dane and Del, the Bryants were proud that they'd earned over one hundred thousand dollars, which would be the equivalent of about nine hundred thousand dollars in today's economy. For every record sold at the time, the publishing house received two cents—one cent for the publisher, one cent to the songwriter. The Bryants' diligent insistence on "quantity" as a guiding principle proved sound. Year after year, their income increased dramatically.[33]

Despite the successful partnership between songwriters and singers, the Bryants' professional association with the Everlys began to decline toward the end of 1961. The songs Boudleaux and Felice wrote for them, of course, live on. The signing of a lucrative recording contract with Warner Brothers in 1960 had not weakened the Everlys' commercial appeal, nor did it end their relationship with the Bryants. But when Don and Phil told Wesley Rose that they no longer wanted to be managed by him, he reacted bitterly.

Wesley's sharp and retributive response proved financially destructive to all concerned. He declared that the Everlys would no longer be permitted to record any of the Acuff-Rose songs, past or present, authored by Felice and Boudleaux or by any of the other Acuff-Rose songwriters. And all of their songs, at Wesley's advice, had come exclusively from Acuff-Rose. Because Don and Phil also wrote their own songs and "were still signed to Acuff-Rose as songwriters, the falling out with Wesley Rose meant that the brothers lost access to their own material as well, and any material they may write in the future."[34] While the Everlys continued to be popular in Canada, Australia, and the United Kingdom, their reign at the top of the American charts effectively ended, curtailing what very likely would have been their continuance as this country's leading duet team. And in 1964, the British Invasion, based in large part on the Bryants' melodies and the Everlys' harmonies, precluded the Everlys from ever again rising to their previous heights. When interviewed later in life, Phil Everly said: "The one thing I know for sure is the songs that Boudleaux would have written for us would have been designed to move us up to the next level. It would have maintained our career a lot longer, I think."[35] Although the Bryants were both extremely disappointed and angry with Wesley Rose, they still honored their ten-year contract. Their trust in Wesley's judgment, however, was never recovered.

★ ★ ★ ★ ★

Chapter 5

LIVING AT THE LAKE AND BUILDING THE HOUSE OF BRYANT

Although the Bryants profited immensely from their association with the Everlys, they never depended solely on them for their economic livelihood. Boudleaux, for his part, was always trying new ways to prosper in the music business. He wrote liner notes, occasionally sat in as a session musician, and in 1959 even directed the band (made up of an assemblage of major Nashville musicians) on an LP of cowboy songs recorded by Johnnie Ray, *On the Trail* (Columbia CL 1385). The Bryants continued to place songs with other artists and occasionally saw some of them win major success on the popularity charts. "Bye Now Baby," in fact, won extensive circulation in 1959 and 1960 as the B-side of Mark Dinning's blockbuster hit, "Teen Angel." Dinning's song chronicled the story of a young girl who died in a stalled car hit by a train. She was trying to retrieve the class ring that her sweetheart had given her. This lachrymose ballad was one of several similar songs of the era, like "Running Bear" and "El Paso," that inspired another Bryant hit, "Let's Think about Living," written in 1960 and recorded that same year by Bob Luman.

Luman was from a little community called Blackjack, near Nacogdoches, Texas. He moved from traditional country music to rockabilly when he saw Elvis Presley in concert in East Texas. He said that was "the last time I tried to sing like Webb Pierce or Lefty Frizzell."[1] When he first heard "Let's Think about Living" in the Bryants' living room, Luman was impressed with its clever "complaint" about the rash of dying-for-love songs but was otherwise indifferent to the song as a whole. But when, from the kitchen, Felice joined in with some joyous responses to Boudleaux's singing, Luman began to recognize the song's potential. Performed with Luman's trademark rockabilly swagger, it became his first No. 1 song.

The Bryant songs of the 1960s—prior to "Rocky Top"—did not all become major hits (at least not immediately), but some of them nevertheless won distinction for other reasons. "Raining in My Heart," for example, first released in 1959 by Charles "Buddy" Holly, began its rise to prominence only after his death. It went on to become one of the Bryants' most recorded and enduring songs, performed by country singers like Ray Price and pop performers ranging from Patti Page and Connie Francis to Don McLean. British singers Graham Nash and Leo Sayers made hit recordings of the song; outside of the United States, it still performs as one of the House of Bryant's largest copyrights.[2] Jimmy Dickens got onto the rockabilly bandwagon in April 1958, with "I Got a Hole in My Pocket," a song successfully recorded years later by Ricky Van Shelton. Boudleaux became involved in the success of "My Last Date with You" in a roundabout way. Based on Floyd Cramer's earlier instrumental hit "Last Date," the song gained renewed life when Skeeter Davis (Mary Frances Penick) recorded it in December 1960, with lyrics provided by Boudleaux and Skeeter.

Leona Douglas made country music history in 1962 when she recorded Felice and Boudleaux's "Too Many Chicks." She was an African American vocalist who called the innovative owner and producer Fred Foster at Monument Records to inquire if he would be willing to record her. Foster, who had become one of the Bryants' best friends, took the gamble and asked them for some appropriate lyrics. Released in 1962, four years before Charley Pride made his first recordings for RCA Victor, "Too Many Chicks" may merit recognition as the first country song to be released by an African American singer in the modern era.[3]

Boudleaux was a well-liked personality in Nashville, with a host of associates, but no one was closer to him than Fred Foster. For the last thirty years of his life, Boudleaux enjoyed the almost constant presence of this genial North Carolinian as a close personal friend, neighbor, musical confidant, and a tenant in the Hendersonville office building that Boudleaux built for him. Born in Rutherford County, North Carolina, in 1931, at the age of seventeen Foster moved to Washington, DC, where he began to work in the Hot Shoppe Restaurant chain.

Music was his real love, however, and he soon began writing songs and making contacts with people like Jimmy Dean in the thriving local music community. He found employment with Mercury and ABC-Paramount and by 1958 had joined with Buddy Deane to found the Monument record label, a title inspired by the Washington Monument that he viewed with awe when flying into the nation's capital. In that same year, while living in Adelphi, Maryland, he was intrigued by an infectious traditional song being played by a neighbor, John Dildine. Dildine, who hosted a folk music show on a local public radio station, had a large collection of ethnic and traditional records. This particular song, later labeled by Foster as "Gotta Travel On," had been put together from older fragments by folk singer Paul Clayton.[4] Foster placed the song with Billy Grammer, formerly a guitarist with Jimmy Dean's Texas Wildcats, and saw it become one of the big hits of the day, and selling over nine hundred thousand copies. Although still located in Maryland, Foster recorded the song in Nashville and began making frequent trips to the city, establishing a reputation there as an astute student of singers and songs. Foster met Boudleaux sometime in 1959 during a visit to Acuff-Rose. The two men were immediately drawn to one another, and given the interest they showed for the teachings of Eastern religions and other esoterica, Foster believed that Boudleaux had an "aura" around him.[5]

Boudleaux soon became Foster's trusted mentor. He encouraged Foster to move to Nashville in July 1960, setting up the Monument office temporarily in an old building in Hendersonville. Boudleaux had promised to erect a building that would house Monument Records, and he had the Bryant Building constructed in downtown Hendersonville. By August 1963, Foster had moved his business operation to the third floor of the new building, with the Bryant office occupying the floor beneath. Boudleaux even found the Foster family a place to live on the lake around the corner from the Bryants.[6] When they weren't fishing—a popular avocation for both men—or engaging in some other social diversion, the Bryant Building served as the site of their frequent meetings with other music industry people. It was not uncommon for young musicians such as Harlan Howard and Willie Nelson to show up for drinks and fellowship.

An encounter in the Bryant Building inspired the writing of one of pop and country music's most famous songs. Foster often came down to Boudleaux's office on the second floor. On one occasion Boudleaux said, teasingly, "Fred, you're not fooling me. You're just coming down to see Bobbie McKee, my good-looking secretary!" Fred carried the story in his head, and said one day to one of his bright young singer-songwriters, Kris Kristofferson, who had been suffering from a temporary writer's block, "I have

Boudleaux and Fred Foster (*seated*); Wesley Rose and Roy Orbison (*standing*).
Courtesy of the Country Music Hall of Fame® and Museum.

a great song title for you, 'Me and Bobbie McKee.'" Fred told him to go
home and write the song. Kristofferson misunderstood the name, and he
was reluctant to write on assignment, but he eventually came up with the
song made famous by Janis Joplin, "Me and Bobby McGee." In gratitude for
the inspiration, Kristofferson put Foster's name on the song as a cowriter.[7]

Kristofferson was only one of many great artists who thrived under the
direction, production, and promotion of Fred Foster. The young Dolly Parton made her first hit records at Monument. Afterward, she was joined by a
lengthy array of performers—such as Ray Stevens, Grandpa Jones, Billy
Walker, Jeannie Seely, and Boots Randolph—who achieved fame while
making Monument records.[8] While these performers constituted an impressive list, the artist who won the greatest success while helping to build the
label an international reputation was Roy Orbison, a young tenor from
Wink, Texas, whose singing ranged from rockabilly to country pop. When
Orbison came to Monument, he was a shy young singer who was reluctant

to test his full vocal powers. But Foster persuaded him to move out of his falsetto and into his natural high tenor and built an instrumental sound that would complement, and not smother, the singer's sound. Under Foster's direction, Orbison moved far beyond the hillbilly style he had grown up with and, with songs like "Only the Lonely," "Pretty Woman," "Blue Bayou," and "Crying," became an elegant vocalist whose music was admired around the world.

Boudleaux was present at many of Monument's finest moments. Foster trusted Boudleaux's musical instincts and was pleased to have him at his recording sessions. Boudleaux even played guitar on a couple of Orbison's sessions on June 26 and 27, 1961, which included "Crying" and "She Wears My Ring," Boudleaux and Felice's rearrangement and rewriting of a classic Mexican song, "La Golondrina." He also occasionally wrote liner notes for Orbison's LPs. While Orbison usually wrote his own songs, Boudleaux contributed a few, including one that has endured as a classic of pop music around the world. After considerable debate at a recording session in 1961, Foster made "Love Hurts" the B-side of a record that featured "Running Scared" as the prominent cut. Orbison's version of "Love Hurts" did become No. 7 on the Australian popular charts, but it received little radio play in the United States. The song's exalted place in history did not come until later.[9]

Boudleaux and Fred also occasionally worked together to produce recordings. They collaborated, for example, with the Hollywood actor Robert Mitchum, who experimented successfully with the country idiom and even wrote a few popular hits like "Ballad of Thunder Road." In 1967 Mitchum recorded an LP for Monument called *That Man, Robert Mitchum, Sings*, with liner notes by Johnny Mercer and four songs written by the Bryants.

Boudleaux and Fred also collaborated on instrumentals. At least two of their productions, "Mexico" and *Polynesian Suite*, explored exotic international themes. The genesis of "Mexico," intriguingly, came out of a trip Foster took to Germany in 1961 to promote some of his recordings on the Continent. A skeptical German producer told Foster that not only would a recording of Roy Orbison there be an exercise in futility, but that no American-produced record could ever be No. 1 in Germany. Foster had no potential hit ready, but he made a wager that he could produce one. He and the German producer agreed that the loser would have to treat the winner to dinner anywhere in the world, at the latter's choosing. The loser of the bet would also have to foot the bill for the transportation and lodging of the winner. On the day of the wager Foster spent time with a driver visiting clubs and bars to see what customers were selecting on jukeboxes. His time was well spent, since he discovered that German people liked "Latin" songs with horns and a strong beat.

When he returned home, Fred immediately asked Boudleaux to write an instrumental piece that met those dictates. Boudleaux delivered a few compositions the next day, and Fred selected "Mexico," which was soon recorded by an all-star group of instrumentalists headed by the bass player Bob Moore, one of the most active session musicians in Nashville. The recording charted in the top ten in the United States—it even inspired Herb Alpert to found his own very successful band, the Tijuana Brass—but it reached the No. 1 status in Germany. The German producer was greatly relieved when Foster asked him to host the winning dinner at a fine local restaurant.[10]

Boudleaux loved the steel guitar and held the master of the instrument, Jerry Byrd, in high esteem. Like Boudleaux, Byrd was born in 1920. He hailed from Lima, Ohio. At the age of thirteen, Byrd first encountered the Hawaiian guitar in a touring Hawaiian tent show and soon began playing the instrument. He built an impressive record as a musician on numerous country music sessions in Detroit, Cincinnati, and Nashville backing up people such as Ernest Tubb and Red Foley. As much as any one person, he made the steel guitar one of the preeminent instruments in country music. Even though he had become one of country music's early session musicians, he was so enamored of Hawaiian styles that he moved to Hawaii in 1971 and became an iconic figure in the music scene there.[11]

Boudleaux's admiration for Byrd inspired him to write *Polynesian Suite*, an ambitious attempt to create a symphony for the instrument. He wrote a series of short pieces with romantic titles reflecting various sites and events in the Hawaiian Islands and then presented them to Byrd to learn. Felice and Boudleaux and Billie and Fred Foster embarked on a combined vacation and business trip, along with Byrd and Bill Justis, a noted musician and arranger. The troupe flew to Mexico City in August 1968, where they added a fifty-eight-member Mexican symphony orchestra. They completed three recording sessions there before a major earthquake forced the evacuation of their hotel. Almost three minutes in duration, the quake was so loud that Fred maintains that he couldn't hear for a week. Three more sessions took place in Nashville. According to reviewer Joseph M.

Boudreau, the production costs topped twenty-five thousand dollars. He lauded the final product as "an entrancing musical quilt, a true symphonic suite consisting of twelve individual segments, including an opening and a finale done in the finest tradition of the Broadway musical stage." With the steel guitar as the centerpiece, Boudreau pronounced it "the most ambitious recording project ever undertaken to showcase the instrument."[12] Unfortunately, *Polynesian Suite* did not achieve commercial success, and many steel guitar aficionados were indifferent at best to what they thought was a waste of Jerry Byrd's talent. Some critics were hostile to an effort that seemed "an oddity" or, at least, too bland or boring to suit their tastes.[13]

The trip to Mexico is only one example of the fellowship shared by the two men. Fred and Boudleaux made one trip to England alone, sometime in 1966, where Fred visited recording contacts, and he and Boudleaux spent most of their free time in antique shops, looking for rugs and instruments.[14] Fred said that an attractive stewardess on the flight to London seemed smitten with Boudleaux and was extremely attentive to his needs, conversing with the two passengers whenever she had ample time between duties. When they reached the hotel, she called, hoping that she and Boudleaux could get together. Flattered, Boudleaux politely refused, telling Fred that he would never do anything to jeopardize his relationship with Felice, the love of his life.

Boudleaux and "the love of his life" found comfort in the lake house that they had built on an expansive, well-situated lot on Old Hickory Lake. Complete with a stone patio and large pool, it also was ideal for their boys and their friends. The Bryants wanted a home that would both serve as a center for their work and socializing and yet keep their sons close by. That meant designing an environment that would be the destination for their sons' social activities. With a pool, fishing, a backyard large enough for football and badminton, and fun-loving "parents who were writing rock 'n' roll hits and would sing them for their kids' friends," 715 Neptune Drive anchored the family.[15]

Del remembered how Felice drove the boys' bowling team, the "Bird Dogs"—aptly named for the Bryants' big Everly hit—to the bowling alley for their weekly league competition. She also liked to don costumes for Valentine's Day and Halloween, making herself up to be extremely beautiful or extremely scary. Although Boudleaux was far more reserved, he was generous to all the neighborhood children, taking them for walks among

The Bryants enjoyed the relaxing comfort of their Old Hickory Lake home.
Courtesy House of Bryant Publications.

the many varieties of trees he had planted while they made leaf collections
for their school projects. Because of their parents' warm welcome that
made their friends feel at home, Dane and Del were very popular. "We were
proud of them; they were supportive."[16] Team Bryant worked on every level.

The big house on the lake had come to be the Bryants' primary and
proud sanctuary. It also served as a popular rendezvous for people in the
Nashville music community. To Felice's great consternation, Boudleaux
frequently invited people home without first consulting her. But she stood
ready to prepare one of her signature Italian dishes for them. After she
voiced her frustration, Dane and Del would get busy cleaning the house
and stirring the tomato sauce. On one especially hectic day, a guest landed
in a pontoon plane, and Eddy Arnold arrived at their lakefront in his large
Chris-Craft. When Boudleaux looked down the long driveway and saw
Jimmy Dickens pulling up in his Cadillac, Felice exclaimed: "My God, now

Felice's open kitchen was more than a cherished family gathering place; it also served as their songwriting nexus. Courtesy House of Bryant Publications.

they're coming by land, sea, and air." She recalled, "We had a houseful all the time."[17]

Apart from impromptu visits, the Bryants became well-known for their Christmas and New Years' parties—marked by Boudleaux's customary southern preparation of black-eyed peas—which were both convivial gatherings and business-networking affairs. Boudleaux believed strongly in maintaining crucial contacts with radio personalities, such as Ralph Emery, as well as musicians, record executives, and music journalists. Some people, though, were particularly special through their long-standing personal friendships: BMI executive Frances Preston, producer and songwriter Joe Allison, Bluegrass musician Sonny Osborne, singer Roy Orbison and his wife, Claudette, Chet Atkins, Phil Everly, and Fred and Billie Foster.

The Fosters' home at 142 Riviera, a circle right off Neptune Drive, was across the slough only a short distance from the Bryants', and they were on constant call for small, intimate gatherings. Visits between the two families occurred often. Boudleaux and Fred joked that if they could only walk on water they could walk from one backyard to the other. On New Year's Day each of them observed what they described as a "Southern tradition," the belief that the first person the male head of household greeted beyond the members of one's own family had to be a male. They maintained this custom by making sure that they saw each other first before greeting anyone else each New Year's Day. If the Bryants' housekeeper Martha Woods showed up for work before Fred or Boudleaux saw one another, she had to wait outside in the carport until the ritual was accomplished.[18] When *Billboard* published an appreciation of the Bryants, called "25 Years of Harmony," Fred took out a full-page advertisement in the issue in his longhand script: "Dear Boudleaux and Felice, All those New Year's Day breakfasts of Black-Eyed Peas and hog jowl have really been working—but so have you. Congratulations and Love, Fred."[19]

Felice and Boudleaux were the unofficial godparents of the Foster children. The youngest Foster daughter, Leah, remembers riding on her bicycle frequently to visit the Bryants unannounced and being welcomed with treats and small talk. She remarked that she had been too young to realize she may have been interrupting their work, because she had never known any man who worked at home. Boudleaux and Felice made her feel comfortable, even if they'd been busy writing songs when she arrived. "They always asked *me* questions, and seemed genuinely interested in me, rather than ever talking about themselves. When you got to their house, you immediately relaxed. It was my safe haven. I tried to model my life after them. I didn't realize that until the other day when I thought of the relationship I share with my husband. Of all my tucked-away memories, being around them would be in my top ten."[20]

Felice counted Billie Foster, who lived only three minutes away by car, as one of her closest friends. Although both were excellent cooks, Billie's style and ingredients reflected her Virginia farm background. Felice taught Billie her special trick for roasting peppers, for example, and Billie shared tips on her special dishes in return. Felice and Billie would drive in Felice's Thunderbird to the bowling alley, where they enjoyed playing in their league, sometimes stopping for lunch before they returned home. The two women loved shoes and enjoyed shopping for them together. Never having had a sister, Billie said that she regarded Felice as a sister from the first time they met. Even though their busy schedules prevented frequent socializing, when they managed to meet the two freely discussed everything—from the practical to the spiritual. They created a prayer circle, conversing periodically as they added to each other's prayer list the names of friends and family who were having some kind of difficulty or medical crisis. Each kept a group of her own friends who would also pray for those on the list, and the prayer circle provided a source of comfort and strength, or a sense of sharing that became a real "bonding experience."[21]

Boudleaux and Fred fished, negotiated, traveled together, and talked at great length. They may have been seasoned music professionals, but they were also southern country boys who relished home-cooked meals at breakfast or special occasions, or for no other reason than getting together. When Fred went back home to North Carolina, he usually returned with cases of his favorite brand of mayonnaise, and he kept a stand of homegrown tomatoes in his backyard, which he shared with the Bryants. He liked to come to their kitchen and meticulously prepare his favorite meals for them. Boudleaux remembered, for example, Fred grating onions and orange juice together "when preparing an utterly fabulous gourmet meal, all the while waving a razor-honed butcher knife like a medieval weapon at a jousting match."[22] Fred admired the Bryants' relationship as well. "When they were showing songs," he said, "it was like a party. He would suggest one thing, and she'd counter with another as she'd serve food and drink. They were just a wonderful team like that."[23]

Exploring the spiritual side of human nature was a favorite enterprise for Boudleaux and Fred. They both liked to think of themselves as "seekers" of the truth, but Boudleaux particularly was ready to talk about many subjects at the drop of a hat, including the realms of mysticism, occultism, clairvoyance, spiritualism, and the varieties of religion. He had talked frequently with Fred Rose about Christian Science. Boudleaux read voluminously, with the facility of a speed reader, and he loved to share his knowledge with others, but only when they seemed receptive to such topics. His earliest interest in these subjects probably predated his involvement in theosophy while he was living in Atlanta. Boudleaux believed that many paths led to God and to spiritual fulfillment, and that the divine purpose was eternal and universal. These beliefs underlay his fascination with the possibility of chance encounters with divine sparks in others or in experiences of enlightenment in the realms of reincarnation and clairvoyance.

Boudleaux's devotion to the works of Edgar Cayce further fueled his investigations into spiritual matters. Cayce (1877–1945) was the Kentucky-born clairvoyant who built an immense following with his tales of diagnosis of illness through self-hypnosis. When he emerged from his "trances," Cayce gave "readings" that told his patients how their problems could be treated. These diagnoses evolved into prophecies of both personal and world events.[24] Boudleaux believed that "Cayce was a genuine prophet" with an "ability to zero in on the eternal truths of the force that operates us." He continued, "When he was in his sleep state, I think he absolutely made contact with the infinite, and I think he got information there that was absolutely right. And I think he shared a lot of that information through his readings with all of us."[25] Del noted that his father was a member of the Association for Research and Enlightenment, founded to further the work of Edgar Cayce and, beyond that, "was always flying psychics in and searching for the meaning of life."[26] Boudleaux apparently never delved into prophecy, but he accepted the validity of clairvoyance, consulted those he perceived as spiritual intermediaries, and practiced hypnosis from time to time. He even hypnotized Felice on at least one occasion, but he abandoned the practice when she emerged from the experience tearful and distraught. He never attempted it with her again.[27]

In the years following the exhilarating and busy Everly Brothers' experience, the Bryants could now spend more time on trips to relax at their favorite vacation haunts—Gatlinburg and the Smoky Mountains. While the Bryants never stopped thinking about nor writing songs, the need to produce new ones now lacked the urgency and demanded less time than it had in their almost-starving era of the early Nashville days. Their son Del, though, said that song-plugging was in his dad's DNA, and that even on vacations he and Felice took along a few records to show DJs along the route as they traveled. While such trips were necessary and restful, Boudleaux could also devote more attention to his passion for fishing, or to spending restful hours with his sons or seizing the moments to discuss esoterica with Fred Foster or other friends. An undated clipping from this period shows Boudleaux and Moon Mullican, the noted barrelhouse piano player, holding a big string of crappie fish weighing about thirty-three pounds.[28]

Songwriting was immensely profitable, but Boudleaux sought further security through the acquisition of tangible property. He did not invest in the stock market, but instead bought cars, instruments, rugs, buildings, and land. His son Del said that his dad was "an acquirer" who did not like to see money lying around being unproductive. He helped both sons find good houses on prime pieces of land once they were ready to put down stakes.[29] Permanently marked by the deprivations of her childhood, Felice happily partook of the joys and glamour of their hard-won prosperity. Their longtime housekeeper, Martha Woods, said that Felice liked to dress well when she went before the public and that she enjoyed new clothes. Like Felice, Woods was a small woman, and Felice passed on the clothes she was no longer wearing, which fit her housekeeper perfectly.[30] And she and Boudleaux both loved their cars—from the 1953 Oldsmobile to the 1958 four-door Cadillac family car and Felice's Thunderbird—for which they took great pride in paying cash *after* moving into the lake house.[31] They also realized that such visible displays of success could lure aspiring musicians to their songs.

Boudleaux carefully studied the classifieds each morning, looking for bargains that might be of interest. In 1965 he ventured into "ranching," buying nineteen hundred acres near Franklin, just a few miles southwest of Nashville. The family referred to the property as a farm, even though the primary purpose of the venture was raising cattle. Boudleaux decided to stock his farm with Santa Gertrudis cattle, a breed of which he had become increasingly aware since they were first offered for public sale in 1951.[32] Developed in South Texas on the King Ranch and named for the Spanish land grant where the ranch was located, the Santa Gertrudis were the first beef breed developed in the United States. They were the product of the mating of Brahman bulls and beef shorthorn cows and were famous for their hardiness and sumptuous beef.[33] With the typical thoroughness that he devoted to every subject that interested him, Boudleaux read all the literature he could find on the cattle and on the lore of South Texas. He also corresponded with the managers and cowboys of the King Ranch and even briefly brought up a small family of Mexican American vaqueros to take care of his cattle. Boudleaux paid meticulous daily attention to the affairs of the farm. He was even inspired to write a song, Bob Luman's hit "Love Worked a Miracle," after seeing the tranquilizing effects wrought on a mean-spirited bull when a pretty young cow was put in the pen with him.[34]

While Boudleaux contemplated a permanent move to the place, Felice was easily spooked by country noises and disliked the solitude. Del and

Dane, on the other hand, loved the idea of retreating to country life, which both of them did after they retired. Del, in fact, planned to build his retirement home on part of the tract that he inherited—until his wife learned of the presence of snakes on that undeveloped property.

Like any devoted husband, Boudleaux never wanted to see Felice unhappy. When Dane and Del were teenagers, Felice's mother called to borrow money, because she wanted to build an addition onto the home she and George Sokas owned in Florida. While the Bryants were doing well and living well, they did not have the cash on hand to lend the amount she wanted. Katherine began berating her daughter on the phone, hurling hurtful insults, and telling her she was sorry Felice had ever been born.

Felice cried hysterically, frightening her sons and Boudleaux. Boudleaux picked up the phone and told his mother-in-law never to call their home again. That conversation was the last time Felice had any contact with Katherine. She did not go to her funeral when she died, mentioning the death to Dane and Del only a couple of years after it occurred. Felice had put her painful Milwaukee past behind her. Even though she had remained closer to her father after she grew up, Felice treated his death the same way, not telling her sons until well past the event.[35]

The severing of ties with Felice's mother presaged another significant break, one that had been gathering strength over time. When the Bryants first signed their ten-year contract with Acuff-Rose, their relationship with Wesley and his family flourished. Their friendship was so close that they generally celebrated Christmas and birthday parties together. Margaret and Wesley babysat Dane and Del while their parents attended the funeral of Felice's grandmother in Milwaukee. Del even mentioned that "the only house that Dane and I ever slept in, other than home, or at Grandmother's, was at Wesley Rose's."[36]

While the Bryants had hated to be caught in the middle of the argument between the Everlys and Wesley, they nevertheless had maintained their contract with Acuff-Rose. But as that contract approached the end of the ten-year agreement, Wesley's displeasure with the arrangement suggested a further deterioration between him and his most highly producing clients. Boudleaux and Felice perceived "chicanery" in Wesley's attempts to renew, update, and change the agreement—which they absolutely did not want. Because the Bryants were held in such stellar regard throughout the Nashville music community, an interviewer in the mid-1980s asked the couple if there was anybody in the music business with whom they did not get along. Felice replied: "Wesley Rose is the one who brought the hate out in me." Boudleaux immediately concurred: "Wesley Rose was the only one whom we definitely disliked, and that was only after seven years of working together."[37]

Songwriter Dennis Morgan drove that point home in a story he learned while he and his wife were driving in England with a friend of Boudleaux's. The friend told him that once when he, Felice, and Boudleaux were touring in England, three of the Bryant songs came over the radio in quick succession. Boudleaux immediately said, "Wesley Rose, that SOB," since Wesley had downplayed the value of the international copyrights, which had been excluded from the ten-year contract.[38]

The Bryants' resentment of Wesley, however, stemmed from other transgressions they believed he had committed. Del explained: "My dad had a huge ego, but he knew his spot in the chain. Fred [Rose] was good at everything; Wesley wasn't good at anything but accounting. He had to act like he was good at everything." Although the Bryant family members had enjoyed socializing with Wesley, Del felt that "he went nuts if his power was challenged," even claiming that Wesley feigned heart attacks to get his way. The Bryants' disappointment also sprang from their belief that Wesley lacked the humanity, magnanimity, and compassion that had distinguished his father. Del argued that Wesley Rose had prospered from the contacts Fred Rose initiated, and that Acuff-Rose moved from "small time success to big-time success: from Hank Williams to the Everlys and Orbison." And in that transformation, "Wesley went from honest and good to mainly shrewd." As the ten-year contract was nearing its end, Felice felt "betrayed" by what she saw as Wesley's avarice and claimed that he was belittling their contributions.[39]

Felice and Boudleaux offered examples of the lengths to which they thought Wesley went in his attempt to diminish and blacken their reputation. As Felice put it: "The love affair was so hot that when he decided he had to do some quick work on us—give us four years of hell to make us resign those contracts—he went totally the other way," trying "to kill us in the newspapers and magazines. He tried to destroy us by saying we weren't writing much anymore, and other writers were coming up, and the material we were writing was passé. Just terrible, terrible PR."[40]

Boudleaux claimed that in a major article in *Billboard* that mentioned both the Bryants and the singer and songwriter John Loudermilk, Wesley implied that Loudermilk was writing "about a hundred songs a month" and Boudleaux and Felice had "almost quit writing." Boudleaux believed that this information came directly from Wesley during an interview with one of the staff writers in which he told everyone that Boudleaux and Felice signed ten-year contracts. "He just didn't tell anyone that we were getting our copyrights back." Felice added that Rose was "the king of half-truths." Wesley knew that other songwriters respected Felice and Boudleaux and their work for Acuff-Rose. By not telling other prospective songwriters that the Bryants' contracts specified an end date, he lured new clients into believing they would be working under similar terms.[41] The breakup with Acuff-Rose left a bitter memory.

On January 1, 1967, Felice and Boudleaux once again established their own publishing company, the House of Bryant, finally achieving the independence they had always wanted, with headquarters on the second floor of the Bryant Building. The House of Bryant profited from the earlier reversion agreement, which permitted the return of their previously published and unpublished songs. Along with their newly composed songs, Felice and Boudleaux now had their own highly competitive business. It remained their publishing house for the rest of their careers and continues with their sons today.

While Felice and Boudleaux could take great satisfaction in their work, which was providing them with economic security, this feeling probably paled next to their pride in their sons. As the boys grew toward manhood, they had already experienced a lifetime apprenticeship in music. They had heard and embraced their parents' music since they were babies. The boys listened from infancy to the negotiations about songs and occasionally made demos for their parents. Sometimes the sons went out on the road with Boudleaux and Felice during their tours of radio stations throughout the South. Dane and Del entered Hendersonville High School as freshmen, but when they reached their junior and sophomore years respectively, their family's economic success enabled them to transfer to one of the finest private high schools in Nashville.

They matriculated and graduated from Peabody Demonstration School (later renamed the University School of Nashville), the laboratory school for the highly regarded George Peabody College for Teachers, now within Vanderbilt University. In the first integrated school in the city, Del and Dane gained a broad liberal arts education taught by highly trained instructors, many of whom were PhDs or graduate students at Vanderbilt. Because of the links between the Demonstration School and Peabody College, the high school's faculty experimented with and implemented new methods to reach students. Both boys encountered outstanding courses as well as a culturally diverse student body. Under such circumstances the Bryant sons gained a solid academic foundation, which both of them appreciated.[42]

When Dane was seventeen and Del sixteen, their parents gave them one briefcase with both sets of the boys' initials lettered on the top. It contained two compartments that housed records for their sons' first solo song-plugging adventure on the road for the House of Bryant. They were replicating the experiences of Felice and Boudleaux, carrying a briefcase stuffed with records and visiting radio stations along the route. Del recalled some of the gimmicks their parents used to popularize records, and in which he and Dane participated. When the House of Bryant published "Georgia Piney Woods," for example, they included pine seedlings when they sent or delivered a record to disc jockeys, and for "Muddy Bottom," they presented the DJs with a little package of dirt and rocks.[43] Having both inherited and grown up in the midst of their parents' business expertise and familiarity with their music, Dane and Del were well equipped to stop at radio stations between Nashville and Knoxville, the first destination of their initial road trip. Like their father, they knew how to establish, build, and nurture relationships with DJs and station managers. Dane, for example, still knows the man who ran the Knoxville station.

The boys met with distributors as well. "We went to every radio station we could until we'd given all the product away. Then we'd offer to buy them lunch. We understood that when records sold, things were better." That memory kindled a much earlier one. Dane recalled being with Del in the yard of the basement house "in those little plaid jackets" when their mother came down to tell them "we had to cinch up our belts when things got tight. And we knew that that meant we couldn't go to the movies and eat buttered popcorn. We knew what belt-tightening meant."[44] This particularly vivid scene and others like it accompanied them into adulthood, undergirding their own understanding of the dedication it took to become successful music business entrepreneurs.

Chapter 6

ASCENDING "ROCKY TOP" AND REACHING OTHER PEAKS

With the founding of the House of Bryant in 1967, Felice and Boudleaux stood at the pinnacle of a remarkable songwriting career, and their songs were now circulating around the world. No one could have blamed them if they had chosen to retire—having gained such success at the ages of forty-two and forty-seven. After all, it had been ten years since "Bye Bye Love" shook up the music world and introduced them to an international audience. A mythical peak in the Smoky Mountains, however, literally took the Bryants on a steep hike to another summit altogether. This ascent began with a request from the country music personality Archie Campbell. He had a summer show in Gatlinburg where he performed every night; Chet Atkins told Boudleaux that Archie was looking for some new material.

Archie asked Boudleaux if he and Felice could come up to Gatlinburg to talk about a "golden years" album he was putting together. Boudleaux replied: "OK, we'll come up there and write some stuff, and we'll be there readily available, and as we get it done, we can show it to you." As usual, the Bryants were ready to run with an assignment. Felice told an interviewer: "You don't have to invite us twice to Gatlinburg. We love it."[1]

Three and a half hours east of Nashville, the Great Smoky Mountains surround Gatlinburg's picturesque valley location. In 1912 a national college women's sorority, Pi Beta Phi, opened a settlement school there, just as similar schools were founded in the Appalachian region to teach mountain children. The earliest such school in Tennessee, Arrowmont, became important in the development of Gatlinburg as a center of mountain handicraft culture.[2] Three years after the Great Smoky Mountains National Park was established in 1934, Gatlinburg Inn opened its doors to visitors even before the park was fully complete. The town began attracting greater numbers of tourists, especially after World War II, and its reputation as a vacation center has only expanded since.[3] Its compelling scenery, park access, and historic charm and its distance from urban and suburban living make it easy to understand why the Bryants so enjoyed their time there, whether they were simply vacationing or busily creating.

On August 28, 1967, Boudleaux and Felice checked into the Gatlinburg Inn. They were already spending more and more time throughout the year at the inn in "their" Room 388, songwriting and relaxing. The inn's proprietors, R. L. and Wilma Maples, permitted them to stay there even during the winter when the place was otherwise closed to guests.

The Bryants began experimenting with possible "golden years" song themes but soon wearied of the assignment, finding it hard to say something original and positive about aging, with its attendant infirmities and concerns about mortality. Felice particularly became exasperated, telling the interviewer Patricia Hall: "The kids are gone, the dog is dead, autumn is here, and the leaves are red, and oh my God, let's go to bed, or some damned thing." She told Boudleaux that she needed a break and something peppy to give her a lift. As the interview continued, the couple's banter revealed just how the two responded to her frustration:

> BOUDLEAUX: I wanted to go ahead with what we're doing, and she just about balked on that whole proposition, and I got about half mad about the whole thing and—
> FELICE: So, he starts beating the guitar, "Well, how about this? Well, how about that?" I said, "God damn it, that sounds good!"
> BOUDLEAUX: And it was "Rocky Top."
> FELICE: And it was "Rocky Top," and it just clicked off.
> BOUDLEAUX: Suddenly, it did sound pretty good, you know.
> FELICE: I mean it just chink-chink-chinked right away in ten minutes.
> BOUDLEAUX: We just both went to work on it.
> FELICE: And there it was.
> BOUDLEAUX: Ten minutes, and we were done.[4]

This interview is the Bryants' recollection of the initial drafting of the song. Its actual shaping and polishing took a bit longer.[5] Regardless of the duration of its composition, "Rocky Top" became the most famous bluegrass song in the world. Coming as it did during one of the most troubling eras in American history—only one year before the Vietnam Tet

Offensive and the assassinations of Robert Kennedy and Martin Luther King Jr.—the song may have appealed because of its vision of a mythically simple life, free from tension:

> Wish that I was on old Rocky Top
> Down in the Tennessee hills,
> Ain't no smoggy smoke on Rocky Top
> Ain't no telephone bills . . .
>
> Rocky Top, you'll always be
> Home sweet home to me
> Good ol' Rocky Top,
> Rocky Top, Tennessee,
> Rocky Top, Tennessee.
>
> I've had years of cramped-up city life
> Caught like a duck in a pen.
> All I know is it's a pity life
> Can't be simple again.

Archie Campbell did eventually complete his album, and it contained four songs written by the Bryant family: "Fall Away," "Love, the Leaves Are Turning," "Love Is a Sparrow," while Del wrote "Young Just Yesterday," all on Side 1. Actor Eddie Albert enjoyed songwriting credits with Boudleaux and Felice on "Love Is a Sparrow," while some of the other songs on the album are familiar standards such as "Memories" and "If I Had My Life to Live Over."[6]

After their sojourn in Gatlinburg, the Bryants returned to their lake home. In November, Sonny Osborne—who with his brother, Bobby, constituted one of the greatest acts in bluegrass music, and who lived near the Bryants on Old Hickory Lake—called Boudleaux requesting a song for their forthcoming recording session. Sonny had been a warm admirer and close friend of Boudleaux since 1952, when they met at a Bill Monroe recording session in Nashville. Not only did Sonny play the five-string banjo for Monroe and his Blue Grass Boys at this particular session, but Boudleaux, who was there presumably plugging songs, was also called into service as a bass singer when the bluegrass quartet did an old African American spiritual, "Walking in Jerusalem."[7]

"Rocky Top" may have been conceived in ten minutes, but it went through various revisions, as shown here on the ledger page. Courtesy of the Country Music Hall of Fame® and Museum.

After Sonny's call, Boudleaux asked Felice what they might have that was appropriate. She said, "How about that thing we did in Gatlinburg, 'Rocky Top,' that bluegrass thing?" Boudleaux replied, "Where the hell is that?" Felice responded, "It's got to be in that briefcase," explaining to Hall, "because we do not travel with the books. So, he goes scrounging through that thing and he finds it." When Sonny came over, Boudleaux began playing it for him. "And," Felice continued: "Sonny says, 'That's fine. That's fine.' He gets on the phone, and he calls Bobby. Now, Boudleaux, mind you, is not through singing the song." Boudleaux added: "First eight bars." Felice popped up: "'But wait a minute, Sonny, he isn't finished.' Bobby comes down and makes a quick chord sheet. Now when you hear Sonny tell the story, Sonny says he heard the song *unfinished*." The Bryants insisted that the *song* was finished, but Sonny never waited for Boudleaux to complete his rendition.[8]

Strangely, in spite of their instant acceptance of "Rocky Top," neither brother seems to have recognized the song's true potential. After they recorded it a few days later, on November 16, 1967, they issued it as the B-side of a record that featured a slower song, "My Favorite Memory." The record was released on Christmas Day. With its initial run selling over one hundred thousand copies—unprecedented in bluegrass music—"Rocky Top" actually did not begin to attain great popularity until a few weeks later, when the Osborne Brothers appeared on Ralph Emery's influential radio program, touting "My Favorite Memory."

Sometime in early 1968 when Sonny and Bobby went on the show, they thought that their newly recorded love song was what the bluegrass community wanted. Later during the program, Emery turned the record over and played "Rocky Top." Distinguished by Bobby Osborne's high and clear tenor, and Sonny's propulsive banjo playing, the song bowled Emery over. He continued to play it nightly. And that's how "Rocky Top" began its rapid ascent to its iconic place in American popular culture. The Osborne version only reached No. 33 on the national country music chart (bluegrass fans were notorious for preferring to tape shows or each other's records), but it soon became known to bluegrass fans and musicians around the world. No bluegrass concert or jam session anywhere was complete without a performance of "Rocky Top." Country superstar Lynn Anderson, famous for her performance of "Rose Garden," also recorded the song, and it climbed even higher in the charts.[9]

While its popularity in the bluegrass community was highly gratifying to the Bryants, they could not have anticipated the levels that "Rocky Top" would eventually reach. The song had not been named for any specific peak in Tennessee, although mountain climber Herrick Brown sent them a picture of a "high peak, almost inaccessible, full of rocks and with a bald top" that bore the name of "Rocky Top."[10] The most surprising and rewarding appropriation of the song came on October 21, 1972, when the University of Tennessee (UT) Pride of the Southland Band played it at halftime in Neyland Stadium at the UT-Alabama football game. At halftime during a 1978 football game, Boudleaux and Felice were on the field, presenting the original copy of "Rocky Top" to the university, and then watching the band play the song as it created the letters of the title in formation as a tribute to the songwriters.[11] Although never officially named the fight song of the University of Tennessee, as music reporter Juli Thanki wrote on the fiftieth

The University of Tennessee's Pride of the Southland Band formed the letters and performed the unofficial fight song "Rocky Top" at halftime at the Neyland Stadium in Knoxville in 1978. Courtesy of the Country Music Hall of Fame® and Museum.

Boudleaux and Felice presented the original copy of "Rocky Top" as part of the halftime performance. Courtesy House of Bryant Publications.

anniversary of the song, the band's playing it succeeded in "pumping up players and fans alike," and it quickly moved front and center in the affection of Volunteer fans.[12]

Donald Ryder, director of bands at UT, later said that it was a tradition for a senior trombone player to keep track of how often the marching band played the song each season. In 2016 they played it 438 times. And at some point, the student body began adding a rousing "whoo" to the song, known by every alumnus of the school. A national poll in 2015 indicated that "Rocky Top" had become the nation's top college fight song, and it has continued to enjoy that distinction.[13]

The House of Bryant struck a contractual partnership with UT in 2005 to extend the copyright use of "Rocky Top" to UT merchandise and to an organization known as the Rocky Top Institute under the Department of Retail, Hospitality, and Tourism Management. This proposal enables students to engage in product development, replicating the functions any marketer would perform in bringing a product to market. The institute's profits are funneled into three benefactors: The House of Bryant; retail, hospitality, and tourism management; and discretionary dollars for UT Band scholarships. In 2014 Brian Hardy, director of development at UT, asked Del Bryant to be the grand marshal at the 2014 Homecoming Parade. Hardy said, "I think 'Rocky Top' is as synonymous with the University of Tennessee as Peyton Manning is. And maybe even more so. Just wherever you go, anywhere in the world and you say University of Tennessee, people think of the orange, the checkerboard and 'Rocky Top.' That's what we're known for."[14]

On February 15, 1982, with the support of the legendary band director W. J. Julian and governor Lamar Alexander, the Tennessee General Assembly voted to adopt the song as one of the official state songs. As Boudleaux and Felice beamed in appreciation, the Osborne Brothers sang it on the floor of the General Assembly of Tennessee. On the fiftieth anniversary of "Rocky Top," the senate of the Tennessee legislature passed a joint resolution calling the song "a crown jewel of our musical and cultural heritage."[15]

The influence of that Tennessee cultural heritage was far reaching, as evidenced by the recollection of Ray Isenburg, a retired UT alumnus and former roommate of Dane's. He described his encounter with "Rocky Top" while on a river cruise in 2007. Having told the onboard entertainment singers about the song, he wrote:

> I cannot begin to convey the utter surprise when the Bulgarian duet team offered three full verses of the song in the lounge on the fifth deck of the Viking Century Sky cruise ship as we sailed down the Yangtze River in the middle of the Peoples Republic of

China. The innovative Bulgarian singers may not have understood the history and significance of "Rocky Top," but they were clever enough to download the words and music from an Internet web site that they accessed while onboard the ship.[16]

Much closer to Gatlinburg, Bluefield Beverage in Bluefield, West Virginia, debuted a soft drink named "Rocky Top." A press conference in 1984 at the Bluefield Industrial Park advertised the drink's availability and incorporated the song, "blaring from a small cassette tape recorder as Boudleaux, holding his poodle named Cassette, and Felice smiled while one flash after another signaled that photographs had been made." In recognition of the Bryants' musical contribution, Bluefield Beverage's Dick Morath presented the couple with a vending machine full of "Rocky Top" soft drinks to be used at the Bryants' Gatlinburg motel—named Rocky Top Village Inn. It included a variety of flavors, such as cherry, grape, strawberry, lemon-lime, orange, and root beer.[17]

Although "Rocky Top" became one of the most important copyrights in the House of Bryant catalogue, the publishing house did not exist solely for the promotion of new material. Above all, like any publishing company, it was designed to protect, preserve, and publicize the entire Bryant catalogue. Boudleaux aggressively asserted ownership over his tunes and challenged any unauthorized use of them, even if such usage may have been unconscious. In 1975 the House of Bryant reached an amicable agreement with Merle Haggard about the tune of his song, "Living with the Shades Pulled Down," which bore a close resemblance to "Rocky Top." After asking what he could do to make things right, Haggard gave Felice and Boudleaux cowriting credits, and the song became part of the House of Bryant catalogue.

"You're the Reason God Made Oklahoma," on the other hand, ignited a contentious battle. Originally credited to Larry Collins and Sandy Pinkard (who actually did write the lyrics), and popularized in 1981 by Shelly West and David Frizzell's rendition for the soundtrack of the Clint Eastwood movie *Any Which Way You Can*, it climbed to No. 1 on *Billboard*'s Hot 100. But the Bryants recognized the melody, and they eventually won a lawsuit that acknowledged them as cocomposers. According to Del Bryant, the attorneys for Warner Brothers tried to make the case that the tune was traditional, but none of their hired musicologists could find a song previous to "Rocky Top" that bore the same melody. Thereafter, the song carried the Bryants' names in its credits, along with Collins and Pinkard, and this, too, is solely published by the House of Bryant.[18]

Other significant accomplishments followed "Rocky Top" in the next decade. One of the most important cover cuts that the House of Bryant ever had was included in Paul Simon and Art Garfunkel's *Bridge over Troubled Water*, recorded in 1970. The only song on the album not written by Simon was "Bye Bye Love." In July of that year, *Billboard* declared: "The great pro, Boudleaux Bryant, scores again. He and his talented, lovely wife Felice, have a pair of songs in the new Bob Dylan album, 'Take Me as I Am' and 'Take a Message to Mary.'"[19] A year or so earlier, Dylan had recorded an album in Nashville. During Dylan's stay in the city, Johnny Cash organized a "guitar pull" at his Old Hickory Lake home in Dylan's honor. Designed in part to permit local songwriters to test their songs among their colleagues, such affairs were popular events.

Reluctant to be influenced by other writers or to have new material unconsciously borrowed or a theme copied by them, Boudleaux usually avoided such occasions. But on this particular evening, strumming his guitar, he sang those two older and reliable songs. He and Felice were pleasantly surprised when they later discovered the songs in Dylan's double-album of folk and country songs, *Self Portrait* (Columbia, 1970). Marked by Dylan's affected efforts to sound country, the album initially was not received warmly by the critics, but it reached No. 4 on charts in the United States, and No. 1 in the United Kingdom.

The Bryants no longer had to promote songs with the same urgency as in the past—they now had field representatives in various parts of the nation. In 1983 Boudleaux explained the structure of his business to Country Music Hall of Fame interviewer John Rumble:

> When we have a new record that seems to show some promise and looks as though it has a chance to be a chart record, we utilize, in the main, three regional prongs that work for us quite often. We have a man in Atlanta, we have a man in Chicago, and we use them almost on a continual basis promoting in their areas. The man in LA handles eleven states, all the main large cities out on the coast and inland as far as Arizona and that sort of area. The guy in Chicago handles about eight states up there, and the man

in Atlanta is a national promo man, and he knows jockeys all over the country. We do hire those people any time we have a record that looks promising.[20]

Boudleaux still occasionally tailored a song to fit the style of an individual performer. Inspired by a sixteenth-century poem written by Christopher Marlowe, Boudleaux wrote "Come Live with Me" with Roy Clark in mind. Along with Buck Owens, Clark cohosted the immensely popular CBS television show *Hee Haw*. Although famous as a comedian and instrumentalist, he was a smooth singer with a taste for pop country songs. In a 1973 interview with John Erling, Roy Clark said, "I got to *Hee Haw* one morning, and Boudleaux Bryant was sitting in the producer's office with a little guitar. 'He said, 'I've been up all night writing you a song.' The first thought that hit me was, 'Lord, what if I don't like it? How do you tell Boudleaux Bryant thanks, but no thanks?' He played a little bit of it, and I took

Boudleaux and Felice performing with Roy Clark on *Hee Haw* in 1982. Courtesy House of Bryant Publications.

the worry out of it and said, 'that's a great song. It was my first number one song.'"[21] In 1982 Boudleaux and Felice appeared on *Hee Haw* with Roy. He accompanied them as they sang some of their best-known hits and he completed the set by singing "Come Live with Me."[22]

While the hits no longer appeared as frequently, the 1970s and early 1980s were nevertheless a period of commercial flowering for the Bryants. With songs like "Georgia Piney Woods" and "Muddy Bottom," both recorded in 1971, and "I Can Hear Kentucky Calling Me" in 1979, each by the Osborne Brothers, the Bryants secured a solid foothold in the bluegrass community that had earlier welcomed "Rocky Top." Felice's paean of love to Boudleaux, "We Could," once again vaulted to the top through a recording by Charley Pride, released in April 1974, in his album, *Country Feelin'*. As a single, it reached No. 3 on the *Billboard* Hot Country Chart and No. 1 on Canada's RPM Country Chart. That prized No. 1 hit from the early 1950s, "Hey Joe," even came back as a popular dance hall number in 1981 when recorded by Moe Bandy and Joe Stampley.

Those years also saw some of the Bryants' songs reaching a new and large audience of young people in both the United States and abroad, who identified themselves increasingly with the hybrid musical styles known as country-rock or alt-country. "Love Hurts," recorded earlier by both the Everly Brothers and Roy Orbison, drew much greater acclaim during the 1970s in two influential covers. The first, a soft and poignant recording by the American country rock duo Gram Parsons and his protégé, Emmylou Harris, proved highly influential but never landed on the country music charts. Born Ingram Cecil Connor in Winter Haven, Florida, Gram Parsons discovered country music at Harvard. Thereafter, he embarked on a crusade to fuse the styles and audiences of country and rock. He and Harris recorded the song in 1973, but it was not released until 1974 on the album *Grievous Angel* after his tragically early death. Gram had already reached young musicians everywhere through his earlier performances with the Byrds and the Flying Burrito Brothers. Now he and Harris lent credibility to such songs as "Love Hurts," "Sleepless Nights," and "Brand New Heartache." Elvis Costello, for example, recorded "Sleepless Nights" in 1981.[23]

The Gram-Emmylou version of "Love Hurts" clearly inspired the Scottish hard-rock band Nazareth, whose version of the song proved to be a

Boudleaux and Felice holding Everly Brothers albums in London in the early 1980s. Courtesy of the Country Music Hall of Fame® and Museum.

commercial powerhouse throughout Europe. It spent sixty-one weeks on the Norwegian Top Ten, peaked at No. 1 there for fourteen weeks, and topped the charts in Belgium, the Netherlands, South Africa, and Canada, as well as being the only recording of the song "to become a hit single in the United States, reaching No. 8 on the *Billboard* Hot 100 in early 1976."[24] The group's lead singer, Dan McCafferty, presented the song with a high-pitched, intense,

Boudleaux took pride in "Love Hurts" and in all of those who continued to record it. Courtesy of the Country Music Hall of Fame® and Museum.

and utterly compelling sound, drawing the listener into its moody and anguished orbit.

"Love Hurts" can be justly praised for its musical construction. The music journalist Franklin Bruno called it a "master class in pop structure"; he sees "majesty in the stoic regularity of its verses' motifs giving way to a soaring, insistently rhymed bridge."[25] The song should be equally valued for the tender poignancy of its text. The words ring true for love at any age, not specifically for teenagers alone, although they may express their angst more passionately. The lyrics of the opening verses immediately acknowledge the depth of that heartache:

> Love hurts, love scars, love wounds and mars
> Any heart not tough nor strong enough
> To take a lot of pain, take a lot of pain,
> Love is like a cloud, holds a lot of rain
> Love hurts, mmm mmm, love hurts.
>
> I'm young, I know, but even so
> I know a thing or two, I learned from you
> I really learned a lot, really learned a lot
> Love is like a stove, burns you when it's hot
> Love hurts, mmm mmm, love hurts.
>
> Some fools dream of happiness
> Blissfulness
> Togetherness
> Some fools fool themselves, I guess
> But they're not fooling me.
>
> I know it isn't true
> I know it isn't true
> Love is just a lie
> Made to make you blue.
>
> Love hurts, mmm mmm, love hurts.

The 1970s also marked the beginning of many awards and recognition of the Bryants' contributions to American music. Boudleaux's and Felice's elections in 1972 to the Nashville Songwriters Hall of Fame was the first of such occasions. Conceived by songwriter Eddie Miller in November 1967, the Nashville Hall of Fame had been a pet project of the Bryants since its inception. The following year Boudleaux was elected to its first board of directors. Using a slogan that was first suggested by Lorene Mann but attributed to Frances Preston—"It All Begins with a Song"—the group successfully worked for an objective that had always been close to the Bryants' hearts: ensuring that the record companies listed the full names of the writers on record labels and album jackets. Their dear friend Frances Preston—who in 1953 was Frances Williams, a receptionist at WSM—was instrumental in persuading BMI to give its first-ever awards to Nashville songwriters.[26]

In a symposium designed by the Songwriters Hall of Fame to encourage fledglings to the field, the Bryants served on a panel moderated by Nashville publicist Patsy Bruce. She sent the couple an outline for the symposium and a list of questions that registrants hoped would be answered by the leading songwriting professionals included on the panel. In the answers that Boudleaux jotted down, one gets a good glimpse of his brand of humor. One questioner wondered "How can I select a collaborator?" to which Boudleaux responded, "Marry talent." Another wrote, "A to Z. I need help in all areas—putting a hooker into the song." Boudleaux answered, "Find a girl singer on lower Broadway. Take a pimp to lunch." A third asked, "What is the best structure for a country song?" and Boudleaux suggested, "Carnegie Hall or the Grand Ole Opry House. Either is good."[27]

On January 26, 1974, *Billboard* magazine printed a twenty-fifth anniversary appreciation of the couple, called "25 Years of Harmony." The unsigned article noted that theirs had been "a marriage made in Milwaukee, but obviously sanctified in Heaven."[28] Then on April 14, 1975, Boudleaux and Felice presented a program in New York City at the Ninety-Second Street YM-YWHA, another milestone in the recognition of their contributions as songwriters. The Bryants' program marked the first time that Nashville or country music had been represented in a series called "Lyrics and Lyricists," conceived by the Y's Music Department in cooperation with the Billy Rose Foundation, under the artistic direction of Maurice Levine. A Yale-trained violinist, Levine worked at the Ninety-Second Street Y for over forty years, conducting the Y's Workshop Orchestra and teaching classic orchestra literature as well as Broadway theater music to the musicians.[29]

After Boudleaux joked that he thought YMHA meant "Young Men's Hill-billy Association," he attempted to define the genre in which he worked:

> The word Country, as applied to music, is roughly on the same level as the word home used to define cooking. Just walk into a restaurant that displays a home cooking sign and order the special of the day. You might just get some surprises. Depending on where you are, you could get anything from lox and eggs to turnip greens and ham hocks and cornbread with a little lox and bagels on the side. Ask your favorite country DJ for a platter of country music and you're likely to get anything from "Tennessee Coon Hunt" by Arthur Fiedler and the Boston Pops to Brahms "Lullaby" featuring three guitars, a washboard and a piccolo. In short, the country music heritage is polyglot, very hazy, extremely diverse and mixed up.[30]

During the course of the evening, Boudleaux and Felice also elaborated on an idea that had always been central to their approach to song-making: the belief that country music, in essence, had always depended on interpretation or performance. With Maurice Levine acting as moderator and interlocutor, they took Gilda's aria from Giuseppe Verdi's opera *Rigoletto* and with the backing of their highly skilled accompanists—Bob Thompson on guitar and banjo and Dave Kirby on guitar—presented it in various ways. First, they did the aria in Italian, according to Boudleaux, "as best we could." Then they took the rock 'n' roll lyrics they had written to the melody and "did a treatment of that as maybe the Everlys would have done, as a nice ballad with a sort of cha-cha beat." Next, the Bryants fashioned "an up-tempo heavy rocking type version," followed by a comedy version, with slightly different lyrics. Boudleaux later told the interviewer Hugh Cherry that "it was a gas to do, and the people just loved it, because it illustrated better than anything that I've been able to come up with, the fact that the performance, the manner in which a song is done, is really what determines what kind of song it is."[31]

Levine and his son Mike interviewed the couple after their performance, questioning them on their approach to songwriting and about the confluence of the fields of country, pop, and rock. The questions had been presented to Boudleaux and Felice ahead of time. To the question "During your twenty-five-year span in songwriting, have you found that there is a change in what the public likes to hear in the lyric of a country song?" they fashioned their response around the enduringly popularity of love: "good love, bad love, hot love, cold love, old love, new love, yesterday's love, tomorrow's love, physical, spiritual, imaginary, real, platonic, sexual—any kind of love. . . . In fact, lyrically, the only changes are those that reflect social changes—sexual permissiveness, etc., plus an occasional 'in' word or phrase that has its day and fades away."[32] Boudleaux and Felice received a standing ovation at the end of the evening.

After the show, a musician and songwriter named Donald J. Darcy went backstage and invited the Bryants to a late supper at Tony's on West Seventy-Ninth. After dinner they hung out at Darcy's house, conversed, and listened to reggae music. Felice and Boudleaux then invited their hosts to visit their lake home in Hendersonville. Some weeks later, while the Darcys were planning their trip to Hendersonville, they learned that Boudleaux's mother and sister, Lafontisse, had been killed instantaneously one year before, on January 15, 1974, on their way home from visiting relatives. Near Americus, Sumter County, Georgia, a truck driver fell asleep at the wheel and caused a head-on collision with their car. Boudleaux was still grieving, even though that tragic accident had occurred well before the event at the Ninety-Second Street Y. Darcy was intrigued that Boudleaux's "main concern was the speed of their transition to the other side. The concept was a little foreign to me." A few days later Boudleaux called Darcy and renewed the invitation to visit.[33]

When they arrived in Hendersonville, as Darcy commented in his book, *Blues to Blood: Doing It the Hard Way: Music, Addiction, and Recovery*, "Boudleaux was drinking quite heavily, but had stopped by the time we left" ten days later. While Darcy may have been aware of Boudleaux's struggle with alcohol because of his own issues, he was more interested in and inspired by Boudleaux's passion for different paths to enlightenment. "The most significant thing to happen while staying there was that Boudleaux hypnotized me," Darcy wrote, "something he had not done in a long time, and gave me a reading list of Edgar Cayce's work. These books were the beginning of a long road of esoteric knowledge that seemed to have no end."[34] Once again, Boudleaux managed to inspire a disciple.

When interviewed by Joe Allison two years after Boudleaux's death, Felice told him that Boudleaux never did gain complete control of his alcoholism. "He got to where he could drink a day out of the week," and although he "stayed sober three, four days in a row, if he had guests for dinner, it was all open house." This revelation surprised Allison, who said "I knew him many, many years, and I've only seen him that way a few times. Because he sure stayed out of the limelight when he was like that." Felice replied, "Oh yeah. We kept under cover." Felice kept the couple focused and disciplined with songwriting. Boudleaux's love for his wife and children and his intense interest in Eastern thought, real estate, and reading on any subject that intrigued him kept him engaged in the world beyond the bottle.

This engagement was duly noted in 1986 when the Bryants received their most prestigious award, their election to the National Songwriters Hall of Fame, an arm of the National Academy of Popular Music, founded in 1969 by Johnny Mercer and a couple of publishers. To both Boudleaux and Felice, this honor validated their forty years of work. The organization had been historically stingy in its selection of country composers, having named only Hank Williams and two protest writers, Woody Guthrie and Pete Seeger, who were only tangentially related to the country idiom. The Bryants, then, were pioneers in the acceptance of mainstream country music as a legitimate art form.[35]

While the Bryants took great delight in having moved one step higher in their ascent to international music fame, they could only have had bittersweet feelings about their sons' imminent departure from Neptune Drive. While Dane and Del were preparing for high school graduation, they were also leaving the warmth and comfort of home. Dane attended Peabody College his freshman year before departing for the University of Tennessee in Knoxville. He stayed there for one year and then decided that he preferred the music publishing business. But because the country was involved in Vietnam and Dane was no longer enrolled in college, he was drafted in April 1968. Like many of America's young men, Dane did not want to go to war, and his parents would have supported his flight to Canada had he chosen to make that decision. "Mom threw a fit because I wouldn't go to Canada. I just wanted to come back and be a music publisher." And Dane was worried that if he left the country he would be arrested after his return. The dream of being a music publisher was more important than avoiding service, even if it meant Vietnam.[36]

Dane was serving in the infantry when a Bryant family friend, singer songwriter Jan Howard lost her son Jimmy in Vietnam when the tank he was driving hit a land mine and killed him. Her older son had committed suicide not long beforehand, and Jan was devastated. Felice was always empathetic when a friend was in need, but her concerns about Dane's vulnerability in the service may have made her even more sensitive to Jan's suffering. When she went to offer Jan her sympathies and comfort, Felice surprised her by arriving with large grocery bags in her arms. She told her grieving friend that while others might bring food and flowers, no one was likely to bring the things she could really use such as paper towels and toilet paper. Jan appreciated that Felice "always made me feel special, and [Felice and Boudleaux] were special to me. They were *friends*." Jan was grateful for Felice's warmth during this particularly stressful time. And because of her own loss Jan also reached out to Felice, recalling, "I understood her fear." Lee Wilson wrote that, during the entire year Dane was in Vietnam, "Felice kept herself in a state of tension. When she got the word, by phone, that he was back in the States, she literally collapsed on the floor, shaking with relief."[37]

Felice's fears were not unfounded. As an infantryman Dane suffered a foot injury while in the dense vegetation of Vietnam's wetlands. When the doctor opened the foot, it got massively infected, and Dane was sent to a hospital in Cam Ranh Bay. One vivid memory he carried away from Vietnam was telling a reporter who asked about his position, "I'm a Nashville publisher." Only after he said it did Dane realize that he had not answered the question as the reporter expected. The reporter was referring to his position in Vietnam. After his foot healed, Dane returned to his company, but he got a reprieve by agreeing to return to the University of Tennessee after his dismissal from active duty. Following his year in Vietnam and three additional months at the university, Dane went right back to the publishing world of the House of Bryant, as he had tried to tell the reporter in Vietnam.[38]

After his graduation from Peabody Demonstration School, Del matriculated at the University of Miami, where he majored in history while taking whatever music business courses were available, since that was his reason for choosing the university. After completing his coursework and graduating from the university Del, too, went to work for the House of Bryant, just as he had planned. When faced with the prospect of being drafted, he joined the Air Force Reserves just before graduating in 1970, but he did not have to go to Vietnam. He did his stint stateside as a parachute rigger, stationed in San Antonio and Wichita Falls, Texas, and then in Charleston,

South Carolina, before returning to the House of Bryant six months later. Once again, the Bryants were realigned as Team Bryant, but this reunion only worked for the next couple of years.[39]

In September 1972, the founder of BMI's Nashville office in 1958 and one of the Bryants' best friends, Frances Preston, called Boudleaux and asked that both he and Felice get on the phone. Born Frances Williams, she married E. J. Preston in 1962, and kept his name after they divorced. Beginning her business experience in the city as a receptionist at radio station WSM, she became the first female executive in Tennessee when named as BMI's vice president in 1964. She recalled that at the time women were not allowed in the main dining room at the powerful downtown Cumberland Club.

Hardworking and dedicated, she rose through the ranks and, by 1986, was named BMI's president and chief executive officer. When Preston called the Bryants, Del and Dane happened to be at their parents' home. Boudleaux answered the phone, then asked Felice to get on the extension. As Del recalled upon his own retirement in June 2014:

> In just a matter of minutes my mother comes down the stairs, sobbing—she said "Frances Preston wants to hire one of my boys, and she doesn't care which one!" My mother was so proud that either of us came up to Frances's standards. "Is anybody interested?" And my brother said, "I'm not"—he had just gotten back from Vietnam and was just happy as could be to be home. And I had married very early and I had a young child and one on the way, as Loretta [Lynn] would say.
>
> So [taking the job at BMI] was primarily a monetary driver, but with my experiences and training—I say training, it was just life: learning how to do demos and what they were; getting the house ready when somebody was coming over for a pitch session. I had been in charge of a lot of the royalties with [the Bryants' publishing company]. I was good with numbers, I understood how a writer was paid, I was the one in the family who could guesstimate what was coming in. It could not have been better schooling to go and work in Nashville with BMI. It was so natural, so easy, so much fun.[40]

Dane described his decision to remain a publisher by saying, "I wanted to pick the awards up, and Del could hand them out."[41] Many years later, a seventy-year-old Del, who followed his mentor Frances as president and CEO of BMI, reflected on the experience of growing up as the son of Felice and Boudleaux. He stated simply, "I grew up in a passion." Their parents' lifelong love, their songwriting, and their music infused every aspect of the Bryants' sons world. They lived and breathed Team Bryant. Del had never assumed he would take a different path in life.[42]

BMI's offer was also too good to refuse, not simply for its immediate financial benefits, but for what it promised. BMI paid three hundred dollars a week and offered a car, while the House of Bryant was paying seventy-five dollars a week. Del went to work for BMI in October 1972, at the age of twenty-three. His first job was to recruit writers and composers and to develop their careers. At the time, the company was bringing in forty million dollars a year; by 2018 the figure had climbed to over a billion. Understanding his parents' struggles to protect their copyrights led to his passion to protect songwriters. "I've really given my life to this because I appreciate so much not only what songwriters do, but what they give up to do what they do. What makes you succeed is mercurial."[43]

Dane stayed with the House of Bryant until the mid-1970s when he began two separate but related ventures. In 1974 he started his own publishing company, Onhisown Music, and signed Billy Ray Reynolds as a songwriter. Fortunately, as with Team Bryant, the first recording was a hit, with Tanya Tucker's cut "Don't Believe My Heart Can Stand Another You." That's when he invited Steve Singleton, an old friend and former classmate of Del's at Peabody Demonstration School, to join him in the business. Steve and Dane also formed a studio, OAS Wild Tracks, shortly afterward. Between the publishing company and the studio, they produced several big songs, such as Anne Murray's "Could I Have This Dance?" by Bob House and Waylon Holyfield, a No. 1 hit for the singer. It was included in the soundtrack of *Urban Cowboy*, along with one Del wrote, "I Cheated on a Good Woman's Love." A recording of it by Crash Craddock hit the top five on the *Billboard* country chart and was featured in the movie *Convoy*, starring Kris Kristofferson.[44]

In a retrospective mood in 1979, Boudleaux and Felice entered Wild Tracks, recording twelve songs for an LP, *A Touch of Bryant*, for CMH Records

Dane, Boudleaux, Felice, and Del at a BMI awards celebration in the early 1980s.
Courtesy of the Country Music Hall of Fame® and Museum.

(CMH 6243). They included "When I Stop Loving You," "Raining in My
Heart," "I Can Hear Kentucky Calling Me," "Why Can't I Leave You Alone,"
"I'll Never Get Tired of Loving You," "Bye, Bye, Love," "Playing in the
Sand," "Rocky Top," "I See, I See," "Keepin' Warm," "No Matter What You
Do to Me," and "All I Have to Do Is Dream." They were accompanied by six
Nashville musicians, plus special guest guitar players Chet Atkins and
Lenny Breau, who played gut string guitars with Boudleaux on "When I
Stop Loving You." Steve Singleton, who produced the album, admired
Boudleaux's immense talent as a musician, referring to him as a "musical
genius." Although Boudleaux had not played his fiddle for twenty-five or
thirty years, Steve talked him into playing it on some of the cuts on the
album. After he played the fiddle, he put it back in the case and never
played it again; Boudleaux could not play the fiddle without drinking, and
this time was no exception. Steve remembers sending out for vodka and
beer before the session started and notes that Boudleaux relaxed after

playing a part by petting his teacup poodle, Cassette, as if the dog were a "worry stone."[45]

In 1982 Dane and Steve moved in different directions, selling their publishing company and catalogue to Tree Music.[46] Dane began another company, Dane Bryant Music. With songwriter Bill Price he published "Do Me Right," recorded by Shelly West and David Frizzell, a chart record, in 1985. But helping his father improve land on the farm—building an accessible road, providing a water supply, and negotiating with other development demands—whetted Dane's appetite for real estate. He enjoyed the work and recognized that financial rewards were more immediately accessible as well. He became licensed and joined the successful firm of Lura Bainbridge & Associates. Michael Kosser, in *How Nashville Became Music City, USA: 50 Years of Music Row*, wrote, "If you're looking for an office to rent on Music Row, or a building to buy in the area, then Dane Bryant is your man. He is Music Row's most popular realtor—he carries a map of Music Row in his head."[47]

During the summer of 1978, Jill Nabarro (then Douglass), daughter of Boudleaux's sister Danise, spent the summer in Nashville after graduating from college. While the House of Bryant's office manager was on vacation, Jill filled in. She remembered that Boudleaux and Felice were writing jingles at the time and that she helped Felice hang up signs around town advertising some kind of future event. And what a vivid memory!

As the two drove around the city, Felice sang the entire time, making up verses about whatever people or places they were passing. As Jill described her aunt, "Whatever she'd see, she'd start making up songs. She sang a lot in the kitchen while she was working." Delighted with Felice's "effervescence," Jill was also impressed with Boudleaux's demeanor; he was "like a gentle giant," and she enjoyed "their very gentle and respectful relationship."[48]

With their sons no longer actively involved in the House of Bryant, Boudleaux and Felice began spending more time in Gatlinburg, where they had luxuriated in serenity and solitude for so many years. But they became resolved to a permanent move to the area after two robbery experiences shattered their illusion of the security of their lovely lake home. While his parents were out of town the evening of the first robbery, Dane went out to the lake house for the weekend. Finding the door open, he called the police. "Mom felt so violated and scared," he said, recalling that

many valuable items had been taken, including some of Felice's jewelry and
furs. She knew she did not want to stay in the house, no matter how much
time, love, and memories the family had invested there. After the second
robbery attempt, they rented the house to the rock star Leon Russell, who
later bought it.[49]

Dealing with family stresses provided another reason that Felice and
Boudleaux may have been relieved to give up the lake house. Del's first
marriage was, in his words, "a disaster." He was a single parent with an
"impossible" former mother-in-law in the Hendersonville area, and his
parents were probably glad to get further away from the scene of this
unpleasantness.

Since his parents were still creating daily, he described them as slightly
"reluctant" grandparents whose idea of grandparenting was therefore "less
involved than otherwise." They were always glad to see their grandchildren—
Boudleaux played with them in the swimming pool, and Felice taught
them to play gin rummy—but they were not enthusiastic about babysitting
or keeping them overnight. Granddaughter Heather (Del's older daughter)
loved the fact that Boudleaux planted a tree for each of his grandchildren.
But she was later dismayed after learning that "Leon Russell paved over the
front for his tour buses, and there went my tree."[50]

Although Boudleaux purchased an older home in the town of Franklin, Felice showed no inclination to spend any time there. Before moving
permanently, they alternated their time at the Gatlinburg Inn with living
briefly at the handsome Rokeby condominiums in Nashville. In 1978 they
found the home they wanted in Gatlinburg, a large older house bordering
the Great Smoky Mountains National Park. They hired a talented local
family of woodworkers and carpenters to remodel it completely to suit their
needs. The four-thousand-square-foot house had hand-carved beams in
the living room, each depicting leaves of a different species of native tree,
such as maple or oak. The garage was a separate building with an apartment above that doubled as a guesthouse.[51]

While they were remodeling the house, Boudleaux was onto his next
real estate venture—purchasing a hotel or motel to renovate and run there
in Gatlinburg. He found the old Hemlock Motel on Historic Nature Trail
(then called Airport Road) and purchased it. When the motel next door to
the parking lot became available, he bought that one, too. Fortunately, the
motel behind the Hemlock also came on the market, allowing Boudleaux

Although the Bryants did not really write while sitting on the steps at their Gatlinburg home, it made for a fine publicity shot. Courtesy House of Bryant Publications.

to become the owner of the entire complex. He renovated the buildings in order to give the appearance of a single property, aptly named the Rocky Top Village Inn. He enjoyed adding "innkeeper" to his vocational profile.[52]

Once Felice and Boudleaux finally moved in 1980, they never looked back. Dane said, "Mom thought that Gatlinburg was the place to retreat from Dad's private battle with alcoholism." Located at the end of a cul-du-sac, the house was a sanctuary where "Mom felt safe, with her dead-bolt on the door." He described the idyllic setting as "a beautiful spot with a back yard that they tried to keep open—until a bear walked across their back porch."[53] Heather remembers visiting her grandparents in Gatlinburg. She could still visualize Boudleaux in the plaid shirts and jeans that he liked to wear, and she appreciated his dry sense of humor. He'd bought Cassette rain boots, but when Heather asked him why the dog never had them on, he told her, "She couldn't put them on, so I got rid of them." She enjoyed listening to him whistle in harmony and relished taking walks with him. His love for automobiles came into play when he bought his Rolls Royce Silver Cloud. When he took Heather driving around Gatlinburg, he told her that they had to roll down the windows and wave to folks. He called it "parading."[54]

Unfortunately, those halcyon days were not to last nearly so long as Felice and Boudleaux anticipated. They were still busy writing and had recently begun developing plays or musicals, one called "Gander's Gap," another that Dane and Del favored called "Plato Jones," and another called "Square Deal," for which they had completed at least six songs.[55] Their recent forays into creating musicals were finally initiating the path to ful-filling Felice's lifelong dream of writing for Broadway. As she told an inter-viewer some years later: "I am New York bound. That's where my heart is and has always been."[56] But sometime during the still wintry months of early 1987, Boudleaux slipped and fell on his back while crossing a foot-bridge to the park across from their home.

He soon began experiencing intense back pain. He took Tylenol, tell-ing his good friend Fred Foster that he intended to go to a chiropractor. But Fred talked him into going to the hospital to get an X-ray. In the first examination, the local doctor found a spot on his lungs and sent Boud-leaux on to the University of Tennessee Hospital in Knoxville. Upon fur-ther examination, another five spots were discovered, and the medical staff advised surgery. Del stayed with his father in the hospital the night before the operation. He massaged his father's feet, which Boudleaux had always appreciated. During surgery the following morning, the doctor found that his lung cancer had spread everywhere, and no further surgery would be effective.[57]

Like many in their generation, Boudleaux and Felice both smoked heavily. Boudleaux's lungs undoubtedly suffered greatly from this habit. He had been able to stop smoking in the early 1950s, but Felice never could do so. Even though she hated it and railed against it, she simply could not give it up. Del's wife, Carolyn, said that he recounted his "strong memories of his mother's red fingernails and lipstick as she took dramatic drags on her cigarettes." Her smoking in the car made Del carsick. He remembered how smoke from his parents' cigarettes would drift through the wall into the bedroom that he and Dane shared. When she wasn't smoking, Heather remembered her grandmother saying, "I can feel my lungs bleaching." Those unforgettable scenes and sensations must have been paramount when the doctor explained the situation to Del and Felice after the surgery. Felice was alarmed that the doctor was not speaking in hushed tones. She was concerned that Boudleaux, not yet beyond the effects of anesthesia, might be troubled by the terrible news and give up hope. Although the doctor reassured her that Boudleaux could not hear what he was saying, both mother and son knew that Boudleaux believed that, even asleep, the brain could absorb information from conversations or even from a television set left on.[58]

Boudleaux had wondered about his lifespan, asking the various mystics whom he called upon to give him any hints about what they might see. Somehow, the number eighty-seven seemed to appear to more than one of them. Even though no one mentioned that Boudleaux might expect to live to be eighty-seven years old, he was under the impression that such an age was implied. Instead, the number now seemed to indicate the year—1987—and he was only sixty-seven years old. Not wanting to feel sick, he refused radiation. Always one to try healthy diets, for a few weeks Boudleaux had a couple prepare macrobiotic meals for Felice and him, but they were of no help.

Like many surprised by the diagnosis of a terminal and quickly debilitating disease Boudleaux, as Del recalled, went through the full range of emotional responses and, uncharacteristically, was sometimes short with Felice. Troubled at seeing their mother's unhappiness, being unprepared to deal with Boudleaux's mood swings, Dane and Del decided they needed to confront their father. When they entered the room to talk with him about the need to be kinder and more considerate of Felice, Del served as the spokesperson. He worried that he was hurting his father's pride while defending his mother.

That conversation, so late in his father's life, still troubles Del, but it did have a positive effect. During the remaining days of his life Boudleaux and Felice huddled together, as he worked hard to remember, forgive, and bless all the people they knew, including Wesley Rose. Boudleaux did not want to die with any rancor or resentment in his heart. For all of the interest he had expressed in Eastern religions and ways of knowledge, he believed that Jesus now seemed to him the "freshest," as he told Del. The teachings of his childhood comforted him as his life was closing.[59]

Boudleaux died on June 25, 1987. The following day Fred Foster was quoted in the *Nashville Tennessean*, saying Boudleaux was "the most talented music man I ever knew. I was closer to him, spent more time with him than some members of my own family. He has just proven to us that he was mortal, though he did have some qualities of the immortal."[60] Fred arranged the music portion of Boudleaux's funeral. It was called a "Requiem for Boudleaux," and it included a string quartet performing some of the Bryants' songs. His sons had made sure that Boudleaux's casket contained some of the "tools" for which he could be remembered: lead sheets for songwriting, plenty of pencils, and a deck of cards, since he and Felice both were avid solitaire players.[61]

Songwriter Thomas Schuyler felt deeply moved that Felice, Dane, and Del wanted him to deliver the eulogy. He eloquently synthesized Boudleaux's achievements, quoting another famous songwriter, Harlan Howard, who called him "'the most professional, talented, humble man' he knew. 'He liked all of us, but his best friend, from beginning to end was Felice. It was like a great love song.'" Schuyler lamented the fact that songwriters' names often remain unknown to most of the listening public, but "to the producers who chanced upon the writing of Boudleaux and Felice Bryant, most notably, Mr. Chet Atkins, that name meant the opportunity to change the course of American popular music. And to the singers who were fortunate enough to have first dibs on a Boudleaux and Felice tune, most notably the Everly Brothers, that name meant a first-class ticket on the train of hits." For songwriters such as Schuyler himself, "The name Boudleaux Bryant was everywhere. It transcended styles and formats. It had no argument with charts or ratings. The name Boudleaux Bryant was simply there. Right next to the name Felice. Representing lyrics that stuck with you like the alphabet: rhythms that automatically made you tap something and melodies that you can hum in the worst of moods. And for these things we thank him." A bagpiper performed "Amazing Grace" while pallbearers—Fred Foster, Chet Atkins, Sonny Osborne, Lonnie Polk, and Jascha and Levigne Bryant—carried out the casket. Among the Bryants' songs performed during the ceremony, mourners heard a haunting, slowed-down version of "Rocky Top."[62]

★ ★ ★ ★ ★

Chapter 7

"WE COULD AND WE DID"
The Legacy of Boudleaux and Felice Bryant

Felice lived for another eighteen years. Boudleaux's death, understandably, severely diminished her creative energy, but it did not diminish her spunky personality. Without Boudleaux, her songwriting no longer contained the magic it once possessed, and life did not seem worth living, even though she told Joe Allison she kept on writing. She summed up the feelings of those days in an unsent letter to songwriter Jimmy Webb (remembered for "Wichita Lineman" and "By the Time I Get to Phoenix"), shortly after Boudleaux's death. "I've tried many times to answer your very tender letter regarding my Boudleaux," she began, "but I can't seem to put my feelings into words at this time. I'm still in a strange place after the loss of my friend, and I'm trying hard to come out of the fog that used to be cloud nine."[1] Some years after his death, Felice told another interviewer, "All I needed in my life was my Boudleaux. Boudleaux needed me. He didn't need me as much as I needed him, but he needed me."[2]

Felice lived long enough to receive the praise of a grateful music industry and the recognition of musicians around the world for the contributions she and Boudleaux had made. In 1991 the Nashville Arts Foundation presented her with their Living Legend Award.[3] That same year, she was named, along with Boudleaux, to the Country Music Association's Hall of Fame, the first full-time songwriters to receive that honor.[4] Nervous, but beaming with delight, she mounted the stage on the arms of her proud sons and accepted the trophy from Barbara Mandrell. She cast aside the remarks she had written, and with her effervescent wit, ad-libbed her acceptance and spoke to Barbara Bush in the front row, telling her, "Thanks for bringing Georgie." The occasion marked Felice's final public appearance before a large audience.[5]

Felice with George Jones at an event at the Country Music Hall of Fame in 1991, the year she and Boudleaux were inducted. Courtesy of the Country Music Hall of Fame® and Museum.

Her sons encouraged her to resume songwriting, and Del suggested that Dennis Morgan, a family friend and the writer of such songs as "I Was Country When Country Wasn't Cool" and "Smoky Mountain Rain," go to Gatlinburg and write with her. Dennis was keen to do it and drove from Nashville, staying in the Rocky Top Village Inn. During the first visit, they worked at the hotel, but on the next trip, Felice invited him to the house, instructing him where to sit. Morgan immediately realized it was Boudleaux's chair, telling Felice, that he was in "Seventh Heaven." That phrase did it. The two took off. "Boom! She handed me a blank ledger and told me, 'Let's put our songs in this.' We were off and running and wrote 'Seventh Heaven' in about ten minutes." Morgan understood that Boudleaux and Felice "had such a special synergy" that when she handed him the ledger "it was a high, high honor." That experience reinforced his impression of Felice as "very quick; she was nobody's fool, obviously. I let her kind of lead. I wanted her to know that I knew that (a) she was a woman, and (b) she was smart." As much as she enjoyed Dennis, she told Del she did not want to do it again. And although the two had filled several pages of the journal with songs, nothing came of it.[6]

Felice had no desire to return to Nashville and continued to live in the big house in Gatlinburg. She could be a gracious host when visitors arrived, showing them the city and providing them with anecdotes about the region's history. The well-respected journalist Chet Flippo interviewed her in Gatlinburg for the online journal *Nashville Skyline* sometime in the early 2000s and included some information from it in an obituary on April 24, 2003. He called her "a very expressive, funny and very compassionate person" with whom he felt "privileged" to work on a project. "I never had more fun and was never made to feel more at home by anyone," Flippo recalled. "I greatly enjoyed being driven around town by this stately woman in her long, green Mercedes 600 Pullman limousine with its elegant side curtains as she gave me a running commentary on the sights and the people we passed. Sometime later I ran into her son Del and I mentioned something about how much I admired that car and how well it suited his mother." Del told Flippo that Felice donated both the Mercedes and Boudleaux's Silver Cloud Rolls Royce to the Ronald McDonald House. Flippo saw that as "very much in character for her to do that." Del joked that his mother got to be a little like Elvis Presley, buying cars for people who helped her. His daughter Heather reiterated that Felice "was giving cars away left and right near the end of her life." Heather was a recipient of her largesse.[7]

But in many respects Felice became reclusive—or what Dane described as "a Sicilian widow." As his wife, Lee Wilson, wrote: "For a girl brought up among Catholic Sicilian women who donned black when their husbands died and spent the rest of their lives in mourning, it was a predictable response." Felice became more strongly Catholic in her behavior and beliefs. She had always been interested in Catholic history and avidly read about the various popes. Del came across a scratch copy of a letter she had written to James Kavanaugh, a former priest, who in 1967 wrote *A Modern Priest Looks at an Outdated Church*. Felice began by telling him: "You truly are a brother to men. You should be wearing white instead of black. (All the good guys wear white.)" Then she wrote about her own religiosity:

> I was raised in the Catholic church, but they never made a Catholic out of me. I asked too many questions. The Catholic church of our time is a twin to the system that Jesus fought against during his time on earth. I am not a member of any organized church. I am a member of God's creation, as is every man. I enjoy the freedom to love God without legal loop hole[s], knot holes & dry holes.[8]

Felice's identification with Kavanaugh's dissatisfaction is the only known testimony of her faith. While the church itself did not touch her spiritually, the folk elements of the religion continued to offer her comfort. Del remembers she always lit candles for all those for whom she was praying, a practice Heather talked about, while also remembering the shrine to Mary that Felice kept in her bedroom. The family made sure that she was buried with a rosary.[9]

Felice enjoyed her independence even as she retreated and lived alone until illness necessitated the employment of caregivers. When her granddaughter Heather, then an incoming freshman at Arizona State University, called to tell Felice she had arrived, her grandmother gave her "a safe-sex talk," suggesting that her granddaughter use condoms. Heather describes her as having been unexpectedly "very straight-to-the-point," further confirming Heather's perception that her grandmother was "a real hoot!" The two would watch television shows together long distance, staying on the phone and discussing the incidents during commercials. After Heather graduated and began work at the House of Bryant early in 2000, she commuted to Gatlinburg for about six months after Felice's diagnosis with pancreatic cancer. Heather drove her to chemotherapy appointments in Knoxville during the week and returned to Nashville on weekends. Although Felice famously liked to remain at home, she had her favorite Gatlinburg restaurants where the two would dine. Felice had a hard time making up

Phil Everly and Felice at a "Rocky Top" celebration in Gatlinburg in the mid-1990s
Courtesy House of Bryant Publications.

her mind about what she wanted to eat so would order two or three entrees at the Red Lobster or the Outback Steak House. Heather found her grandmother's last days particularly difficult. Like Boudleaux, Felice's emotional states were erratic during her much longer bout with cancer, and she was often angry or withdrawn, the kind of final passage that her family hated to witness.[10]

Felice died on April 22, 2003. Obituaries appeared all over the world. Chet Flippo's appreciative appraisal of her significance is illustrative: "Felice Bryant was the first woman who moved to Nashville to be a songwriter. Consider the implications of that, for a town and a music industry that were built on songs. Without Felice Bryant, there would have been no Loretta Lynn, no Tammy Wynette, no Dolly Parton, or the many other women writers and artists who have followed them. Felice was truly a pioneer. In an industry that has been male-dominated from the start, Felice Bryant took no crap."[11]

Visitations were held for her in Sevierville, Tennessee, at the Atchley Funeral Home on April 23 and in Nashville on April 24 at Woodlawn Funeral Home.[12] In addition to Dane and Del, she was survived by four grandchildren, two great-grandchildren, and her sister, Kitty. Del gave a eulogy in the form of a loving letter to his mother, beginning with an idyllic childhood memory: "When I was a young schoolboy, Mama, I used to think you were THE MOST beautiful woman in the world. You were always dressed to the nines just to pick us up from school." He moved on to the more painful recent past, apologizing for encouraging her to be less reclusive after Boudleaux's death. "Dane and I never quit trying to get you out of the house, and for this I ask your forgiveness. Forgive me for trying to change that part of your personality." Del recognized that she had never "quite got over" losing his father, and he conjured up a sweet fantasy: "I'm sure you and Dad are collaborating. Dad's strumming the guitar, you're singing catchy little lines to go with his melody. He's probably about to spring it on you that he's invited all of Heaven over for dinner tonight, and you're cooking!" Finally, he shared a painful insight: "I realize that because you had such a rough childhood, you never quite felt worthy of the love and adoration you received."[13] She and Boudleaux are interred side by side in a mausoleum at the Woodlawn Cemetery in Nashville.

Songwriter Tom Schuyler, famous for his musical homage to the Nashville writers, "Sixteenth Avenue," gave the principal eulogy at her service, just as he had done earlier for Boudleaux. Schuyler did not know the Bryants well, but it was very fitting that he should present the eulogies. Although they had done most of their writing at home, in a very real sense, their careers had inspired and fulfilled the dreams of the hundreds of men and women who had inhabited Sixteenth Avenue. One of Schuyler's most poignant stanzas succinctly epitomizes the dilemma of the typical songwriter who, "after years of being nothing," miraculously conjures up a hit and now, "for a while," goes "in style on Sixteenth Avenue."[14] But Felice and Boudleaux were blessed with so many golden words and melodies to match, they went "in style" far longer than most. Their "a while," in some measure, remains, since many of their best-known songs—and even those previously unrecorded—continue to be recorded and sung.

Their contributions were enormous, and their legacy worldwide. But when they first came to Nashville in 1950, they lived in a trailer court, struggling to survive with a growing young family. They entered a music community that was still seeking identity and commercial viability. Timing was everything. Lyric-centric country music needed the Bryants, who tirelessly worked to provide memorable lyrics wrapped around, at their best, beautifully replicable melodies. Boudleaux and Felice helped broaden that music community, since, as Schuyler said, "Although songs were being crafted before they arrived, the idea of a songwriters' community in Nashville really began with their example." Because they became "powerful for what they accomplished, [they] therefore had a powerful voice in shaping the music of Nashville."[15] Near the end of Schuyler's eulogy, he suggested that, because of Felice's "talent, because of her strength, because of her drive and personality, because of her perseverance and passion for her work, [she] cut a new road through Music City. She cut the original road for women. She was strong and fierce, and it is reasonable to suspect that the Bryants would not have achieved such lofty success without her determination."[16]

Their being among the inaugural inductees to the Walk of Fame in Nashville is a fitting commemoration of their role in the making of Music City, USA. Del and Dane were on hand in November 2006 to celebrate the permanent sidewalk medallions made of stainless steel and terrazzo. Each honoree's name is displayed in a star-and-guitar design along Music Mile, the roughly one-mile stretch of Demonbreun Street from Fourth Avenue South to the Music Row Roundabout at Sixteenth Avenue South.[17]

By 1980, when the Bryants moved to their traditionally crafted and renovated home in scenic Gatlinburg, they could point to both the abundant evidence of their contributions to Nashville's music industry—a thriving publishing house with copyrights all over the world—and a musical city teeming with songwriters. While they were certainly not the only songwriters working in Nashville, they were, as Ralph Emery called them, "the spiritual godparents of thousands who make their living today."[18] They had contributed immeasurably to the broadening of country music's horizons. They taught songwriters and musicians that an extra chord or an unorthodox harmonic progression would not necessarily destroy the integrity or purity of a country song. While Harlan Howard had once praised country music for its simplicity and ability to convey total honesty in a song called "Three Chords and the Truth," Boudleaux and Felice informed us that *truth* could also be conveyed in a song that contained more than three chords.

Through their highly visible success, they had also done much to establish the legitimacy of songwriting, while protecting and publicizing the identities of writers. As members of the Nashville Songwriters Association, they lobbied to ensure that country songwriters' names would appear on records, CDs, and albums. Their election to the National Songwriters Hall of Fame and to the Country Music Hall of Fame not only cemented their own reputations but promoted those of other country songwriters as well. Still, their repertoire has to be considered their most important legacy.

In their wildest dreams during their earliest days in Nashville, they could not have anticipated the longevity achieved by many of their songs. In the early days they wrote in great quantity, assuming that only a few songs would garner chart status during their short shelf lives. While both were still alive, however, they witnessed again and again the revival of such songs as "It's a Lovely Lovely World," "I Got a Hole in My Pocket," "Bye Bye Love," "All I Have to Do Is Dream," "We Could," "Sleepless Nights," "Devoted to You," "Raining in My Heart," and "Love Hurts." In 1999 John Prine and Iris DeMent recorded "We Could," and Alison Krauss's and James Taylor's exquisite version of "How's the World Treating You," recorded the year of Felice's death, provide further evidence of the staying power of their songs.[19] Financially, the House of Bryant catalogue more than sustains itself. As Del said:

> Standards such as "Bye Bye Love," "Love Hurts," "All I Have to Do Is Dream," and "Rocky Top" earn more each year than they did in the initial decade of their earning history. Most of this income is derived from synchronization rights when used in movies, commercials, television and cable shows across all platforms. The yearly performing rights income from BMI generated domestically and around the world today far outstrips any of the most successful years the Bryants experienced during their lifetimes. Since their deaths, new artists continue to pick songs from the Bryant catalogue—both old standards and those never before recorded— and are introducing or reintroducing them to the public.[20]

In a tribute to the Bryants, music historian Peter Guralnick wrote: "For all of their diversity, for all the broadness of their subject matter—from low comedy to deep emotion—all of the best songs from the House of Bryant had two things in common: They could not be reduced to formula; and they always retained a simplicity and directness of approach, however sophisticated the harmonic structure, however witty (or corny) the word-play." Paul Simon alluded to the magic wrought by "All I Have to Do Is Dream" when the Everly Brothers sang it in 2003 during their guest performances with Simon and Garfunkel: "You could hear a collective sigh from the audience, which means it was a great song."[21]

Although the ultimate fate of their songs cannot be predicted, at least one of them, "Rocky Top," seems to have won immortal fame. We learned about its ubiquity when we went with Del one Friday night in early March 2018 to Puckett's Grocery and Barbecue, in Franklin, Tennessee. Almost as we walked through the door, we heard a local bluegrass band playing the song and everyone in the restaurant singing along. A couple of hours later, as we prepared to leave, the band played the song once more as their finale, again with audience accompaniment. And Thomas Schuyler mentioned that he had recently attended a wedding in which the bride and groom were both proud graduates of the University of Tennessee. A string quartet played classical selections before the ceremony began, but as the bride walked down the aisle, the musicians broke into a slow and stately rendition of "Rocky Top."[22] All one has to do is look up "Rocky Top" on YouTube to find children of all ages and abilities performing the song on their fiddles, banjos, and guitars and belting out the lyrics with all the fervor of Volunteers fans.

Probably the greatest revelation that we learned during our research is the degree of affection, and even downright awe, inspired by Boudleaux and Felice Bryant among musicians throughout the world, particularly in the United Kingdom. Del even noted that Paul and Linda McCartney asked to write songs with Boudleaux, but he declined because he felt that Felice was his ideal partner.[23] The best affirmation of that acclaim came in a DVD produced in England in 2016 titled *Harmonies from Heaven*. This was a salute to the Everly Brothers, but the names of Boudleaux and Felice Bryant appeared repeatedly. In case after case, there and in subsequent interviews with us, British musicians attested to the mystique of their names and the songs they provided to the Everlys, just as Paul Simon had. Musicians like Sir Tim Rice, Keith Richards, Graham Nash, Peter Asher, Elvis Costello, Donovan, and Eric Clapton fell in love not only with the exotic names of the Bryants but also with the direct and deceptively simple words of their songs and the elaborate harmonic structures in which they were couched. Keith Richards said: "I don't think you'll ever find another pair that can match 'em." And in an interview conducted in 2004, Elvis Costello talked about one of his own songs called "Heart-Shaped Bruise": "It's very much styled after a Felice and Boudleaux Bryant song. It has this very unusual harmonic change at the top of the bridge, which is a characteristic of their writing." He went on to say: "they would write these heartbreak ballads largely inside the country idiom, and at some stage they would just surprise you."[24]

For most of these musicians, encounters with the songs of Felice and Boudleaux Bryant and the harmonies of the Everly Brothers were the beginnings of their own illustrious careers. The so-called British Invasion of the early 1960s was, in no small measure, a consequence of that moment in history when then-young musicians like the Beatles heard the harmonies of the Everly Brothers, a sound dramatically unlike anything in their British experience. This reverence was brought home to Del and Dane many years later in a seriocomic way. The two of them were walking on the Upper East Side of New York City, and they passed a restaurant where Del

Felice and Boudleaux remained sweethearts as they aged. Courtesy House of Bryant Publications.

saw a friend—the songwriter and record producer Russ Titelman—eating dinner with someone at a table near the window. Del tapped on the window and waved hello, as he and Dane walked on. Then they could hear, as Del told it, "scuffling at a fast pace behind us, calling my name. When we stopped and turned around," a fellow had dropped to one knee, telling them how much their parents' songs had meant to him. It was Eric Clapton.[25]

Clapton's sidewalk appreciation surprised Dane and Del. But they may also have found it poignant that Boudleaux's hometown of Shellman, Georgia, commissioned mural artist Chris Johnson to paint their father's portrait with his fiddle on the side of one of three huge grain elevators leading into Shellman. The murals, which took two years to execute, were completed in 2017 in time for the town's annual Boudleaux Bryant Festival. Shellman's mayor, Paul Langford, and Johnson both envisioned the murals as a way to revitalize the community and demonstrate and encourage economic development.[26]

Although their names do not carry the glamour of a British rock star, Dane and Del Bryant nevertheless may embody the most satisfying human aspect of the Bryant legacy. Their lives and careers have been enduring testimonies to the strengths of their famous family and of the ability of their parents to raise two healthy and aspiring boys amid the stress of an aggressive songwriting business. In a telephone conversation with Del in the fall of 2018, we told him that we were working on his folks' legacy, and he remarked that we could call it "We Could and We Did." We decided he was right. When Felice saw Boudleaux coming toward the water fountain where she was stationed at the Schroeder Hotel in Milwaukee on Valentine's Day 1945, she knew that her future was approaching, even if she had no idea what that future might be. Once they earnestly pursued what was, essentially, *her* dream, both Felice and Boudleaux were as relentless as Julius Caesar's claim *veni, vidi, vici*. They could, and they did. Amen.

★ ★ ★ ★ ★

LYRICS TO FOURTEEN CLASSIC BRYANT HITS

All I Have to Do Is Dream
Dream, dream, dream, dream, dream
Dream, dream, dream, dream, dream.
When I want you in my arms,
When I want you and all your charms,
Whenever I want you all I have to do is
Dream, dream, dream, dream.

When I feel blue in the night
And I need you to hold me tight,
Whenever I want you all I have to do is
Dream.

I can make you mine, taste your lips of wine,
Anytime, night or day.
Only trouble is, Gee Whiz,
I'm dreaming my life away.

I need you so that I could die,
I love you so and that is why,
Whenever I want you all I have to do is
Dream, dream, dream, dream. Dream.

> Boudleaux Bryant, 1958
> House of Bryant

Bye Bye Love

Bye bye love, bye bye happiness.
Hello loneliness, I'm think I'm gonna cry.
Bye bye love, bye bye sweet caress,
Hello emptiness, I feel like I could die.
Bye bye my love goodbye.

There goes my baby with someone new.
She sure looks happy, I sure am blue.
She was my baby till he stepped in.
Goodbye to romance that might have been.

I'm through with romance, I'm through with love.
I'm through with counting the stars above.
And here's the reason that I'm so free,
My loving baby is through with me.

> Boudleaux and Felice Bryant, 1957
> House of Bryant

Come Live with Me

Come live with me and be my love.
Share my bread and wine.
Be wife to me, be life to me, be mine.

Come live with me and be my love.
Let our dreams combine.
Be mate to me, be fate to me, be mine.

With these hands I'll build a roof
To shield your head
And with these hands
I'll carve the wood for a baby bed.

Come live with me and be my love.
Share my bread and wine.
Be part of me, the heart of me, be mine.

I'll try to do my best for you.
I promise you,
I'll laugh with you, I'll cry with you,
My whole life through.

Come live with me and be my love.
Share my bread and wine,
Be part of me, the heart of me, be mine.

Boudleaux and Felice Bryant, 1973
House of Bryant

Country Boy

Now I'm just a simple guy, but there's one thing sure as
    shootin'
I hate those folks that think they're so doggone high falutin'
I'd be the same in Hollywood, or right in my own kitchen
I believe in fussin' when you're mad
And scratchin' when you're itchin'.

I'm a plain old country boy, a cornbread lovin' country boy.
I raise Cain on Saturday, but I go to church on Sunday.
I'm a plain old country boy, a cornbread lovin' country boy.
I'll be lookin' over that old grey mule when the sun comes up
    on Monday.

Where I come from opportunities, they never were too good.
We never had much money, but we done the best we could.
Ma doctored me from youngun-hood with Epsom salts and
    iodine.
Made my diapers out of old feed sacks, my ' spenders out of
    plow lines.

Every time the preacher called, Ma always fixed a chicken
If I reached for a drumstick, I was sure to get a lickin'.
She always saved two parts for me, but I had to shut my
    mouth.
'Twas the gizzard and the north end of a chicken flyin' south.

        Boudleaux and Felice Bryant, 1948
        Sony

Devoted to You

Darling you can count on me
Till the sun dries up the sea
Until then I'll always be
Devoted to you.

I'll be yours through endless time
I'll adore your charms sublime
Guess by now you know that I'm
Devoted to you.

I'll never hurt you, I'll never lie
I'll never be untrue
I'll never give you reason to cry
I'd be unhappy if you were blue.

Through the years my love will grow
Like a river it will flow.
It can't die because I'm so
Devoted to you.

> Boudleaux Bryant, 1958
> House of Bryant

Let's Think about Living
In every other song that I've heard lately
some fellow gets shot
And his baby and his best friend both die with him
as likely as not.
In half of the other songs
some Cat's crying or ready to die.
We've lost most of our happy people
and I'm wondering why.

Let's think about living,
let's think about loving.
Let's think about the whoopin' and hoppin' and boppin'
And the lovie lovie dovin'
Let's forget about the whinin' and the cryin'
And the shooting and the dying
And the fellow with a switchblade knife
Let's think about living, let's think about life.

We lost old Marty Robbins
down in El Paso a little while back,
And now Miss Patti Page or one of them is
a-wearing black.
And Cathy's Clown has Don and Phil
where they feel like they could die.
If we keep on a-losing our singers like that
I'll be the only one you can buy.

Boudleaux Bryant, 1960
House of Bryant

Love Hurts

Love hurts, love scars, love wounds and mars
Any heart not tough nor strong enough
To take a lot of pain, take a lot of pain
Love is like a cloud, holds a lot of rain.
Love hurts, oh, love hurts.

I'm young, I know, but even so
I know a thing or two, I learned from you
I really learned a lot, really learned a lot.
Love is like a stove, burns you when it's hot.
Love hurts, oh, love hurts.

Some fools dream of happiness
Blissfulness, togetherness
Some fools fool themselves I guess
But they're not fooling me.
I know it isn't true, know it isn't true,
Love is just a lie, made to make you blue.
Love hurts, oh, love hurts.

> Boudleaux Bryant, 1960
> House of Bryant

Making the Rounds

I'm making the rounds with someone new now that you've
    gone away
But making the rounds is not the fun it was with you
The glamour is gone from all those spots that seemed so
    bright and gay
But making the rounds is all that's left for me to do.

I never go home 'til the last lone hid-away place has closed its
    door
There's too much at home to remind me that we're through
I laugh and pretend that I'm not wishing for a bygone day
When we were in love and I was making the rounds with you.

      Boudleaux Bryant, 1957
      House of Bryant

Raining in My Heart

The sun is out, the sky is blue
There's not a cloud to spoil the blue,
But it's raining, raining in my heart.

The weatherman says clear today
He doesn't know you've gone away,
And it's raining, raining in my heart.

Oh misery, misery,
What's gonna become of me?
I tell my blues they mustn't show,
But soon these tears are bound to flow
Cause it's raining, raining in my heart.

> Boudleaux and Felice Bryant, 1958
> House of Bryant

Richest Man in the World

I got a humpback mule, a plow and a tater patch
Eggs that are gonna hatch someday
I got my Lord above and a good girl to love me
I'm the richest man in the world.

Thank you thank you Lord above for smiling down on me
I'm richer now than any man has any right to be
Health and love and happiness have been my cup of tea
The richest man in all creation surely envies me.

I've got water in my well and heaven in my heart
I have a perfect woman I can trust when we're apart
Cash enough to see a show and eat out now and then
A roof, a bed, a fishing pole, and folks who call me friend.

I don't have much bank account; my cash on hand is small.
But tell me what are riches but contentment after all.
Other folks may think I'm poor but I know it's not so
Cause when I count my blessings I'm the richest man I know.

      Boudleaux Bryant, 1955
      House of Bryant

Rocky Top
Wish that I was on old Rocky Top
down in the Tennessee hills
Ain't no smoggy smoke on Rocky Top,
ain't no telephone bills.

Once I had a girl on Rocky Top,
half bear, the other half cat.
Wild as a mink but sweet as soda pop,
I still dream about that.

Rocky Top, you'll always be
home sweet home to me.
Good old Rocky Top, Rocky Top, Tennessee,
Rocky Top, Tennessee.

Once two strangers climbed old Rocky Top,
Looking for a moonshine still
Strangers ain't come down from Rocky Top,
Reckon they never will.

Corn won't grow at all on Rocky Top,
Dirt's too rocky by far.
That's why all the folks on Rocky Top
Drink their corn from a jar.

I've had years of cramped-up city life
Trapped like a duck in a pen.
All I know is it's a pity life
Can't be simple again.

>   Boudleaux and Felice Bryant, 1967
>   House of Bryant

Sleepless Nights
Through the sleepless nights I cry for you
And wonder who is kissing you.
Oh these sleepless nights will break my heart in two.

Somehow through the days I don't give in
I hide the tears that wait within
Oh, but then through sleepless nights I cry again.

Why did you go? Why did you go?
Don't you know? Don't you know I need you?
I keep hoping you'll come back to me
Oh let it be, please let it be,
Oh my love, please end these sleepless nights for me.

Through the sleepless nights I cry for you
And wonder who is kissing you.
Oh these sleepless nights will break my heart in two.

Boudleaux and Felice Bryant, 1960
House of Bryant

Take a Message to Mary

These are the words of a frontier lad
Who lost his love when he turned bad.

Take a message to Mary
But don't tell her where I am
Take a message to Mary
But don't say I'm in a jam.
You can tell her that I had to see the world
Tell her that my ship set sail.
You can say she'd better not wait for me
But don't tell her I'm in jail, oh
Don't tell her I'm in jail.

Take a message to Mary
But don't tell her what I've done
Please, don't mention the stage coach
And the shot from a careless gun.
You better tell her that I had to change my plans
And cancel out the wedding day.
But please don't mention my lonely cell
Where I'm gonna pine away, until my dying day.

Take a message to Mary
But don't tell her all you know.
My heart is aching for Mary
Lord knows I miss her so.
Just tell her that I went to Timbukto
Tell her I'm searching for gold.
You can say she better find someone new
To cherish and to hold, oh Lord,
This cell is cold.

       Boudleaux and Felice Bryant, 1959
       House of Bryant

Wake Up Little Susie

Wake up little Susie, wake up
Wake up little Susie, wake up.
We've both been sound asleep
Wake up little Susie and weep
The movie's over, it's four o'clock and
We're in trouble deep.
Wake up little Susie, wake up little Susie

What are we gonna tell your momma
What are we gonna tell your pa
What are we gonna tell our friends
When they say ooh-la-la
Wake up little Susie, wake up little Susie

I told your mama that you'd be in by ten
Well Susie baby looks like we goofed again
Wake up little Susie, wake up little Susie,
We gotta go home.

Wake up little Susie wake up
Wake up little Susie wake up
The movie wasn't so hot
It didn't have much of a plot
We fell asleep our goose is cooked
Our reputation is shot.
Wake up little Susie, wake up little Susie.

          Boudleaux and Felice Bryant, 1957
          House of Bryant

We Could

If anyone could find the joy
That true love brings a girl and boy
We could, we could, you and I.
If anyone could ever say
That their true love is here to stay,
We could, we could, you and I

When you're in my arms
I know you're happy to be there
And just as long as I'm with you
I'm happy anywhere.

If anyone could pray each night
And thank the Lord that all is right,
We could, we could, you and I.

Felice Bryant, 1954
House of Bryant

Appendix B

A GUIDE TO THE RECORDINGS OF BOUDLEAUX AND FELICE BRYANT SONGS

Felice and Boudleaux wrote thousands of songs, and at least nine hundred of them have been recorded on 78s, 45s, and LPs, formats that have all become extinct or at best obsolescent. Thanks to dedicated fans and collectors, most of these recordings can be found on websites, particularly on YouTube where they can be freely heard. The would-be listener, of course, must have access to a computer and the awareness that even YouTube reproductions may not always be available. Otherwise, while older recordings do frequently appear on CDs (now also an endangered species) or on some digital format, one cannot be sure that they will remain in print for any great length of time. The collections described below, therefore, are listed with those caveats in mind.

The most valuable source for material from the recorded Bryant catalogue is *All I Have to Do Is Dream: The Boudleaux and Felice Bryant Story,* a box set compiled and organized by Lee Wilson and Dane Bryant, with notes written by Wilson, and published by the House of Bryant in Gatlinburg, Tennessee. In addition to a short, reliable, and colorfully produced biography of the Bryants, the beautifully illustrated box set includes a DVD documentary and an invaluable collection of over fifty recordings of their songs by various entertainers, including Boudleaux and Felice themselves (performing both commercial numbers and twenty-one demos). The credits for these recordings are important because they include artists, recording dates and places, and session musicians. The book also has a section called "The Bryant Hit Parade," that lists sixty-nine songs along with many of the people who recorded them.

The box collections of American roots music produced by the Bear Family label in Germany are state-of-the-art productions, highly valued for their cleanly mastered cuts, copious photographs and graphics, and informed commentary. Material not otherwise available in the United States can be found on these box sets. Bear collections that are relevant to this book include Jimmy Dickens, *Country Boy* (BCD 15848), four CDs covering the period from 1949 to 1957, and consisting of at least seventeen songs written by the Bryants; Carl Smith, *Satisfaction Guaranteed* (Bear Family BCD 15849), five CDs, with eight songs from the Bryants; and the Everly Brothers, *Classic Everly Brothers* (Bear Family BCD 15618), three CDs. This collection contains all of their Columbia and Cadence recordings, 1955–1960.

Also relevant to the Everly Brothers' career is *Heartaches and Harmonies* (Rhino R2 71779), four CDs produced in 1991, and a magnificent DVD collection produced in 2016 by BBC, *Harmonies from Heaven,* two DVDs consisting of some of their songs, including a concert in Australia, and a wealth of testimony taken from various British entertainers. This collection makes clear just how important the names of Felice and Boudleaux Bryant continue to be in the United Kingdom.

The Bryants themselves made an LP in 1979, released in 1980 and titled *A Touch of Bryant* (CMH LP 6243). The album was released again in March 2018 by CMH in digital format: Audiophile 96KHz/24bit.

The epochal recording of "Rocky Top" was made by the Osborne Brothers in December 1967. Since that time, the song has been recorded by scores of musicians around the world. The original Osborne recording was subsequently included in the Smithsonian collection *Classic Country Music,* originally released in 1981. The song also appears from time to time in other anthologies.

The album of Osborne Brothers bluegrass interpretations of Bryant songs, *From Rocky Top to Muddy Bottom: The Songs of Boudleaux and Felice Bryant,* was originally recorded in 1977 (CMH 9008) as two LPs and was released on CD in 1991.

Scholars of American music can find elaborate data about the recordings mentioned in this book on a website called *Praguefrank's Country Discography*. This remarkable website includes dates and places of recording, sessions' personnel, names of songs, writers, producers, and engineers, providing a full account of a singer's recording experience. Deep researchers can go to BMI Repertoire Search and look under the names "Boudleaux Bryant" and "Felice Bryant" to obtain a detailed list of titles.

NOTES

PREFACE

1. Robert Edelstein, "President and CEO, BMI: Del Bryant," *Broadcasting and Cable*, October 25, 2010, https://www.broadcastingcable.com/news/president -and-ceo-bmi-del-bryant-111320.

2. Lee Wilson, *All I Have to Do Is Dream: The Boudleaux and Felice Bryant Story* (Nashville: House of Bryant, 2011). The book will be cited as Wilson, *All I Have to Do Is Dream*. If citations are taken from the filmed interviews, the reference will be *All I Have to Do Is Dream* DVD. The book is now available as a stand-alone paperback; the boxed set can only be purchased as a used copy. The boxed set also includes CDs, which are audios of songs only, some sung by the Bryants as demos and some recorded by the artists who made them famous.

3. The Bryants penned thousands of songs, including novelty pieces, and some social commentary did appear in a few items, such as "The Sixties," "When the Green Berets Come Home," "A Gun Don't Make a Man," and "The Russian Bear," but these were neither memorable nor among their best efforts, even though they were recorded.

4. Franklin Bruno, "The Honeymooners," in Alex Ross, ed., *Best Music Writing 2011* (De Capo Press, 2012), 197. The song "You Never Even Call Me by My Name," written by Steve Goodman and John Prine, was recorded in 1975 and can be heard on YouTube, https://www.youtube.com/watch?v=vAOVRkSCWmg.

ACKNOWLEDGMENTS

1. We began interviewing the Bryant sons—Del in November 2017 by telephone and both brothers in person in Nashville in March 2018. After those initial interviews, we talked to them frequently both by phone from Madison and in person on subsequent visits to Nashville. We recorded our in-person interviews and took notes on others made by phone. We have—and will retain—written records of both, which we cite.

2. These House of Bryant interviews were originally taped to be used by Lee Wilson in writing the book *All I Have to Do Is Dream*. They are kept on CDs in the House of Bryant private collection in Nashville. They will be cited with the

name of the person being interviewed and the House of Bryant CD number. The general public has no access to them.

Chapter 1. **LOVE AT FIRST SPLASH**

1. Del and Dane heard the story from their father their whole lives, as Del retold it in a telephone conversation, November 21, 2018. An alternative narrative exists, however, in the article "Duke and Duchess of Country Minstrelsy," in *Billboard,* November 23, 1959, 8. Boudleaux is quoted as saying: "When my father was in the front lines in World War I, he couldn't pull the pin on a hand grenade properly. He was trying to knock out a machine gun next [*sic*] before he got knocked out. A Frenchman finally showed him how, and he lived to name me after the fellow, whose name was Boudleaux."

2. Danise Bryant Nabarro, telephone interview with authors, December 7, 2017, in which she mentioned, "My parents liked names different from everybody else's in the world." Thanks to Ann Boyer for suggesting La Fontaine.

3. Del and Dane, who have both undergone genealogical mouth-swabbing to determine ancestry, remain skeptical about any American Indian origins.

4. Diadorius Boudleaux Bryant birth certificate, Boudleaux and Felice Bryant Collection, Frist Library and Archives, Country Music Hall of Fame (hereafter the B&FB Collection).

5. Much of this information comes from Jamil S. Zainaldin, "The Great Depression," *New Georgia Encyclopedia,* April 17, 2018, http://www.georgiaencyclopedia.org/articles/history-archaeology/great-depression/.

6. Danise Bryant Nabarro, interview with Lee Wilson and Dane Bryant, Atlanta, Georgia, April 6, 2006, recording in the House of Bryant Collection (hereafter Danise Bryant Nabarro, Wilson and Bryant interview).

7. Elizabeth B. Cooksey, "Colquitt County," *New Georgia Encyclopedia,* March 15, 2019, http://www.georgiaencyclopedia.org/articles/counties-cities-neighborhoods/colquitt-county/.

8. Danise Bryant Nabarro, Wilson and Bryant interview, April 6, 2006.

9. Boudleaux quoted from "Duke and Duchess of Country Minstrelsy," *Billboard,* November 23, 1959, 4. "The Sages," handwritten music and words by Daniel G. Bryant, in the B&FB Collection.

10. Gail Love May, telephone conversation with authors, July 2, 2018, notes in authors' possession.

11. Wayne W. Daniel, "Georgia Old-Time Fiddler Conventions," *New Georgia Encyclopedia,* February 19, 2017, http://www.georgiaencyclopedia.org/articles/arts-culture/georgia-old-time-fiddlers-conventions/.

12. *Tennesseean Magazine,* January 8, 1956, 76.

13. Boudleaux Bryant interview, *All I Have to Do Is Dream* DVD.

14. Danise Bryant Nabarro, telephone interview with authors, December 7, 2017.

15. "Billboard's 25th Anniversary Appreciation of Boudleaux and Felice Bryant: Twenty-Five Years of Harmony," *Billboard,* January 26, 1974, 46.

16. Danise Bryant Nabarro, Wilson and Bryant interview, April 6, 2006. Danise thought that the African American musician Boudleaux encountered in Atlanta was Erroll Garner, but Del thought it must have been someone else. He believed that Boudleaux met Garner somewhat later. Del Bryant, telephone conversation with authors, January 5, 2019.

17. Stripling went on the air on September 27, 1953, on WMA-TV in Macon (the station's first operating day). He died at the age of forty-two on October 18, 1958. See "2012 Legacy Inductee: Lowry 'Uncle Ned' Stripling," Georgia Radio Museum and Hall of Fame (accessed December 15, 2018), http://www .grhof.com/2012LGACYStripling.htm.

18. Boudleaux and Felice Bryant, interview with John Rumble (transcript), Country Music Oral History Project, Gatlinburg, Tennessee, March 26, 1983, Frist Library and Archives, Country Music Hall of Fame, Nashville, Tennessee (hereafter B&FB, Rumble interview), 10.

19. For more information about Hank Penny (September 18, 1918–April 17, 1992), see Rich Kienzle, *Southwest Shuffle: Pioneers of Honky-Tonk, Western Swing, and Country Jazz* (New York: Routledge, 2003). Unfortunately, Milton Brown died in April 1936, from injuries suffered in an automobile accident.

20. B&FB, Rumble interview, 5; Rich Kienzle, "The Checkered Career of Hank Penny," *Journal of Country Music* 8, no. 2 (1980): 48.

21. B&FB, Rumble interview, 15.

22. B&FB, Rumble interview, 17.

23. Kelland Clark, "Memories of Boudleaux, circa early 1940s, recorded in late 1987" (tape), B&FB Collection (hereafter Clark, "Memories of Boudleaux"). Clark sent the tape to the Bryant family after Boudleaux's death.

24. Clark, "Memories of Boudleaux."

25. Penny played guitar on all sessions, used a six-piece band in the first two sessions, and a five-piece on the others. Noel Boggs played electric steel guitar on the first two sessions, and Eddie Duncan played on others. For Penny's recordings, see the compilation made by Tony Russell, *Country Music Records: A Discography, 1921–1942* (New York: Oxford University Press, 2004), 686; and the LP by Hank Penny and His Radio Cowboys, *Tobacco State Swing* (Rambler 103), 1980.

26. B&FB, Rumble interview, 11–12; Russell, *Country Music Records*, 697.

27. After Boudleaux's days with the band, Penny moved to Los Angeles. On the West Coast he played in large ballrooms such as Venice Pier in Santa Monica and worked with Spade Cooley. Penny joined Cooley and Amand Gautier in 1949 to cofound the famous Palomino Club. In Los Angeles he became well known for his role as a hayseed character called "The Plain Old Country Boy," a phrase that was identical to a line in Felice and Boudleaux's first big hit. In the 1960s Penny's wife, Sue Thompson (born Eva Sue McKee), recorded some of Boudleaux's songs after he obtained a contract for her with Hickory Records.

28. Clark, "Memories of Boudleaux."

29. Danise Bryant Nabarro, Wilson and Bryant interview, April 6, 2006.

30. Danise Bryant Nabarro, Wilson and Bryant interview, April 6, 2006.

31. Photo of Gene Steele's Sunny Southerners in B&FB Collection.
32. Clark, "Memories of Boudleaux."
33. B&FB, Rumble interview, 20.
34. The question was never resolved, according to Kelland, who said that during a visit to Gatlinburg not long before Boudleaux's death, the latter decided that the closest thing to true altruism was a mother's love for a child. Clark, "Memories of Boudleaux."
35. B&FB, Rumble interview, 15.
36. Del Bryant, telephone conversation with authors, August 19, 2018; Boudleaux and Felice Bryant, interview, House of Bryant, Gatlinburg, Tennessee, mid-1980s, Dane and Del Bryant Collection CD 2 (hereafter cited as B&FB interview, House of Bryant CD 2).
37. B&FB, Rumble interview, 18.
38. B&FB, Rumble interview, 17–20.
39. Wilson, *All I Have to Do Is Dream*, 16.
40. The Scadutos lived at 787 Humboldt Street at the time of their second daughter's birth. State of Wisconsin birth certificate in B&FB Collection. Their older daughter, Katherine (Kitty) Terrissa, was born on November 11, 1923. Wilson, *All I Have to Do Is Dream*, 17.
41. Felice understood that her parents divorced because of Sam's philandering. After the divorce, Katherine Loverdi retrieved her maiden name, using her prowess in the kitchen to cook in several restaurants. Felice's sister, Kitty, said that, after cooking elsewhere in the city, her mother opened her own restaurant in the historic White Horse Tavern. According to her family, she was popularly known as Spaghetti Kate. Del and Dane Bryant interviews, March 1–2, 2018; Wilson, *All I Have to Do Is Dream*, 19; Kitty Scaduto Cole, interview with Lee Wilson and Dane Bryant, Tyler, Texas, April 13, 2005, House of Bryant CD 1 (hereafter Kitty Scaduto Cole interview with CD number).
42. John Gurda, "Milwaukee's Immigration Connection with Sicilian Region Continues Today," *Milwaukee Journal-Sentinel*, April 5, 2013, http://archive.jsonline.com/features/travel/milwaukees-immigrant-connection-with-sicilian-region-continues-today-201637211.html.
43. Kitty Scaduto Cole interview, House of Bryant CD 1. See also Del Bryant, conversations with authors, 2017–2019; Wilson, *All I Have to Do Is Dream*, 18.
44. Along with the tenets of Catholicism, both Kitty and Felice seem to have believed in some aspects of occultism and the psychic world. Del told a story about his mother calling him up when he was away at college and accurately discerning that he was very ill. Del and Dane Bryant interviews, Nashville, March 1–2, 2018; Wilson, *All I Have to Do Is Dream*, 19.
45. John Gurda, *Milwaukee: City of Neighborhoods* (Milwaukee: Historic Milwaukee, 2015), 211–12. "The 1932 annual school census shows the same trend as was started in the 1920s of newly arriving Italians to the First Ward living on streets where other Italians resided. Moreover, the trend of blood relatives pooling

their money in order to purchase a two-flat house is also indicated." See "Italians in Milwaukee's Labor Force: The Even Years, 1926–1940," compiled by Mario Carini (Milwaukee County Historical Society, January 2000).

46. Felice Bryant interview, *All I Have to Do Is Dream*, DVD.
47. Pete Balistrieri, a barber himself in Milwaukee's Shorewood neighborhood, shared a memory: "Salvatore Scaduto used to come to our restaurant in the 1950s, and he'd always order a big plate of spaghetti and meatballs. He asked me to sit with him because he knew I had signed up for barber school. He'd tell me that if I became a barber, I would live like a king. I think he's related to our family, perhaps on my father's side. He was a real gentleman, as I remember." Pete Balistrieri, telephone conversation with authors, August 2018.
48. B&FB, Rumble interview, 2.
49. Del Bryant phone interview, November 29, 2017.
50. Felice Bryant, interview with Greg Tornquist, Gatlinburg, Tennessee, 1994 (recording), B&FB Collection (hereafter Felice Bryant, Tornquist interview, B&FB Collection); Greg Tornquist, typed memo to Even Stevens about his interview with Felice Bryant, August 12, 1994, 8, sent to authors by Del Bryant, March 8, 2019, House of Bryant Collection (hereafter Tornquist memo, with page number, House of Bryant Collection).
51. Wilson, *All I Have to Do Is Dream*, 20.
52. "Historic Designation Study Report, St. Casimir Church Complex," Archdiocese of Milwaukee Archives, St. Francis, Wisconsin.
53. B&FB, Rumble interview, 2–3.
54. Dane and Del Bryant, interviews, March 1, 2018; Kitty Scaduto Cole, interview, House of Bryant CD 3.
55. Kitty Scaduto Cole, interview, House of Bryant CD 2.
56. Boudleaux and Felice Bryant, interview with Patricia A. Hall (transcript), Country Music Foundation Oral History Project, November 19, 1975, Nashville, Tennessee (hereafter B&FB, Hall interview), 4.
57. Lee Wilson, email to authors, October 9, 2018.
58. Kitty Scaduto Cole interviews, House of Bryant CD 2 and CD 5.
59. Wilson, *All I Have to Do Is Dream*, 22–23. See also Del Bryant, telephone interview, November 29, 2017; *Variety*, September 18, 1935, 58; Obituary of Gertrude Stemper, a former jazz singer who performed on *Cousin Betty's* when she was fourteen, *Milwaukee State Journal* archive (accessed October 1, 2018), http://archive.jsonline.com/news/obituaries/43705147.html/,.
60. "Recording Academy Living Histories: Felice Bryant" (transcript) Tape T1692, 6, June 7, 1999.
61. Dane and Del Bryant, interview, Nashville, March 2, 2018; Kitty Scaduto Cole interviews, House of Bryant CD 2 and CD 5.
62. Wilson email to authors, October 9, 2018.
63. According to "Italians in Milwaukee's Labor Force: The Even Years, 1926–1940," compiled by Mario Carini in January 2000, Salvatore's shop was listed

as Modern Service Barber Shop (Milwaukee Historical Society), Milwaukee City Directory, 1940.

64. Dane and Del Bryant, interviews, Nashville, March 1, 2018.

65. Del Bryant, phone interview, November 29, 2017; Wilson, *All I Have to Do Is Dream*, 24; Kitty Scaduto Cole, interview, House of Bryant CD 1; US Census, 1940.

66. Dane Bryant, interview, Nashville, March 2, 2018.

67. Excerpt from Del Bryant, interview, Smithsonian National Museum of American History, April 6, 2017, http://americanhistory.si.edu/american-scene/del-bryant/.

68. Wilson, *All I Have to Do Is Dream*, 22.

69. B&FB, Rumble interview, 21; "Felice Bryant Interview," by Joe Allison, December 7, 1989 (transcript), 3, in B&FB Collection (hereafter Felice Bryant, Allison interview).

70. Kitty Scaduto Cole, interview, House of Bryant CD 2.

71. Kitty Scaduto Cole, interview, House of Bryant CD 1. Kitty mentioned that the sisters both also worked in a defense plant: Felice only briefly, and Kitty for much longer.

72. Wilson, *All I Have to Do Is Dream*, 26–27.

73. Felice Bryant, interview (transcript), Recording Academy Living Histories, Tape T1691, 3.

74. B&FB, Rumble interview, 22–23.

75. Wilson, *All I Have to Do Is Dream*, 28; B&FB interview, House of Bryant CD 1.

76. Theosophy concerns "that higher intuition acquired by Theosophia, or God-knowledge, which carried the mind from the world of form into that of formless spirit," sometimes enabling humankind "to perceive things in the interior or invisible world." H. P. Blavatsky, "What Is Theosophy?" Theosophy Library Online (accessed August 8, 2019), https://www.theosophy.org/.

77. B&FB interview, House of Bryant CD 1.

78. Wilson, *All I Have to Do Is Dream*, 24, 26–27; Felice Bryant, interview with Archie Campbell, *All I Have to Do Is Dream* [DVD]; B&FB interview, House of Bryant CD 1; Felice Bryant, Allison interview, 5.

79. B&FB, Hall interview, 73.

80. B&FB, Rumble interview, 22.

Chapter 2. **"WHAT DID THE LITTLE LADY DO TODAY?"**

1. Wilson, *All I Have to Do Is Dream*, 31–32.

2. Del Bryant, interview, March 1, 2018.

3. Wilson, *All I Have to Do Is Dream*, 29; B&FB, Rumble interview, 22.

4. Wilson, *All I Have to Do Is Dream*, 29; Kitty Scaduto Cole, interview, House of Bryant CD 1.

5. Wilson, *All I Have to Do Is Dream*, 31; B&FB, interview, House of Bryant CD 1.

6. *Tennessean Magazine,* January 8, 1956, 76.

7. B&FB, interview, House of Bryant.

8. Wilson, *All I Have to Do Is Dream,* 31; Danise Bryant Nabarro, phone interview with authors, December 12, 2017; Gail Love May, phone interview, July 2, 2018; Danise Bryant Nabarro, Wilson and Bryant interview.

9. B&FB, Rumble interview, 23.

10. Felice Bryant, interview, House of Bryant CD 1; B&FB, Hall interview, 12.

11. *Billboard,* January 26, 1974, 46.

12. B&FB, Hall interview, 4.

13. Felice Bryant, interview, House of Bryant CD 1.

14. *All I Have to Do Is Dream* DVD; Felice Bryant, interview, House of Bryant CD 1.

15. Boudleaux and Felice Bryant, recorded television interview with Ralph Emery in a video montage presentation at the Blair School of Music, Vanderbilt University, September 28, 2007.

16. Felice Bryant from Tornquist memo, 8, House of Bryant Collection.

17. Boudleaux Bryant, recorded interview, in video montage presentation at the Blair School of Music, Vanderbilt University, September 28, 2007; B&FB, Hall interview, 5.

18. The list of songs recorded in Moultrie can be found online in the *Catalog of Copyright Entries,* 1946, 41:131, at https://babel.hathitrust.org/cgi/pt?id=uc1 .b3421224;view=1up;seq=141/.

19. Wilson, *All I Have to Do Is Dream,* 41–42.

20. Del Bryant, telephone conversation, January 12, 2019.

21. B&FB interview, House of Bryant CD 1.

22. *Billboard,* January 26, 1974, 47.

23. B&FB, Hall interview, 6, 17.

24. B&FB, Hall interview, 8–9.

25. Felice Bryant from Tornquist memo, 16, House of Bryant Collection.

26. Betty Gallup typescript, dated August 2 (no year indicated), to Boudleaux and Felice Bryant, sent to authors by Del Bryant, February 1, 2019, House of Bryant Collection.

27. *Billboard,* November 23, 1959, 8.

28. Boudleaux Bryant, Moultrie, Georgia, to Kelland Clark at Radio Station KFAB, Lincoln, Nebraska, June 20, 1946, B&FB Collection.

29. *Billboard,* September 14, 1946, 36.

30. B&FB interview, House of Bryant CD 1; Dane Bryant, conversation, Nashville, March 3, 2018; Del Bryant, telephone conversation, January 12, 2019.

31. Coldiron's band eventually evolved into the Sundowners, which was long a centerpiece of country music in Chicago.

32. B&FB interview, House of Bryant CD 1; B&FB, Rumble interview, 25.

33. B&FB, Rumble interview, 25.

34. "Country Boy," Columbia 40685.

35. "Rome Johnson," Hillbilly-Music.com; *Country Song Roundup* 25 (August 1953). He moved to California in 1953 and became active on the local scene, eventually joining the legendary western group, the Sons of the Pioneers.

36. Felice's comment in a television interview by Bobby Bare, captured in the video at the Blair School of Music Tribute to Boudleaux and Felice Bryant, Ingram Hall, Vanderbilt University, September 28, 2007, Del Bryant Collection. See also B&FB, Rumble interview, 26–27.

37. For information on Fred Rose, see John Rumble, "Fred Rose and the Development of the Nashville Music Industry, 1942–1954," (PhD dissertation, Vanderbilt University, 1980); "Fred Rose," Nashville Songwriters Hall of Fame (accessed August 8, 2019), http://nashvillesongwritersfoundation.com/Site/inductee?entry_id=4567/; "Fred Rose," Country Music Hall of Fame (accessed August 8, 2019), https://countrymusichalloffame.org/Inductees/InducteeDetail/fred-rose/.

38. Correspondence between Fred Rose and Boudleaux Bryant, B&FB Collection.

39. "Living Histories: Felice Bryant," Recording Academy, June 7, 1999, Tape T1692 transcription, 10; Fred Rose, letter to Boudleaux Bryant, March 28, 1949, B&FB Collection. The next surviving letter from Rose, dated June 1, 1949, told the Bryants that Dickens planned to sell copies of "Country Boy" at his personal appearances as long as "we will sell him the copies at half price." Such an arrangement would require Boudleaux and Felice to accept "half royalty" of the copies sold to Dickens at that cut rate, after which the Bryants could split the money equally. "I think we could sell Jimmie a mess of copies and pick up some extra if it is agreeable with you."

40. Fred Rose, letter to Boudleaux Bryant, June 1, 1949; B&FB, Rumble interview, 30.

41. B&FB interview, House of Bryant CD 2.

42. Felice Bryant, Allison interview.

43. B&FB, Rumble interview, 34.

44. B&FB, Rumble interview; B&FB interview, House of Bryant CD 1.

45. House of Bryant, CD 1.

46. Ibid.

47. Felice Bryant interview, House of Bryant CD 1.

48. Felice Bryant interview, House of Bryant CD 1.

49. Felice Bryant, Allison interview, 14. See also Dane Bryant, quoted in Michael Kosser, *How Nashville Became Music City, USA: 50 Years of Music Row* (Milwaukee: Hal Leonard, 2006), 88.

50. Gail Love May, telephone interview, July 2, 2018.

51. Wilson, *All I Have to Do Is Dream*, 34; B&FB, Rumble interview, 36.

52. Music columnist, Johnny Sippel, announced in *Billboard*, February 4, 1950, 33, that Tannen had hired Boudleaux Bryant to be his "representative out of Nashville."

53. *Billboard*, March 15, 1947, 108; March 26, 1949, 22; July 30, 1949, 17; December 31, 1949, 14; February 4, 1950, 33; August 26, 1950, 18; December 5, 1953, 73; August 2, 2003, 48.

54. B&FB, Rumble interview, 42.

55. Nat Tannen, letter to Boudleaux Bryant, May 22, 1950, House of Bryant Collection.

56. See an obituary by Thomas Brown, "Peanut Faircloth—Comedy Giant, Singer, Emcee, Songwriter, and Flush-a-Phone Virtuoso," chattanoogan.com, August 25, 2006, http://www.chattanoogan.com/2006/8/25/91581/Peanut -Faircloth—-Comedy-Giant.aspx/. A fuller account has been provided by Robert K. Oermann, "Peanut Faircloth Passes," *MusicRow: Nashville's Music Industry Publication*, March 22, 2010.

Chapter 3. **SPAGHETTI AND SONG-PLUGGING**

1. Check stub from Boudleaux Bryant, provided by Del Bryant, October 1, 2018; Although a much older song, Tex Ritter's version of "The Ballad of the Boll Weevil" (Capitol 40084) was recorded in 1948.

2. Felice Bryant, interview, *All I Have to Do Is Dream* DVD; Randy Fox, "Hillbilly East: A Short History of Nashville's Eastside," *Muddy Roots Music News*, March 21, 2016, http://muddyrootsrecords.com/mr_news/article.php?nid=hillbilly-east -a-short-country-music-history-of-nashvilles-eastside#.W8gSwS_MwWo/. Books that discuss trailer park country music culture include Jeanne Pruett, *Miss Satin Sheets, I Remember* (New York: Page, 2017); Willie Nelson and Bud Shrake, *Willie: An Autobiography* (New York: Simon and Schuster, 1988).

3. Examples of Boudleaux's expenses and correspondence while working for Nat Tannen can be found in the B&FB Collection.

4. B&FB, Hall interview, 33.

5. B&FB, Rumble interview, 33; Del Bryant, telephone conversation, January 27, 2019.

6. Benjamin Houston, *The Nashville Way: Racial Etiquette and the Struggle for Social Justice in a Southern City* (Athens: University of Georgia Press, 2012), 3.

7. "Living Histories: Felice Bryant," Recording Academy, June 7, 1999, Transcript Tape T1692, 5.

8. Martin Hawkins, *A Shot in the Dark: Making Records in Nashville, 1945–1955* (Nashville: Vanderbilt University Press and Country Music Foundation Press, 2006).

9. For a discussion of Nashville's growth as a music center, see Hawkins, *A Shot in the Dark*; Craig Havighurst, *Air Castle of the South: WSM and the Making of Music City* (Urbana: University of Illinois Press, 2007); Brian Dempsey, "Music Row, Nashville," *Tennessee Encyclopedia of History and Culture* (accessed September 20, 2018), http://tennesseeencyclopedi.net/entry.php?rec:1634/; Lacy J. Dalton recorded the definitive version of "Sixteenth Avenue" (Columbia B003XX883C), 1982.

10. Correspondence between Boudleaux Bryant and Nat Tannen, B&FB Collection.

11. Chet Atkins, reminiscence, *Billboard*, January 26, 1974, 53.

12. For information on the Nashville Sound, see Paul Hemphill, *The Nashville Sound* (Everthemore Books, 2005).

13. Chet Atkins, interview, *All I Have to Do Is Dream* DVD.

14. Felice Bryant, Rumble interview, 46. See also Dane and Del Bryant, conversations, Nashville, March 1–2, 2018; Wilson, *All I Have to Do Is Dream*, 111; Del Bryant, telephone conversation, October 20, 2018.

15. Dane and Del Bryant quotes from *All I Have to Do Is Dream* DVD; Dane and Del Bryant, conversations, Nashville, March 1, 2, 2018; Del Bryant, telephone conversation, January 21, 2019.

16. Dane and Del Bryant, conversations, Nashville, March 1, 2018.

17. Felice inscribed more than one ledger on the inside of the front cover with an endearing note to Boudleaux: "To my adorable husband on his 31st birthday. You're a wonderful father and a very loving husband. I thank God for you, Felice," February 13, 1951, Ledger 1, B&FB Collection; Del Bryant, telephone conversation, January 27, 2019.

18. A selection of the Bryants' demos have been collected and presented on CDs in the *All I Have to Do Is Dream* Box Set, House of Bryant Publications, 2011.

19. B&FB, Rumble interview, 47; Ray Stevens, telephone interview, September 4, 2018.

20. Felice Bryant, from Tornquist memo, 12, House of Bryant Collection.

21. Del Bryant, telephone conversation, August 1, 2018; Felice Bryant, Allison interview, 13.

22. Felice Bryant, interview, House of Bryant CD 2.

23. Dane and Del Bryant, conversations, Nashville, March 1–2, 2018; "25th Anniversary Appreciation of Felice and Boudleaux Bryant: 25 Years of Harmony," *Billboard*, January 26, 1974, 48.

24. Dane's note in the brochure, "BMI Salutes Boudleaux and Felice Bryant, Named to the Songwriters Hall of Fame, March 3, 1986, by the National Academy of Popular Music," B&FB Collection; also Dane and Del Bryant, conversations, Nashville, March 1–2, 2018.

25. *All I Have to Do is Dream* DVD.

26. House of Bryant interview, CD 5.

27. Felice Bryant, Tornquist interview, B&FB Collection.

28. Del Bryant, email to Bobbie Malone, April 30, 2018.

29. Felice Bryant, Tornquist memo, 18–19, House of Bryant Collection.

30. Del Bryant, telephone conversation, June 30, 2918.

31. Felice Bryant, Allison interview, 26.

32. Felice Bryant, Tornquist memo, 19, House of Bryant Collection.

33. Lee Wilson, email to Bobbie Malone, October 9, 2018.

34. B&FB, Rumble interview, 47.

35. Nat Tannen, New York, to Boudleaux Bryant, Nashville, September 7, 1950, House of Bryant Collection, Nashville.

36. House of Bryant interviews, CD 3. In this interview, Boudleaux said that Fred Rose advised going along with the cut-ins, saying, "I don't believe in it, and this is totally up to you," essentially reinforcing what Tannen suggested in the letter.

37. Gail Love May, telephone interview, July 2, 2018.

38. Del Bryant, interview, *All I Have to Do Is Dream* DVD.

39. Boudleaux Bryant, interview, House of Bryant CD 2.

40. Price recorded such songs as "Take Me as I Am" and "Raining in My Heart." A good biographical profile of Price has been written by Rich Kienzle for the Bear Family box set, *Ray Price and the Cherokee Cowboys* (BCD 15843 JK).

41. "Felice and Boudleaux Bryant," interview with Hugh Cherry for *Heroes of Country Music* (transcript dated July 1, 1981, B&FB Collection), 26.

42. The Fred Rose–Mitch Miller relationship is discussed in John Rumble's dissertation on Rose.

43. Quoted in Chet Flippo's obituary of Mitch Miller, "He Took Hank Williams to the World," *Nashville Skyline*, August 5, 2010, http://www.cmt.com/news/1645179 /nashville-skyline-he-took-hank-williams-to-the-world/. A helpful obituary is Spencer Leigh, "Mitch Miller: Producer, Composer, and Conductor Who Made an Enduring Impact on American Popular Music," *Independent*, August 4, 2010, https://www.independent.co.uk/news/obituaries/mitch-miller-producer -composer-and-conductor-who-made-an-enduring-impact-on-american -popular-music-2042353.html/, and Michael Friedland, "Mitch Miller Obituary: US Record Producer, Bandleader and Star of His Own Popular TV Show of the 1960s," *Guardian*, August 3, 2010, https://www.theguardian.com/music/2010 /aug/03/mitch-miller-obituary/.

44. Boudleaux Bryant, interview, *Country Song Roundup Magazine*, November 1964, 14.

45. Hillary Mantel, "On the Edge," review of Gordon Burn's novel *Alma*, which contains an insightful biographical sketch of Alma Cogan, *New York Review of Books*, September 24, 1992, https://www.nybooks.com/articles/1992/09/24 /on-the-edge/.

46. Dane and Del Bryant, interview, Nashville, March 1, 2018.

47. Dane and Del Bryant, interview, Nashville, March 1, 2018. According to Lee Wilson, "Loretta and Mooney Lynn later credited the Bryants with giving them the idea for their own similar promotion trips," which Mooney learned about by reading *Billboard*. Wilson, *All I Have to Do Is Dream*, 66, 68.

48. There is no general history of country disc jockeys, but Craig Havighurst provides a good capsule discussion, in *Air Castle of the South: WSM and the Making of Music City* (Urbana: University of Illinois Press, 2007), 178–84. Paul Kallinger,

the famous DJ on XERF, is profiled in Gene Fowler and Bill Crawford, *Border Radio: Quacks, Yodelers, Pitchmen, Psychics, and Other Amazing Broadcasters of the American Airways* (Austin: University of Texas Press, 2002). Other good profiles include Charles Schroeder's essay on Nelson King in *The Biographical Encyclopedia of American Radio* (New York: Routledge, 2011); an essay with no author or title listed, "Randy Blake," Hillbilly-Music dawt com (accessed August 8, 2019), http://www.hillbilly-music.com/dj/story/index.php?id=14769/; and "Tom Perryman Talks about Jim," on the web page, "Tom Perryman Talks about Jim," John Rex Reeves (accessed August 8, 2019), http://www.johnrexreeves.com /tom1.html/.

49. Ralph Emery in Blair School of Music Tribute to Boudleaux and Felice Bryant, September 28, 2007, Ingram Hall, Vanderbilt University, Nashville DVD, House of Bryant Collection.

50. Ralph Emery, telephone interview with authors, March 7, 2018. For a fuller picture, see Ralph Emery and Tom Carter, *Memories: The Autobiography of Ralph Emery* (New York: MacMillan, 1991).

51. B&FB, Rumble interview, 49.

52. Dorothy Horstman quotes Frank Loesser's wife, Lynn, who said that "he had respect for whatever form of song he wrote, which is probably the reason he had success with so many different types of songs." Horstman, *Sing Your Heart Out, Country Boy* (New York: Dutton, 1975), 275.

53. Felice Bryant, Allison interview, 22–24. See also B&FB, Hall interview, 20.

54. Del Bryant, telephone conversation, August 19, 2018. Del talked about recently finding, among his parents' papers, several versions of "We Could," which demonstrate just how much Felice was capable of polishing songs herself. Del Bryant, telephone conversation, January 27, 2019.

55. Horstman, *Sing Your Heart Out*, 47.

56. Felice Bryant, Allison interview, 18. Felice recorded "We Could," for Hickory Records in 1960, https://www.youtube.com/watch?v=VsvGR_Bo-aE/.

57. Felice Bryant, Allison interview, 11; House of Bryant interviews, CD 4.

58. B&FB, Hall interview, 46.

59. B&FB, Hall interview, 46; B&FB, Rumble interview, 23–24.

60. The foreign copyrights, which Wesley had downplayed, did not affect the Bryants at the time. But Boudleaux admitted to John Rumble that being "pretty green" when signing the contract, he hadn't realized what those copyrights were to yield just a few years later. B&FB, Rumble interview, 24.

61. The data for the Bryants' brief forays into the recording studio can be found at the website, Praguefrank (accessed August 8, 2019), http://countrydisco ghraphy2.blogspot.com/2014/08/boudleaux-and-felice-bryant.html/.

62. Ginger Willis, *Country Song Roundup Magazine*, November 1964, 14–15.

63. Dane Bryant, telephone interview, Nashville, March 8, 2018.

64. Teddy Bart, *Inside Music City USA* (Nashville: Aurora Publishers, 1970), 18, 20–21.

65. Donald J. Darcy, *Blues to Blood: Doing It the Hard Way: Music, Addiction, and Recovery* (Bloomington: iuniverse, 2009), 109.
66. *All I Have to Do Is Dream* DVD.

Chapter 4. **"BYE BYE LOVE" AND HELLO WORLD**

1. B&FB, Hall interview, 57; Wilson, *All I Have to Do Is Dream*, 82; *All I Have to Do Is Dream*, DVD; Del and Dane Bryant, conversation with authors, Nashville, March 1, 2018; House of Bryant interviews, CD 5. Del quoted in *The Everly Brothers: Harmonies from Heaven* (England: Eagle Rock, 2016), DVD.
2. Compiled by the authors from B&FB, Hall interview, 57; Wilson, *All I Have to Do Is Dream*, 82; *All I Have to Do Is Dream*, DVD.
3. Del's statement to authors about Ledger 3 was made while they were examining it at the B&FB Collection, September 13, 2018. Other songs in this ledger include "Blue Boy," "Brand New Heartache," "Wake Up Little Susie," and the original version of "Take a Message to Mary."
4. For more on the Muhlenberg style of guitar playing, see Bobby Anderson, *That Muhlenberg Sound* (Beechmont, KY: Muhlbut Press, 1993); Michael Depp, "Musicians Are All Thumbs in Muhlenberg," March 3, 2002, https://americanprofile.com/articles/muhlenberg-county-kentucky-home-to-thumb-picking/.
5. "The Everly Brothers," ClassicBands.com (accessed August 8, 2019), https://www.classicbands.com/; Paula Jean Bishop, "The Roots and Influences of the Everly Brothers" (PhD dissertation, Boston University, 2011), 102.
6. Del Bryant, telephone conversation, September 25, 2018.
7. Boudleaux from Cherry, "Felice and Boudleaux Bryant," 18; Phil Everly interview in *Harmonies from Heaven*, DVD; Felice quote from House of Bryant interviews, CD 5; Thomas Schulyer quoted Felice in the eulogy he gave at her funeral, copy scanned and emailed to authors.
8. Felice Bryant quoted in Wilson, *All I Have to Do Is Dream*, 87.
9. "Bo Diddley, The Originator of Rock and Roll, & Huge Influence on the EBs," EverlyBrothers.net http://www.everlybrothers.net/forum/thread/380/bo-diddley-quot-the-originator-quot-of-rock-and-roll-huge-influence-on-the-/ (accessed October 7, 2018); Dave Simons, "'That's Old Fashioned,'": Capturing the Sound of the Everly Brothers," *Music World*, November 20, 2012, https://www.bmi.com/news/entry/thats_old_fashioned_capturing_the_sound_of_the_everly_brothers/; "Don Edenton," *Everlypedia*, December 2012, http://www.hillmanweb.com/everly/refs/everlypedia2.pdf.
10. "Review Spotlight on Talent," *Billboard*, April 20, 1957, 59, in Bishop, "Everly Brothers," 115, also 105; Kurt Loder, "The Everly Brothers, the Rolling Stone Interview: Thirty Years of Heart-Melting Music and Heart-Wrenching Sadness," *Rolling Stone*, May 8, 1986, 2–3, https://www.rollingstone.com/music/music-news/the-everly-brothers-the-rolling-stone-interview-110028/.

11. Paul Simon, telephone interview with authors, May 11, 2018; Art Garfunkel interviewed in *Harmonies from Heaven*, DVD. See also Robert Hilburn, *Paul Simon: A Life* (New York: Simon & Schuster, 2018), 25.

12. Graham Nash, *Wild Tales: A Rock & Roll Life* (New York: Crown Archetype, 2013), 31–32; Graham Nash, telephone interview with authors, October 3, 2018.

13. Nash, *Wild Tales*, 32; Graham Nash, telephone interview with authors, October 3, 2018.

14. B&FB, Cherry interview, 11.

15. Felice quoted from Dave Simons, "That's Old Fashioned: Capturing the Sound of the Everly Brothers," *MusicWorld*, November 20, 2012, 2, https://www.bmi .com/news/entry/thats_old_fashioned_capturing_the_sound_of_the_everly _brothers/.

16. Felice Bryant, interview, *Harmonies from Heaven*, DVD.

17. Bishop, "Everly Brothers," 119–20.

18. Bob Greene, in his column, "A Wakeup Call for Little Susie," quotes Rickie Solinger's *Wake Up Little Susie: Single Pregnancy and Race before Roe vs Wade* (New York: Routledge, 1992), and references his interview with Felice Bryant for the *Chicago Tribune*, May 18, 1992, http://www.chicagotribune.com/news/ct-xpm -1992–05–19–9202140895-story.html/.

19. B&FB, Cherry interview, 11.

20. Felice Bryant, Allison interview, 33–34.

21. Felice Bryant, Tornquist memo, 9–10, House of Bryant Collection.

22. Kosser, *Music City*, 92–93; Felice Bryant, interview, *Harmonies from Heaven*, DVD; Felice Bryant, Allison interview, 34; B&FB Ledgers 3 and 5, B&FB Collection, September 14, 2018; other hits in Ledger 3 include "Bye Bye Love," "Blue Boy," "Brand New Heartache," and "Wake Up Little Susie."

23. Felice Bryant, Allison interview, 34.

24. "Saga songs" was actually a term used by the Columbia label to describe such songs as "El Paso" and "Battle of New Orleans," but the description was soon attached to similar songs on other labels.

25. Don Everly, from Lydia Hutchinson, "Felice and Boudleaux Bryant," *Performing Songwriter*, January 14, 2015, http://performingsongwriter.com/felice -and-boudleaux-bryant/; Phil Everly interview, in *All I Have to Do Is Dream* DVD. For the Everlys' evolution as singers, see Bishop, "Everly Brothers"; and the booklet that accompanied the 1994 box set, *Heartaches and Harmonies* (Rhino 71779).

26. B&FB, Hall interview, 13.

27. Del Bryant, telephone conversation, January 24, 2019.

28. Boudleaux Bryant, House of Bryant interviews, CD 3

29. Sir Tim Rice, telephone interview, August 22, 2018.

30. See Harlan Howard, "Country Music Is Three Chords and the Truth," Harlan Howard.com (accessed August 8, 2019), https://www.harlanhoward.com/.

31. Peter Asher, telephone interview, September 6, 2018.

32. Rice, Asher, and Gordon, interviews with authors; Sir Tim Rice and Keith Richards interviews in *Harmonies from Heaven*, DVD.

33. Del Bryant, telephone conversation, January 24, 2019.

34. "How Music Row & Acuff-Rose Killed the Everly Brothers," SavingCountryMusic.com, January 4, 2014, https://www.savingcountrymusic.com/how-music-row-acuff-rose-killed-the-everly-brothers/.

35. Phil Everly, interview in *All I Have to Do Is Dream* DVD.

Chapter 5. LIVING AT THE LAKE AND BUILDING THE HOUSE OF BRYANT

1. Peter Guralnick, *Last Train to Memphis: The Rise of Elvis Presley* (New York: Little, Brown, 1994), 183.

2. Del Bryant, telephone interview, January 24, 2019.

3. Before Douglas cut her record, Charley Pride had cut some recordings for the Sun label, which were not immediately released. DeFord Bailey had performed with the Grand Ole Opry back in its earliest days and made a number of recordings. The boxed collection *From Where I Stand: The Black Experience in Country Music* (Nashville: Country Music Foundation, 1998), includes an excellent short essay on Bailey, 26–28, and one on Charley Pride, 46–47. Also useful is David C. Morton and Charles K. Wolfe, *Black Star of Country Music: DeFord Bailey* (Knoxville: University of Tennessee Press, 1993).

4. For more information on Paul Clayton, see Bob Coltman, *Paul Clayton and the Folk Song Revival* (New York: Scarecrow, 2008). On John Dildine, see Bill C. Malone, *Music from the True Vine: Mike Seeger's Life and Musical Journey* (Chapel Hill: University of North Carolina Press, 2011), 79–80; Ray Allen, *Gone to the Country: The New Lost City Ramblers and the Folk Music Revival* (Urbana: University of Illinois Press, 2010).

5. Fred Foster interview, Nashville, March 2, 2018.

6. Bill Williams, "Foster Creates a Monument," *Billboard*, December 21, 1968.

7. Fred Foster enjoys telling this story, as he did when interviewed in March 2018, but it exists in print as well. One of the most reliable accounts is Dorothy Horstman, *Sing Your Heart Out, Country Boy* (New York: Dutton, 1975), 368.

8. Bruce Sylvester, "Fred Foster's Monument Had the Right Artists for Success," *Goldmine Magazine*, May 1, 2011.

9. The song was first recorded by the Everly Brothers on their 1960 album, *A Date with the Everly Brothers*, but was never released as a single.

10. Fred Foster interview, March 2, 2018.

11. For a good summary of Byrd's career, see "Jerry Byrd," Hillbilly-Music dawt com (accessed August 8, 2019), http://www.hillbilly-music.com/artists/story/index.php?id=10027/, and Byrd wrote a memoir, *It Was a Trip, On Wings of Music* (Anaheim, CA: Centerstream Publishing, 2003).

12. Joseph M. Boudreau, "The Polynesian Suite," in Lorene Ruymar, ed., *The Hawaiian Steel Guitar and Its Great Hawaiian Musicians* (Anaheim Hills, CA: Centerstream Publications, 1996), 165–66.

13. For examples of the reaction made to *Polynesian Suite* by steel guitarists, see the online talk on The Steel Guitar Forum (accessed August 8, 2019), https://bb .steelguitarforum.com/viewtopic.php?t=215588/.

14. Fred Foster interview.

15. Del Bryant, telephone conversation, October 25, 2018.

16. Del Bryant, telephone conversation, October 25, 2018.

17. B&FB, *All I Have to Do is Dream* DVD. See also Del Bryant, telephone conversation, January 24, 2019.

18. Fred Foster interview; Dale Bryant, telephone conversation, October 23, 2018.

19. *Billboard's 25th Anniversary Appreciation of Felice and Boudleaux Bryant:* "25 Years of Harmony," January 26, 1974, 46.

20. Leah Foster Alderman, telephone interview, March 4, 2018.

21. Billie Foster, telephone interview, March 12, 2018.

22. These memories are found in an essay written by Boudleaux, "The Personal Side of Fred Foster," *Billboard*, December 21, 1968, 45.

23. Fred Foster, *All I Have to Do Is Dream*, DVD.

24. See Edgar Cayce, *What I Believe* (Virginia Beach: A.R.E. Press, 1946); Thomas Sugrue, *There Is a River: The Story of Edgar Cayce* (New York: Holt, Rinehart and Winston, 1942); Manly P. Hall, *The Secret Teachings of All Ages* (American Philosophical Society, 1928).

25. Boudleaux Bryant, interview, House of Bryant CD 5.

26. Del Bryant, telephone conversation, November 29, 2017.

27. Dane and Del Bryant, conversation, Nashville, March 1, 2018.

28. Photo in red scrapbook in the B&FB Collection.

29. Del Bryant, conversation, Nashville, March 2, 2018; Dane Bryant, telephone interview, March 8, 2018.

30. Martha Woods, telephone interview, March 19, 2018.

31. According to Del, not only could his parents afford to pay cash, at that time local banks were often unwilling to take the risk of lending money to country music songwriters. Del Bryant, telephone conversation, January 24, 2019.

32. Dane insists that in Tennessee there are no ranches, only farms. The Bryants always referred to the property as "the farm." Dane Bryant, telephone conversation, November 30, 2018.

33. See Art Leatherwood, "Santa Gertrudis Cattle," *Handbook of Texas*, State Historical Association, https://tshaonline.org/handbook/online/articles /ats01/.

34. Elton Whisenhunt, "Nashville Scene," *Billboard*, October 23, 1965, 3.

35. Del Bryant, telephone conversation, October 22, 2018.

36. Del Bryant, interview, March 1, 2018.

37. B&FB interview, House of Bryant CD 4.

38. Dennis Morgan, telephone interview, April 6, 2018.

39. Dane and Del Bryant, interviews, March 1–2, 2018. See also Del Bryant, multiple telephone conversations; B&FB interview, House of Bryant CD 4.

40. Felice Bryant interview, House of Bryant CD 4.

41. B&FB interview, House of Bryant CD 4.

42. Del Bryant, telephone conversation, October 21, 2018. For background on Peabody Demonstration School, see "History of PDS and USN," University School of Nashville (accessed August 9, 2019), https://www.usn.org/page/about/history-of-pds-and-usn/.

43. Del Bryant, telephone conversation, March 17, 2018.

44. Dane Bryant, telephone conversation, April 17, 2018.

Chapter 6. **ASCENDING "ROCKY TOP" AND REACHING OTHER PEAKS**

1. B&FB, Hall interview, 51–52.

2. For more information about settlement schools in Appalachia, similar to Arrowmont's origins, see "Settlement Schools of Appalachia," KET Eduction (accessed August 8, 2019), https://www.ket.org/education/resources/settlement-schools-appalachia/.

3. Pi Beta Phi Settlement School, https://www.history.pibetaphi.org/exhibits/settlement-school/; Gatlinburg History and Culture, https://www.gatlinburg.com/explore/why-gatlinburg/history-culture/; Arrowmont History, https://www.arrowmont.org/about/history/; Gatlinburg History, http://gatlinburginn.com/history/.

4. B&FB, Hall interview, 51–53.

5. Having seen the scrap of paper on which the lyrics were first jotted down, Del noted it was not yet a complete song. Del Bryant, telephone conversation, January 25, 2019.

6. Archie Campbell, *The Golden Years*, RCA Victor LPM 3892, 1968.

7. Neil V. Rosenberg and Charles K. Wolfe, *The Music of Bill Monroe* (Champaign-Urbana: University of Illinois Press, 2005), 92.

8. B&FB, Hall interview, 54.

9. Osborne Brothers, *From Rocky Top to Muddy Bottom: The Songs of Felice and Boudleaux Bryant* (CMH-9008), 1977.

10. Horstman, *Sing Your Heart Out*, 22.

11. Wilson, *All I Have to Do Is Dream*, 118.

12. Juli Thanki, "Rocky Top at 50: How a 'Throw-in' Tune Became Tennessee's Most Beloved Anthem," USA Today Network, September 3, 2017, https://www.tennessean.com/story/entertainment/music/2017/09/03/rocky-top-50-how-throw-in-tune-became-tennessees-most-beloved-anthem/492263001/.

13. Alan Siegel, "Rocky Top Ranked No. 1 in USA Today Poll," *USA Today*, October 27, 2015; https://ftw.usatoday.com/2017/10/10-best-fight-songs-in-college-football. For further information about the evolution of "Rocky Top"'s popularity, and of its adoption by the University of Tennessee, see Garret K.

Woodward, "'Rocky Top' Celebrates 50 Years," in *Smoky Mountain Living: Celebrating the Southern Appalachians*, August 1, 2017, http://www.smliv.com/features/youll-always-be-home-sweet-home-to-me/.

14. Heidi Hill, "Grand Marshal Del Bryant Returns Home Sweet Home," *University of Tennessee Daily Beacon*, October 10, 2014, http://www.utdailybeacon.com/news/grand-marshal-del-bryant-returns-home-sweet-home/article_76234b49–3c1c-521d-9bdd-7c2e5ea3ac25.html/. Peyton Manning was an All-American quarterback at the university and a longtime professional football star.

15. "Senate Joint Resolution 322," Tennessee General Assembly (accessed August 8, 2019), http://www.capitol.tn.gov/Bills/110/Bill/SJR0322.pdf/.

16. Ray Isenburg, "Rocky Top on the Yangtze," *Tennessee Alumnus Magazine* (accessed August 8, 2019), https://alumnus.tennessee.edu/2007/rocky-top-on-the-yangtze/.

17. Karen Kaplan, *Bluefield West Virginia Telegraph*, May 1, 1984.

18. Del Bryant, telephone conversation, March 1, 2018.

19. *Billboard*, July 18, 1970, 48.

20. Boudleaux Bryant, Rumble interview, 27.

21. "Roy Clark" (transcript), 21–22, Voices of Oklahoma (accessed August 8, 2019), http://www.voicesofoklahoma.com/interview/clark-roy/.

22. Boudleaux and Felice appeared on *Hee Haw*, October 23, 1982, http://www.tv.com/shows/hee-haw/ed-bruce-john-schneider-big-al-downing-felice-and-boudleaux-1144008/.

23. For excellent books on Gram Parsons, see Ben-Fong Torres, *Hickory Wind: The Life and Times of Gram Parsons* (New York: St. Martin's Press, 1991), and Jessica Hundley with Polly Parsons, *Grievous Angel: An Intimate Biography of Gram Parsons* (New York: Thunder's Mouth Press, 2005); "Bryant Catalog Flourishes," *Billboard*, September 19, 1981, 34.

24. "Nazareth—Love Hurts (Song)," norwegiancharts.com (accessed August 8, 2019), https://norwegiancharts.com/showitem.asp?interpret=Nazareth&titel=LOVE+HURTS&cat=s/; Joe Blevins, "Nazareth—Love Hurts," December 14, 2017, https://www.youtube.com/watch?v=wIttq4DQhWE/. In a telephone conversation on November 5, 2018, Del Bryant mentioned that the Nazareth version bounced from South Africa to the United States.

25. Franklin Bruno, "The Honeymooners: The Husband-and-Wife Team that Crafted Several Thousand Pop Gems," *Oxford American 12th Annual Southern Music Issue* (May 2011): 30–31.

26. See "Felice Bryant," Nashville Songwriters Hall of Fame (accessed August 8, 2019), http://nashvillesongwritersfoundation.com/Site/inductee?entry_id=3428/; "Boudleaux Bryant," Nashville Songwriters Hall of Fame (accessed August 8, 2019), http://nashvillesongwritersfoundation.com/Site/inductee?entry_id=3133/; Havighurst, *Air Castle of the South*, 182.

27. Typed note with attachments from Patsy Bruce to Felice Bryant, January 24, 1979, sent to the authors by Del Bryant, House of Bryant, February 1, 2019.

28. *Billboard*, January 26, 1974, 46.

29. "Maurice Levine, American Conductor, Teacher, Producer, Director, Writer for Television and Theater: Madeline's Monthly Musical Tips Blogg/Article for February 2018," Dr. Madeleine Frank's Music and Math Learning System, https://www.madelinefrankviola.com/maurice-levine-american-conductor -teacher-producer-director-writer-for-television-and-theater-madelines -monthly-musical-tips-blog-article-for-february-2018/.

30. The event was described in a BMI publication, "Nashville in New York" (1975), which included Boudleaux's remarks. In a scratch copy of his remarks, Boud-leaux auditioned several iterations of YMHA—such as "Yehuda Metropolitan Hillbilly Association," "Yiddish Meshugge Hillbilly Association," and "Yodelin' Willie's Harmonica Academy," sent to authors by Del Bryant, February 1, 2019, House of Bryant Collection.

31. Cherry, "Felice and Boudleaux Bryant," 6–7.

32. Typed list of questions and scratch copy of remarks mailed to authors.

33. Donald J. Darcy, *Blues to Blood: Doing It the Hard Way: Music, Addiction, and Recovery* (Bloomington, Indiana: Universe, 2009), 109.

34. Darcy, *Blues to Blood*, 109–10.

35. "Boudleau Bryant," Songwriters Hall of Fame (accessed August 8, 2019), https:// www.songhall.org/profile/Boudleaux_Bryant/; "Felice Bryant," Songwriters Hall of Fame (accessed August 8, 2019), https://www.songhall.org/profile/Felice _Bryant/.

36. Wilson, *All I Have to Do Is Dream*, 111; Dane Bryant, telephone conversation, October 23, 2018.

37. Jan Howard, telephone interview, November 13, 2018; email from Lee Wilson, October 9, 2018.

38. Dane Bryant, telephone conversation, October 23, 2018.

39. Del Bryant, telephone conversation, November 2, 2018.

40. Jem Aswad, "Del Bryant, Music's Royal Son, Looks Back Ahead of His Retire-ment," Billboard, June 9, 2014, https://www.billboard.com/biz/articles/news /legal-and-management/6114089/del-bryant-musics-royal-son-looks-back -ahead-of-his?utm_source=Yahoo&utm_campaign=Syndication&utm _medium=Morning+Fix%3A+Today%27s+Licensing+Hearings%3B+Del+Bry ant%27s+Legacy%3B+Azoff%27s+Comedy+Play/.

41. Dane Bryant, telephone conversation, April 17, 2018.

42. Del Bryant, telephone conversation, November 13, 2018.

43. Del Bryant quoted in Carol Galligan, "Island Profile: Roots in Nashville Roy-alty with a Shelter Island Foothold," *Shelter Island Reporter*, June 22, 2012, https://shelterislandreporter.timesreview.com/2012/06/22/island-profile -roots-in-nashville-royalty-with-a-shelter-island-foothold/.

44. Dane Bryant, telephone conversation, November 20, 2018.

45. Steve Singleton, telephone interview, April 16, 2018.

46. Steve bought Dane out of the studio and began a new publishing venture, but then EMI offered him a position that he accepted, and he sold the studio to Harold Shedd. Text from Steve Singleton, November 27, 2018.

47. Dane Bryant, telephone conversation, March 8, 2018; Kosser, *Music City*, 8.

48. Jill Nabarro Douglass telephone interview with authors, February 10, 2018.

49. Dane Bryant, telephone conversation, April 17, 2018.

50. Del Bryant, telephone conversation, October 21, 2018; Heather Bryant Creech, telephone interview, October 24, 2018.

51. Dane Bryant, conversations, November 23, 27, 2018.

52. Dane Bryant, telephone conversation, November 27, 2018.

53. Wilson, *All I Have to Do Is Dream*, 119, 122; Dane Bryant, telephone conversations, March 8, November 27, 2018.

54. Heather Bryant Creech, telephone interview, October 24, 2018.

55. The songs can be found on a cassette located in the B&FB Collection. They include such titles as "Let Me Ride the Bull in Gilley's Bar" and "I'm Going Home to Bogalusa."

56. Felice Bryant, Tornquist memo, 21, House of Bryant Collection.

57. Fred Foster interview, Nashville, March 4, 2018; Dane Bryant, telephone conversation, March 8, 2018; Del Bryant, telephone conversation, November 23, 2018.

58. Text message from Carolyn Bryant, November 23, 2018; Heather Bryant Creech, telephone interview, October 24, 2018. See also Fred Foster interview, Nashville, March 4, 2018; Del Bryant, telephone conversation, November 23, 2018.

59. Fred Foster interview, March 4, 2018; Del Bryant, telephone conversation, November 23, 2018.

60. *Nashville Tennessean,* June 26, 1987, 53.

61. Dane and Del Bryant, telephone conversations, November 2018.

62. Photocopy of Schuyler's eulogy sent to Del Bryant and made available to the authors, the House of Bryant Collection; *Nashville Tennessean,* June 28, 1987.

Chapter 7. "WE COULD AND WE DID"

1. Felice Bryant, Allison interview, 42; Wilson, *All I Have to Do Is Dream*, 128–29.

2. Felice Bryant, Tornquist memo, 17, House of Bryant Collection.

3. "Felice Bryant: Co-writer of Such Hits as 'Bye Bye Love," *Independent*, April 24, 2003, https://www.independent.co.uk/news/obituaries/felice-bryant-36467 .html/.

4. Fred Rose had been elected to the Country Music Hall of Fame in 1961, but songwriting was only one of many significant roles he played in the world of country music.

5. Country Music Hall of Fame Award Ceremony, 1991, video captured on the *All I Have to Do Is Dream* DVD; Wilson, *All I Have to Do Is Dream*, 133.

6. Dennis Morgan, telephone interview, April 16, 2018; Del Bryant, telephone conversation, April 25, 2018.

7. Chet Flippo, "Felice Bryant: A Well-Spent Life," *Nashville Skyline*, April 24, 2003, https://www.cmt.com/news/1471510/nashville-skyline-felice-bryant-a-well-spent-life/; Heather Bryant Creech, telephone interview, October 24, 2018; Del Bryant, telephone interview, October 25, 2018.

8. Photograph of Felice's note to James Kavanaugh, c/o Simon & Schuster, undated, texted by Del Bryant, January 28, 2019.

9. Wilson, *All I Have to Do Is Dream*, 128; Heather Bryant Creech, telephone interview, October 24, 2018.

10. Heather Bryant Creech, telephone interview, October 24, 2018.

11. Flippo, "Felice Bryant."

12. "Renowned Songwriter Felice Bryant Dies at 77," *BMI News*, April 21, 2003, https://www.bmi.com/news/entry/20030422_renowned_songwriter_felice_bryant_dies_at_77/.

13. Del Bryant eulogy for Felice Bryant, copy sent to authors.

14. Lacy J. Dalton recorded the definitive version of "Sixteenth Avenue" (Columbia B003XX883C), 1982.

15. Thomas Schuyler, telephone interview, November 26, 2018.

16. Copy of Thomas Schuyler's eulogy for Felice Bryant, emailed to authors, January 8, 2019.

17. "McEntire, Milsap, Orbison, among First Walk of Fame Inductees," *CMT News*, October 16, 2006, http://www.cmt.com/news/1543255/mcentire-milsap-orbison-among-first-walk-of-fame-inductees/.

18. Remarks made at the Blair School of Music at Vanderbilt, September 30, 2007, at an event honoring the fiftieth anniversary of "Bye Bye Love," "Wake Up Little Suzie," and "All I Have to Do Is Dream."

19. "We Could" appeared on the CD *In Spite of Ourselves* on Oh Boy Records and "How's the World Treating You," is on *Livin', Lovin', and Losin': Songs of the Louvin Brothers*, a 2003 tribute album on the Universal label.

20. Del Bryant, telephone conversation, January 24, 2019.

21. Copy of Peter Guralnick tribute to Felice and Boudleaux Bryant for the presentation at Blair School of Music at Vanderbilt, September 30, 2007, honoring the fiftieth anniversary of "Bye Bye Love," "Wake Up Little Susie," and "All I Have to Do Is Dream," sent to authors, August 21, 2018; Paul Simon, telephone interview, May 11, 2018.

22. Schuyler, telephone interview, November 26, 2018.

23. Kelly Gilfillan, "Willco Arts Artist Q&A: Del Bryant," Brentwood Home Page, August 16, 2014, https://www.brentwoodhomepage.com/willco-arts-art-q-a-del-bryant/.

24. Brian Wise, "Elvis Costello Interview," *ABC Dig*, October 4, 2004, http://www
   .elviscostello.info/articles/a-c/abc_dig.041004.php/.
25. Del Bryant, telephone conversation, October 2, 2018.
26. Amanda Hoskins, "Artwork Brings Light to Shellman," WALB News, October 11, 2018, https://www.walb.com/story/36575449/artwork-brings-light
   -to-shellman/.

SUGGESTED READING

Bart, Teddy. *Inside Music City, USA.* New York: Aurora, 1970.
> Teddy Bart was a popular singer and radio and television personality in Nashville who knew most of the country musicians in the city. He hosted them on his shows and interviewed a large number of them. His essay on the Bryants in this book takes you inside their lake house, providing insight into their individual personalities and their intimate relationship.

Bishop, Paula. "The Roots and Influences of the Everly Brothers." PhD dissertation, Boston University, 2010.
> This study presents significant pieces of biographical information, but its chief contribution lies in its musicological studies of the Everlys/Bryants songs.

Bufwack, Mary A., and Robert K. Oermann. *Finding Her Voice: The Saga of Women in Country Music, 1800–2000.* Nashville: Vanderbilt University and Country Music Foundation Press, 2003.
> This is the only comprehensive study of the role played by women in country music culture and in the southern society that preceded the commercialization of the music.

Daniel, Wayne. *Pickin' on Peachtree: A History of Country Music in Atlanta, Georgia.* Urbana: University of Illinois Press 1990.
> Wayne Daniel is a competent and prolific historian of country music, with a concentration primarily on the years before 1950. This book provides context for the setting in which the young Boudleaux worked in Georgia.

Doyle, Don H. *Nashville since the 1920s.* Knoxville: University of Tennessee Press, 1985.
> Doyle is the recognized historian of Nashville.

Eiland, William U. *Nashville's Mother Church: The History of the Ryman Auditorium.* Nashville: Opryland USA, 1992.
> Eiland discusses much more than country music; he provides a history of the building that once served as the site for the evangelism of such preachers as

Sam Jones. The Grand Ole Opry moved into the Ryman in 1943, and it was there, backstage, that Boudleaux first promoted his newly written songs.

Emery, Ralph, with Tom Carter. *Memories: The Autobiography of Ralph Emery.* New York: Macmillan, 1991.
The longtime radio and television personality Ralph Emery knew everyone in the music business in Nashville. He played an influential role in the careers of Felice and Boudleaux.

The Everly Brothers: Harmonies from Heaven DVD. England: Eagle Rock, 2016.
This is an insightful and enlightening documentary, with many of the musicians originally smitten by the Everlys talking about the lasting impact of the brothers and the Bryants' songs in England.

Havighurst, Craig. *Air Castle of the South: WSM and the Making of Music City.* Urbana: University of Illinois Press, 2007.
This is a very good, well-researched history of WSM, introducing readers to the city and music culture that provided context for the Bryants' emergence as songwriters.

Hawkins, Martin. *A Shot in the Dark: Making Records in Nashville, 1945–1955.* Nashville: Vanderbilt University and Country Music Foundation Press, 2006.
This is an outstanding account of the role played by record companies, producers, and publishing houses in the making of the music business in Nashville, well before the city became Music City, USA. Hawkins is one of the world's greatest researchers of American roots music.

Hemphill, Paul. *The Nashville Sound: Bright Lights and Country Music.* New York: Simon and Schuster, 1970.
Concentrating on the 1960s and clearly influenced by the political events of that decade, Hemphill presents a series of vignettes and biographical portraits that explain country music's rise to fame in American culture.

Horstman, Dorothy. *Sing Your Heart Out, Country Boy.* Nashville: Country Music Foundation Press, 1986.
This is an indispensable book with a unique perspective. Horstman describes slices of country music through song lyrics, asking writers to explain why they wrote their particular songs. The Bryants provide short commentaries on three songs: "Rocky Top," "Out Behind the Barn," and "We Could."

Houston, Benjamin. *The Nashville Way: Racial Etiquette and the Struggle for Social Justice in a Southern City.* Athens: University of Georgia Press, 2012.
Although Don Doyle continues to be the principal historian of Nashville, we found Houston's book to be useful for understanding the social context in which country music rose to prominence there after World War II. He presents Nashville as a city of contrasts, an environment that fostered an equally paradoxical music.

Kienzle, Rich. *Southwest Shuffle: Pioneers of Honky-Tonk, Western Swing, and Country Jazz.* New York: Routledge, 2003.
Kienzle is the principal historian of western swing and has written prolifically on honky-tonk culture, the influence of jazz, and the electrification of instruments. His discussion of Hank Penny profited from numerous interviews with this influential musician.

Kingsbury, Paul. ed. *The Encyclopedia of Country Music.* New York: Oxford University Press, 1998.
No one book can encompass the entire history of country music, but this exhaustive collection of performers, business people, and songwriters comes about as close as we might want. The editor of the collection, Paul Kingsbury, has included a short but reliable biography of Felice and Boudleaux Bryant.

Kosser, Michael. *How Nashville Became Music City, USA: 50 Years of Music Row.* Milwaukee: Hal Leonard, 2006.
Kosser does not pretend to have written a full account of Nashville's rise to musical prominence. He has instead concentrated on key events in the music culture's history. His remarks on Dane Bryant are particularly discerning.

Malone, Bill C., and Tracey E. W. Laird, *Country Music, USA*, revised edition. Austin: University of Texas Press, 2018.
This book was the first academic history of country music, and this much revised 2018 edition celebrates its fiftieth anniversary. A new chapter, written by Tracey E. W. Laird, covers the years since 2000.

Rinks, Jerry W. "We Shield Millions: A History of WSM, 1925–1950." PhD dissertation, University of Tennessee, Knoxville, 1993.
This dissertation covers much more than country music, but it provides a good history of the powerful radio station that gave the music an ever-enlarging voice. It concludes in the year that the Bryants came to the city.

Rumble, John Woodruff. "Fred Rose and the Development of the Nashville Music Industry, 1942–1954." PhD dissertation, Vanderbilt University, Nashville, 1980.
This dissertation should have been published long ago. It is the only comprehensive study of the writer, publisher, and promoter Fred Rose, who was in the vanguard of Nashville's rise to music supremacy, and of country music's evolution to international significance. It is much more than a biography; it is an explication of the commercialization and flowering of a major American art form.

Wilson, Lee. *All I Have to Do Is Dream: The Boudleaux and Felice Bryant Story.* Nashville: House of Bryant, 2011.
Captivatingly written and designed, this colorful and beautifully produced book—with its accompanying CDs and DVD—highlights the romance of Boudleaux and Felice's personal story, while describing their musical contributions

to the world. Wilson has also published a full-color paperback edition of the book itself (Nashville: Two Creeks Press, 2017) which is more readily obtainable.

Wolfe, Charles. *A Good-Natured Riot: The Birth of the Grand Opry.* Nashville: Country Music Foundation Press and Vanderbilt University Press, 1999.
Wolfe was a prolific student of country music, in all of its manifestations, and the major chronicler of the Grand Ole Opry. His exhaustively researched history of the Opry takes its story only up to 1940, but he lays the groundwork for understanding the scene in which Boudleaux and Felice flourished after they arrived in 1950.

SONG INDEX

GENERAL INDEX